Kevin Brownlow

Winstanley
Warts and All

UKA PRESS

Published by UKA Press

First published in Great Britain in 2009 by
UKA PRESS PUBLISHING
London & Yorkshire, UK
Olympiaweg 102-hs, 1076 XG, Amsterdam, Holland
St. A, 108, Shida, Fujieda, Shizuoka 426-0071, Japan

A CIP catalogue record for this book is available
at the British Library

ISBN : 978-1-905796-22-9
[1-905796-22-6]

This book was prepared for print by UKA Press
and printed in Great Britain

In memory of Miles Halliwell
(1931 — 2004)

Andrew Mollo and Kevin Brownlow

Table of Contents

Introduction

I wrote this account soon after the film was finished. The technique was to keep a notebook in my pocket and as soon as the car door slammed and my wife drove me away from the location, I would write down everything that had happened. Other encounters were recorded as soon as I could get pen to paper. In those days, I could memorise conversations. (Now I have difficulty remembering names.)

What happened to the film? Apart from a steady distribution to film societies, its subsequent career began with the battle scene becoming part of a display at the National Army Museum in London.

When I joined Thames Television, I was asked to show the film to producer Jeremy Isaacs. My future partner David Gill watched it with him and told me that much as they had enjoyed it, the reels were in the wrong order. This proved to be a frequently-repeated curse; years later, I introduced the film at the Munich Filmmuseum and discovered that even there the print was in the wrong order. The French prints, with their beautifully-translated subtitles, disappeared altogether and have never been seen again.

The BBC refused to screen it. In my argument with them, I pointed out that they had been obliged to transmit many bad films, why not show one more in a good cause by supporting the brave new Production Board? That got me nowhere. Jeremy Isaacs, Controller of Channel 4, described it in his book as just the sort of film that ought to be shown on Channel 4, but Channel 4, once he had left, took an unconscionable time to show it.

From time to time, I have been asked to introduce it at film societies. The most stimulating discussion followed a screening (on videotape!) at a former Victorian veterinary establishment called The Horse Hospital, just off Russell Square.

Extracts were shown in Simon Schama's documentary *A History of Britain*. At a lecture entitled *Television and the Trouble with History* held at the Banqueting Hall, Schama included the battle sequence among sequences from historical films he admired.

The film was eventually released on VHS by the BFI and on DVD by Dennis Doros of Milestone Films in the United States. Dennis secured theatrical showings both for *Winstanley* and our previous film, *It Happened Here*, and we got the sort of reviews that – had we got them when the films first appeared – might have made all the difference to our careers.

Andrew Mollo went on to work as production designer or technical adviser on a number of outstanding features, including *The Pianist* and *Downfall*, while I concentrated on documentaries on film history. But when we meet, I discover that Andrew is still working on scripts.

One final drama occurred when the original camera negative was made available by the British Film Institute to Humphries Laboratories but was not returned. The laboratory went into receivership and most of the cans were chucked into a skip. (Humphries' Revenge? See pages 251-257)

Thus it was necessary for the BFI to restore the film. I was delighted to attend the grading sessions, and when I requested alterations, even more delighted to see the results before my eyes. At last the tyranny of the laboratory had been broken. But now comes the DVD, which I have not yet seen. Will it match what we did?

Sadly, many of the friends who helped us make the film have died, not only players like Miles Halliwell, David Bramley, and Terry and Muriel Higgins, but consultants like Russell Robinson and Madeleine Ginsberg.

Andrew and I are now old age pensioners; we joined forces as teenagers in the fifties, convinced we would have a career in the film industry. Two features may not be much to show for a career, but neither of us would have missed the extraordinary experiences that came our way – most of which I have recorded in *How it Happened Here* and in this book.

Kevin Brownlow
London, April 2009

Chapter One

Andrew Mollo and I celebrated 20 years of working together in 1976. It was a gratifying, if sobering moment. We had started with *It Happened Here* and finished with *Winstanley*, and that was all. Just two titles – meagre return for all those years of investment. But it was not for want of trying. Immediately after we had dubbed *It Happened Here* and checked the combined print, we began to think of our next project. We naively expected that the men who ran the picture business would be only too glad to finance two young filmmakers who had proved their ability by writing, producing and directing a 96-minute feature film for a mere £7,000.

But we rapidly learned that the film industry did not welcome such idiosyncrasy. Had we spent seven million, we should have been warmly embraced, for we would thus have been a conduit to the source of the money. And in the surreal thought-processes of the film industry, a producer who sets out to make a film for seven million and succeeds is less of a producer than one who overspends by a hundred per cent. The first is forgotten. The second is the producer of a 14 million pound production. Once you have proved you can spend that sort of money, your next budget will be proportionately higher.

United Artists bought *It Happened Here* (hereafter *IHH*) from Woodfall Films, who part-financed it, for £10,000. Theoretically, that should have given us all our production costs back plus a modest profit. In fact, the overall cost of the film rose simply because it had been sold. Sebastian Shaw, the actor who played Dr Fletcher, had agreed to work for a nominal sum, unless the film was sold, in which case he had to be paid his full fee. Perfectly reasonable. The same went for Woodfall's accountants and solicitors. By the time they had been paid off, the budget was nearer £12,000, which meant we were already in the red.

George 'Bud' Ornstein, head of United Artists in Great Britain, had covered himself with glory over *Tom Jones*. This Woodfall epic had been directed by Tony Richardson in an eccentric style which the United Artists board did not appreciate. Baffled, they invited their secretaries and telephone girls and other representatives of the youthful, cinema-going public and ran it to them. They loved it. Ornstein, fuelled by their enthusiasm, supported the film, gave it a full publicity campaign and booked it into the London Pavilion, where it ran for a year. The profits were enormous, but Tony Richardson ensured that the money reached those whose efforts had deserved it. I have a poor memory for figures, but one series sticks in my mind. Susannah York, the female lead, was offered 2.5 per cent and her agent, Al Parker, turned it down in favour of an outright payment. This was sensible advice, for none of Woodfall's earlier films had been box-office sensations (except, perhaps, for *Saturday Night and Sunday Morning*) and 2.5 per cent of nothing is still nothing. The outright payment amounted to a couple of thousand but in accepting it she sacrificed something like £17,000.

The success of *Tom Jones* gave Ornstein enormous prestige. United Artists now trusted his decisions implicitly. The picture came out in 1963. *IHH* was ready in 1964, and it came to Ornstein's attention by the same route – Woodfall, Tony Richardson, Oscar Lewenstein etc. Unhesitatingly, aided by a good review in *Variety*, Ornstein accepted it for UA release.

At the end of *IHH*, I had made a swift trip to New York and had begun a series of interviews with silent film stars. I left George Fisher, the sound editor, struggling with all the tracks; upon my return we dubbed the film.

Some months later, after we had almost concluded a deal with the Academy Cinema and Connoisseur Films, Andrew and I were summoned to a London hotel to meet George Ornstein. The very day that the United Artists people had viewed the film, I called at their Wardour Street offices. An American was talking to one of the secretaries and said he had just seen a picture.

'One of ours?'

'I hope not. I didn't like it. It was called *It Happened Here*.'

When Andrew and I arrived at the hotel, the door was opened by this same American. His name was Walter Boxer. We were introduced to George Ornstein, an ebullient and amusing man, disarmingly frank (we learned later) and while our tastes were unlikely to coincide, he had a genuine enthusiasm for pictures. He was American and had, I think, been born and brought up in Los Angeles. He once told me that he had been turned on to films by a friend of his, an assistant in a casting office in the thirties, who would lead the hopeful – and invariably beautiful –

It Happened Here

young girls from the casting office to a nearby hotel where he and George had set up an 'office'. With such a background, it was inevitable he would become a producer. Producers are not a breed I care for, but Bud Ornstein was one of the more likeable varieties.

During the conversation, I mentioned my trip to America and my interest in silent films, and Ornstein revealed that his wife was Mary Pickford's niece. If I would like to meet Mary Pickford, he would fix it for me. Ah, said I, but she lives in Hollywood and I can only afford to travel as far as New York.

Oscar Lewenstein said if that was the case, Woodfall would finance my trip from New York to Hollywood and back. Ornstein said he would write to Pickfair, Mary Pickford's residence in Beverly Hills. Poor Andrew didn't get much out of this display of generosity – Lewenstein joked that he would have to find him a battlefield – but in any case, he was due to leave for Spain to act as military adviser on *Dr Zhivago*.

In New York, I met the main controllers of the United Artists empire: David Picker, a young, handsome executive who showered me with theatre tickets, and Arnold Picker, an older, more aggressive character, who demanded to know how I would handle the exploitation and, when I told him, took immense pleasure in telling me what an idiot I was.

I reached Hollywood, and in ten days of furious interviewing, I talked to 26 people, including Buster Keaton. Although I was able to visit Pickfair, Mary Pickford herself was not available.

The Hollywood trip was the only tangible dividend to result from *IHH*, and I am only sorry that Andrew had no similar experience. Of course, there were innumerable dividends in the abstract sense. But as we made no money out of the picture, and never worked as directors in a professional capacity, one is left with a stark impression of profit and loss.

United Artists changed leadership. George Ornstein departed, and we were faced with the daunting task of securing releases from everyone who appeared in the picture. UA insisted on this and there was even a proviso in the contract; they feared 'invasion of privacy' suits. We pointed out that actors dressed in German uniform could hardly accuse us of having surprised them with our cameras while they were strolling with another man's wife. With nagging demands like this, they managed to keep the film on the shelf for months, and the widespread publicity resulting from the London Film Festival screening had been forgotten.

The 1960s were the years of Swinging London, a largely imaginary phenomenon invented by *Time* magazine. The financial structure of the British film industry, with its Eady fund for films made in England, appealed to American producers, and young British directors were being sought to make titillating stories about Swinging London.

With what I suppose will be regarded as typical intransigence, Andrew and I had grown enthusiastic about another film about the invasion of England – this time, the Norman invasion. We wanted a historical subject, and after a broadcast we had made about *IHH*, we had been contacted by an author called Hope Muntz, who had written a book about William the Conqueror and King Harold called *The Golden Warrior*. She had published it originally in 1940, and the book had aroused a great deal of interest over the years. Of course, the scale of such a film put it outside our scope, but Andrew was convinced we could still handle it, and he convinced me.

We realised that our names carried such little weight with producers that a more commercially reassuring name should be attached to any script. We had acquired an agent, an encouraging and charming man called John Redway. He introduced us to his associate, a lady called Robin Dalton. She in turn produced what she assured us would be the answer to our problems – a writer with the big MGM epic *Mutiny on the Bounty* to his credit, Howard Clewes. To our delight, Clewes was highly enthusiastic about the project and proclaimed *The Golden Warrior* his favourite historical novel.

Hope Muntz was very particular, but all her demands were met, and the way was clear for Howard Clewes to proceed. For a week we heard nothing. When I tried to contact him, he was evasive and awkward. As well he might have been. We discovered that a producer called Thomas Clyde had announced a project on *William the Conqueror* called *The Golden Warrior*, from a screenplay by Howard Clewes. I have never worked out exactly what happened, but it is clear that we were ditched from the outset. Hope Muntz wanted us and she had to be persuaded that her project stood no chance of survival if she insisted on our directing it. I met Howard Clewes once more at a Writers' Guild Award dinner, when Andrew and I received a plaque for Best Original Screenplay for *IHH* in 1966. He was taken aback to be confronted so unexpectedly by us, and we felt it unfair to put him on the spot with an interrogation. But I did not feel so charitable a short time ago when I encountered Robin Dalton again and she declared that she couldn't remember a thing about it. Thomas Clyde told me that he had paid a great deal for the screenplay – 'If it's any comfort to you, it was no easy job to get the money to pay Howard.' The project reappeared once or twice, to be directed by Michael Winner…to star Richard Burton…but eventually it disappeared into that thickly populated Forest of Forgotten Films.

United Artists invited us to submit a project. We sketched an outline for a film entitled *All Over Bar the Shouting* which followed the career of a young man in the North from 1913 through the First World War, which he greatly enjoys, into the post-war slump and his eager enlistment into the Black and Tans in Ireland. The framework was the BBC's Great War series; our chief character, now grown old, is summoned to Television Centre to be interviewed about his experiences. The current mood was opposed to war, and the old man told his audience what he thought they wanted to hear. We saw how his phrases disguised his true feelings about war, which he regarded as the best time of his life.

Andrew and I had a meeting with David Picker, which hinged on the fact that Picker was disappointed with our outline; he thought the idea 'downbeat'. I clearly recall my anger at his use of this word, and I accused him of using it as a euphemism for 'serious'. I know that my angry response was intensified by the memories, the very fresh memories, of how UA had treated us, and by the feeling that we were being patronised. My next memory is of the current head of UA England, David Chasman, pursuing us down the corridor and informing me, with grave intensity, that the outburst had been the most ill-advised of my life. And yet it seemed to pay dividends. Three days later, our agent informed us that UA would pay £2000 so that we could develop any project of our choice, including *All Over Bar the Shouting*. And *IHH* would come on at the London Pavilion after *Thunderball*! Sure enough, a cheque for £2,000 duly arrived. But someone at UA added a postscript; the £2,000 was to be returned if they didn't like the script. You could hardly hedge your bets more closely than that, but they did. They added interest to their loan. Andrew was even more furious than I was, and we rejected the offer, which, no doubt, was their plan all along.

They then faced us with another bombshell; the president of United Artists had at last seen the film, and his political connections (he was to be the next American ambassador to Israel) caused him to blanch when he saw and heard the sequence in which our authentic Nazis discussed their beliefs. He called London and instructed them to cut the scene or forget about releasing the picture.

We called upon support from Israel, in the person of Wim van Leer, and received unsolicited help from Alexander Walker in the *Evening Standard*, and ten other critics, who signed a letter to The *Times* objecting to UA's censorship. This served merely to infuriate UA, who could hardly have cared less whether the film was released or not, but were concerned about their liberal reputation. Realising that the picture was about to be dropped, its rights still belonging to UA, we reluctantly agreed that the sequence could be cut. Like lawyers in a purge court, UA demanded that we sign a document saying that the cut was made with our full agreement. Fortunately, we were never made to sign such a confession.

The picture opened in May 1966, and the takings in the first weeks rivalled those of *Tom Jones*. UA were astonished and admitted they had underestimated the film's money-making potential. Attendance was eventually affected by a severe heatwave, and UA took *IHH* from the London Pavilion after six weeks.

It had grossed £23,000 (I checked the figures every night at the box office) and Andrew and I did some mental arithmetic and naively assumed we would make at least £1,000 each. No such luck. UA's returns claimed that they had spent £22,000 on advertising and the London Pavilion charged £5,000 a week rental, so that we owed them money. The film had short runs in specialised cinemas in big towns, but so unspectacular was the release pattern that I was not surprised when the UA returns came in with larger and larger losses. I have since realised that once a film begins to lose money, it is in the distributors' interests to heap all sorts of other costs on to it. It is some kind of tax loss arrangement. George Ornstein commiserated with us when we met him a few months later. UA had given us a very raw deal, and no one knew it better than he. When he joined Harry Saltzman on the James Bond films, he had set up a group of accountants simply to check UA's figures. He knew, from personal experience, how wildly inaccurate they could be. On the first Bond film, he told us, the accountants had checked the figures from Tokyo with the World Bank and found that they were something like $56,000 short. The yen had been exchanged when the rate was especially favourable, but UA had concealed that fact.

UA's returns came in steadily, showing losses from screenings in all parts of the world. I sometimes received reviews from friends in outlying places, yet those places seldom appeared on the returns. When the losses reached the staggering figure of $127,000, we thought we should note the mournful occasion with a gala dernière at the Tolmer, Tottenham Court Road, in the absence of HM the Queen, for the benefit of our creditors, United Artists (black armbands). UA evidently decided to save postage at this point, and the returns stopped arriving.

Yet Ken Troy, their 16mm sales head in England, told me that the film was doing fantastic business. I managed to restore the censored sequence to the 16mm prints, and upon the evidence of people who have run UA's prints, both 16mm and 35mm, they display an incredible amount of wear and tear, indicating a great many screenings.

Andrew and I tried several approaches to United Artists, asking them for a return of the English distribution rights. They were not co-operative. To our delight, in 1976 Stanley Kubrick set his lawyer to try to recover the rights for us, for it was a film he regarded highly. But even Kubrick met with stalemate.

The interest in young British directors from American producers was at its height in 1966. Paramount asked us to write down ten ideas for their inspection – and, no doubt, internal consumption. No one actually offered to pay for any of this work. We became canny to the ways of producers and ensured that meetings were arranged just before lunch. We were summoned to meet the heads of most of the big companies, but to our agent's dismay, none of our ideas met with their approval. Poor John Redway. We must have been the most disappointing pair of likely lads; his only firm offer during the period of our association was second-unit direction on *The Viking Queen*.

United Artists forgot about us after our affaire de scandale. Both of us were working on other things, fortunately. Andrew was operating the Historical Research Unit, and was acting as technical adviser to feature films with military backgrounds. I was editing for a documentary company, appropriately called Samaritan Films. Otherwise, we would both have starved to death.

Chapter Two

I had never heard of Gerrard Winstanley. I knew virtually nothing about the Civil War, beyond a childhood reading of *Children of the New Forest*, a Cavaliers and Roundhead yarn by Captain Marryat. The first time I saw the name was in a paperback novel called *Comrade Jacob*. Miles Halliwell, an old friend of the Mollos who had played a small part in *It Happened Here*, had given it to Andrew and recommended it for a film. Andrew had passed it, with a pile of other books, to Oscar Lewenstein, the Woodfall producer, who, sympathetic to our plight, had occasionally passed us scripts. One was called *The Knack*. We couldn't imagine how this stage play could be converted into a picture. Andrew went so far as to say he did not believe it would benefit from being made into a film. The next time we visited Woodfall, we met Dick Lester, coming down the narrow stairs, clutching the same script. With a great many changes, he converted it into a smash hit which won top prize at the Cannes Film Festival. In any case, outstanding as it was, it was not a film we could have made.

Comrade Jacob appealed to Oscar Lewenstein. It had therefore better appeal to me, suggested Andrew. I opened it and began reading:

'The General was tired of war, yet war had made him what he was, and in its absence he wandered into labyrinths of uncertainty...'

Promising! The opening paragraphs described the journey of General Fairfax and his troopers to St George's Hill. The author, David Caute, was clearly a historian with a rich, almost rococo style in dealing with this austere, Puritan period. On the following page, another hint of the story:

'It was hardly a month since he had received these peasant leaders at his headquarters at Hounslow. They had refused to remove their hats, but he clung to the reins of his temper, admonishing them gently, respecting their religious beliefs, but warning them that in digging up the common land they were breaking the law, and that it must stop.

Their long, involved dissertation about Jacob and Esau and the Norman Yoke he had endured patiently, well knowing how the poor people had suffered in the wars. Fairfax was no tyrant.'

The characters, the political background, had been sketched in my head in the first couple of pages. Now came the clinching element – the atmosphere:

'This is St George's Hill. Dismounted, cursing their feeble mission, beset with doubts, the soldiers began to pick their way up the endless vales and ridges of the hill. Through the tall elms, oaks and beeches the steady rain fell, gradually eating through the layers of their clothing. Pattering on the heather, denying the spring, whispering in these dark silent spaces of shadow like all the ghosts of the wars, it drowned their footsteps.'

That paragraph sold me. If the rest of the book contained such beautifully evocative writing then surely it would be possible to make an equally beautiful and evocative film.

The subject was not likely to appeal to producers and distributors, more concerned with purveying Swinging London than recreating Ancient England. Caute's novel described the brief existence of a remarkable community called the Diggers, who occupied St George's Hill, Weybridge, Surrey, for the year between the spring of 1649 and that of 1650. Led by Gerrard Winstanley, they were a utopian group, opposed to private ownership and the injustice of privilege, who set out to offer what would now be called an alternative society – a non-violent, hard-working community who sought nobody's destruction, but who cultivated the commons and wasteland in order to survive. Unfortunately, even the commons belonged to someone – and local landowners managed to enlist military support to destroy the Diggers.

Gerrard Winstanley has been described as a Christian communist. I only discovered from his obituary that Oscar Lewenstein was a member of the British Communist Party. So when we suggested the subject to Woodfall, we were given the go-ahead to purchase an option. The date was 1 August 1966. An option was an essential precaution; it gave the filmmaker a clear period – usually six months or a year – in which to make plans, free of competition. Woodfall purchased a six-month option for little more than a hundred pounds. *Comrade Jacob* was already five years old, and it was unlikely that another producer would try to develop it, but one could never be sure. Within two years, another producer was developing it.

While we had the option, and while there seemed a strong chance we would make the picture, we gave a great deal of thought to casting, locations and style. One of the big production problems was posed by the location. The Diggers had occupied St George's Hill; it may have been common land in 1649, but three centuries later it had become, ironically, the most exclusive part of the stockbroker belt. Ten peers of the realm lived there, together with several pop stars, and the parts of the hill not occupied by mock-Tudor mansions were taken up by golf courses. St George's Hill was out of the question.

By one of the coincidences that were to occur all through the making of *Winstanley*, Andrew's father, Eugene Mollo, had bought a house in Churt, about 30 miles down the A3 from St George's Hill. One weekend, Andrew invited me down because he thought he had found an ideal hill.

Larchfield was an ancient house – the central section probably went back to the sixteenth century – but it had twentieth-century additions. It was set back from a quiet road, surrounded by a vast lawn which in turn was surrounded by larch and fir trees. If you walked

Larchfield

further, you came to an almost impenetrable wood of silver birches which the Mollo brothers seemed to spend their lives clearing.

In the centre of the birch wood was a lake, and beyond the lake you climbed over the fence on to the road again. Walk along the road and just a few hundred yards away was a bridle path which dipped down to Hambleden Common. Andrew led me along a muddy path lined with pine trees through which, after a long walk, was suddenly revealed The Hill. It was so unexpected in that smooth and unruffled part of the countryside that it made me laugh. Children drew hills like that; it resembled an illustration from a fairy tale. It was perfect for the film – a hill unlike the broad slopes of St George's Hill, which would never have given much of an impression of height, but a symbolic hill, which could be clearly shown in one shot.

We panted our way up the slippery sand-and-heather coated slope and surveyed the surrounding countryside. I expected a cluster of housing estates and pylons but I misread Andrew's triumphant expres-

Parson Platt (David Bramley) leads the villagers up the hill

sion. The view from the top was exactly the view the Diggers would have seen from the top of St George's Hill. A panorama of virgin countryside; a windblown heath bisected by rough paths, a lake and rough woods extending to the horizon. You could hear cars and an occasional aircraft, but shut your ears and the scene was hallucinatory. Here we were, a mere hour and a quarter from London, confronted by one of the last sizeable stretches of unspoiled and unenclosed common land in England.

Andrew and I felt that the presence of such a stunning location so close to Larchfield was indication enough that we would make the film. I couldn't wait to bring cameras down there and listened for the first possible excuse.

But casting was our next consideration. Andrew suggested Miles Halliwell for Winstanley. Miles had played a Nazi lecturer with eerie skill in *IHH*. He was a schoolmaster, at ease before the camera, and that was about the only thing in his favour as far as I was concerned. I had no mental picture of Winstanley, but I could never fit Miles's ascetic features into the character described in Caute's book. Andrew seemed so positive that I suggested we did a test. We would rent a camera for one day, and test a series of film stocks and developing processes on location at the hill – which, incidentally, rejoiced in the name of the Devil's Jumps. Cameraman Chris Menges was a close friend of mine, and we had worked together on a particularly miserable ATV documentary. He had not done any features before, but he was a brilliant cameraman and I was determined he should photograph this picture as his first feature assignment. He and I had spent many hours looking at the work of the great Hollywood cameramen and discussing their methods. We were very keen on diffusion, a lost art in 1966. The old-fashioned gauze, which cameramen in the 1920s used to mount in front of the lens, was no longer obtainable. My image of Chris Menges will always be of an intense young man in a department store picking up pieces of nylon and staring through them at the light. The correct kind of gauze softens the picture, and causes highlights to form a cross. For aesthetic, if not symbolic reasons, we felt diffusion to be essential on *Comrade Jacob*. It would assist the recreation of another epoch and it would soften the harshness of black and white.

Andrew, however, was not sold on the idea of black and white and suggested we shot some colour, too. Chris Menges brought along his assistant, a young Hungarian called Ernest Vincze, together with a boxful of nets and filters and short ends – lengths of black and white and colour film which had been discarded from professional productions as too short to be usable. Miles was fitted out with a costumier's idea of a seventeenth-century costume, which caused Andrew some anguish, since it was far from accurate, and Andrew's brother, Boris, volunteered to play a Cromwellian officer. We shot about ten takes on each setup, testing various stocks to be developed at different timings and graded for different densities. We did one or two scenes in colour, as we could not afford more than a hundred feet. Andrew himself played a trooper in a glistening silver helmet, and since we had plenty of time (for once) I experimented with a style of shooting which was currently intriguing me. This involved a multiple pull-focus; it was very difficult to time it correctly, but assuming that slow stock was used on exteriors, and the shot began in big closeup, the background would be completely soft. A kind of haze would be visible behind the head. At a signal, the foreground head would turn and the focus would shift to middle distance. Suddenly the haze would resolve into a crisp mid-shot of the character in the middle distance and the foreground closeup would disappear. The background would still be a haze, thanks to the slow stock and the correspondingly wide aperture reducing the depth of focus. Then, on another signal, the central character would vanish and a third plane would be revealed – the far distant background, in this case the hill, with a character in a flowing cloak on top of it.

As it happened, I never returned to this complicated style of shooting, although I still think it has possibilities. As film stock gets faster and more sensitive, however (or the more cameramen switch to high-definition tape), the less chance one has for trying it. You need an overcast day, several planes of action, and, more importantly, enormous reserves of patience.

I was apprehensive about working with Andrew again, for he had been involved for months on the multi-million dollar David Lean epic *Dr Zhivago*, and the experience could well have changed his attitudes. The chances of our partnership surviving *IHH* had always been put at zero by mutual friends. They demanded to know how it was possible for two people to have equal creative say in the making of a film. Neither of us could answer that, although I used to quote the precedent of Merian C Cooper and Ernest B Schoedsack, who made *Grass*,

Chang and *King Kong*. Andrew used to say that you could not analyse a partnership: 'We are as difficult to explain as Laurel and Hardy.'

Fortunately, as I wrote in my diary for 30 August 1966: 'It's magical how the old combination works. But it does. A wonderful afternoon on the hill, despite the trippers. Miles hilarious in costume (kept losing hat in wind). Boris superb. Chris and Ernie work hard but progress slow. Finish – return to Larchfield and run comedies to the exhausted assemblage.'

The tests were developed by Studio Film Labs. One section was incorrectly developed, and produced the kind of accident one prays for. It seemed to be a real breakthrough; the photographic image had lost its bland, slightly grainy texture, and through over-development had become surprisingly harsh. It resembled an engraving as much as a photograph. That, we decided, should set the style.

Miles Halliwell's test for the role of Winstanley

The colour was disappointing. Shot with gauze or without, it exaggerated the intensity of the foliage and the effect was pure chocolate box. But just before we packed up, Chris shot a low angle closeup of Miles, in colour. When I saw that on the screen I nearly fell out of my seat. Miles was transformed by the camera, and there wasn't the slightest doubt that he would be perfect for Winstanley.

We were so encouraged by these tests that we arranged to meet David Caute and run them for him. Andrew had already met him, in arranging the option. I was slightly nervous, for his reaction to us and to the footage could colour all our future dealings. But Caute was relaxed and pleasant. He was not much older than we were, despite his distinguished literary record, and to my surprise, he looked slightly like Miles. He had a lively sense of humour, was easy to talk to and he seemed to approve our choice for Winstanley.

Oscar Lewenstein agreed to pay us to write a script from the book. We hoped for the standard fee, £2,000, and I believe we had the temerity to ask for that amount. He said he would give us £400. At that point, any payment was encouraging. *Variety* had just reported that *IHH* was 'pale' in New York. (Coincidentally, I received a letter from the Philippines, offering me studio space on the island because it was understood I had made many motion pictures – 'some outside of the United States'.)

Andrew took the book with him to the Canary Islands, where he was spending his honeymoon. He had met a Spanish girl, Carmen, as he was returning from location on *Dr Zhivago*, which was shot in Spain, and the wedding had taken place at a church in Surrey (not, regrettably, Parson Platt's). The wedding reception had been held on the lawn at Larchfield.

Andrew adapted the book into scenario form, and since his typing was worse than his spelling, I retyped it. We had the usual arguments about how the script should develop. We thought of a title – 'This Fire Will Spread' – feeling that *Comrade Jacob* was meaningless to the general public. 'Jacob' referred to the Jacob and Esau legend; Esau, the younger brother, oppressed by Jacob, the elder brother, was an image referred to throughout Caute's book, He had added the 'Comrade' as an ironical reference to the communism of the Diggers.

Our script was a straightforward feature film adaptation, the dialogue directly from the book, with a few lines invented for dramatic convenience. A great deal of the quality of the book lay in its descriptive writing, and the feeling that lay behind the words. Much of this had to be sacrificed, but we felt we had retained the spirit of the book. (That's what all adapters say!) I particularly liked Andrew's prologue, which posed dozens of fascinating production problems and which I wish we'd been able to include somewhere.

Chapter Three

The trouble with an account of this sort is that one has to reconcile memory with the facts scribbled down at the time in notebooks and on scraps of paper. A few days after I had finished retyping, my diary recorded: 'Andrew says he has lost all interest in the script.' I cannot remember why, for he had initiated the project, and had worked hard on the adaptation. And I hadn't altered it much. But if he had lost interest, so had Oscar Lewenstein. When he had read the script, he called us into his office and told us that it was, regrettably, something on which he could never secure a deal. Why? It was faithful enough to the book, and the book he had liked. Coincidentally, Tony Richardson offered me the job of editing his new film, *The Charge of the Light Brigade*, 'should *Comrade Jacob* not go'.

This was generous of him, but I had abandoned editing. I felt it was providing me with too much security, and preventing me from doing my utmost to become a feature director. Also, my working on a long-term project would hardly do much for Andrew, and we were determined to keep the partnership going. Returning from the American trip, I remember feeling a sense of the deepest gloom at the thought of spending any more time editing. I loved the job, but the more I edited other people's films, the less chance I would have of directing my own. I regretfully turned Tony Richardson's offer down, and we sent him the *Comrade Jacob* script. On 13 December 1966 he wrote:

'I have read the script very quickly and I think a lot of it is very impressive and it could be extremely powerful. However, I don't think it is going to be at all easy to raise the money, especially at the moment when everything is affected by the squeeze. Let's talk about it next week and see what we can do.'

I took the letter round to Andrew. Miles came to supper, and he said he loved the script. A few days later, we discussed the problem with Richardson and he told us he would send it to David Picker at United Artists.

Meanwhile, Andrew worked out a budget with the Woodfall accountant, and came up with a figure of £72,000 – the lowest reasonable figure for a full professional production. (In our terms that meant one on which everyone was paid.)

Miles drew our attention to a little-known book, *The Digger Movement* by Lewis Berens, first published in 1906, and reissued by Holland Press, London, in 1961, the same year that David Caute had published *Comrade Jacob*. The book was quite startling, for it quoted extensively from Winstanley's pamphlets, claimed that he had a decisive influence on the Quakers, quoted examples of his communist thinking and laid out, from original records, the precise series of events that David Caute had used and elaborated on for his novel.

Seventeenth-century prose, for those unaccustomed to it, is hard going, and I must admit that the book did not have the impact that it should have done. It stood on my bookshelf, a kind of unexploded bomb, due to go off in my brain some years later.

Andrew came up with another idea, to make use of the resources Tony Richardson would have at his command in Turkey for *Charge*; he suggested a version of *Hadji Murat* by Tolstoy. But Richardson felt he was going to have a difficult enough time with the Turks as it was. Andrew, his brother John and the Historical Research Unit began working on the research for *Charge*.

David Picker turned *Comrade Jacob* down, and when I conveyed the news to Andrew, he made the first mention of doing it on our own. I was fairly horrified at the idea. *IHH* was fresh in my memory and the thought of another struggle like that one made me feel like a front-line soldier having his leave cancelled.

When we next met Tony Richardson, on his return from America, he told us that Picker had used the following reasoning to turn the picture down: *Hawaii*, in which Max von Sydow had played a religious fanatic, had failed financially. Therefore 'religious fanatic pictures are death at the box office.'

Andrew and I had a meal that night, and took a sad and forlorn look at the future. We decided that the script should be sent to as many possible sources of finance as we could locate. Naturally, we expected a catalogue of rejections, and we got it, but the way the film was rejected proved so fascinating that details might forewarn prospective filmmakers following the same route today.

Wrote one man, whose job it was to select the product of a powerful new corporation: 'I think there is a strong dramatic picture here, but I know I could never sell it to this company. Regardless of how convincingly I could talk about it, I know these people well enough to realise that they would insist on seeing it as 'a depressingly arty subject' and that would be that…These people are just too new and conservative in film production to risk sticking their neck out on making interesting films.'

It is seldom one receives such a trenchant view from a prospective purchaser of a script. Of course, the fact was, the film fitted all too well into the bracket of 'depressingly arty', and it was helpful of this corre-spondent to indicate what was in store for us. The head of Universal Pictures in London was rather less direct. Jay Kanter was a diffident character, small and nervous, a doleful expression on his face.

'I read your script. Now, I must get this clear. I mean, I liked the character of…of…the parson…'

'Parson Platt,' I prompted.

'Yes, Parson Platt. He was well-written and added considerably to the picture. But the other one…er…the…er…'

'Gerrard Winstanley?'

'Yes, right. Now, as I saw it, he was a man who didn't really know where he was going. He seemed to be a kind of failure. I don't know whether I read this right, but…'

I endeavoured to make the character sound a little more dynamic.

'Well,' he said. 'I don't want to give you boys a "no" right away. I can't say "yes" as of this moment. But I don't want to sit on the fence. So you boys will have to give me a day or two to think about it.'

We never heard from him again.

Actually, we learned that it was rare to hear anything at all from anyone to whom we sent the script. Scripts cost money and it was frustrating to feel one was dropping them down a bottomless well, denied even the satisfaction of hearing the splash.

Occasionally, a script was returned with a routine rejection note: 'Many thanks for letting me read this – I look forward to seeing any other ideas you may have.'

And it is only fair to point out that in their rejection of our script, the commercial producers were quite right. They sensed it would make no money, and sure enough, it did precisely that. Nevertheless, our experiences are an indication of the obstacles ahead for anyone trying to set up a film within the industry.

Robert Solo, later associated with the Ken Russell films, was brief and to the point: 'I'm sorry, but this man Winstanley – I just don't like him. Now I admit that you don't have to like the central character. In Henry Levin's picture you don't like Genghis Khan – but he has a fine relationship with a girl.'

Lukas Heller, screenwriter turned producer, contacted us from California and asked to read the script. 'My current contract,' he wrote when he returned it, 'is one that would make them anxious to waste dollars in the millions rather than in the hundreds of thousands required by a project like this, and any recommendation from me at this moment would probably have the effect opposite to the one we would be hoping for.'

Andrew and I were occasionally sent scripts or presented with story ideas, and we weren't being over-particular when we rejected them. You needed to have been in the top income bracket of film director to be sent first-class scripts. At our level, we received the dross that everyone else had passed up. We tried to make sense of one particularly embarrassing story (*Eye Witness*) which the producer assured us had been turned down by Carol Reed. He imagined this gave the project prestige by association. We struggled to turn it into something reasonably watchable, but we found we were rewriting the entire thing and gave up.

I was still determined to direct, and I turned down another offer to cut *Charge*. I was glad that I did, because a day or so later, John Heyman, agent for Richard Burton and Elizabeth Taylor, said that he had read the script, found it 'delightful' (a term that worried us slightly) and he intended to set it up with Paramount. Heyman was still in his thirties, a powerfully built, striking-looking man, rather like the Hollywood idea of a Good German in a war film, a connection denied by his Jewish background. He was, however, German, having come over before the war and been brought up here. He had once been a speechwriter for Aneurin Bevan, and he had a fund of hilarious stories. I remember one from a speech of Bevan's proposing the National Health Service; a voice from the hall yelled 'And what about the bloody nig-nogs?' Bevan sighed and then declared 'As I always say, you can't put a half-crown idea into a twopenny halfpenny mind.' Heyman was currently backing Peter Watkins' first feature after his sensationally successful *The War Game*. It was called *Privilege*, and it starred Paul

Jones and Jean Shrimpton. Peter Watkins had started with us, years before, on *IHH*. Having made amateur films, he was hired by James Carr of World Wide Pictures, my boss at the time, and assigned to be my assistant in the cutting room. He was very invigorating company; we used to have fantastic arguments about filmmaking, and in between arguing he would help out as an assistant director-cum-stills photographer on *IHH*. It was not surprising that when Watkins left World Wide, he set out to make the kind of picture that most interested us, and tried equally hard to preserve his independence. To his credit, he managed to make a lot more pictures than we did.

The fact that Watkins was working with Heyman was a good omen, but we knew that brilliant opportunities were like light bulbs; the brighter they shone, the shorter they lasted. So we rushed another script round to Philip Mackie, who had been entrusted with the formation of Granada Films, an offshoot of the TV company. Mackie turned the thing down instantly; he wanted a modern subject. And a few weeks later, Heyman informed us that Paramount had rejected it, too. But they were interested in anything else we might have to offer that could be contained within a budget of £50,000.

We had to find another subject – or else. We toured the bookshops. There were some great subjects – or rather subjects which excited us, but they were all historical. There was even one on the Easter Rising. We talked to various agents. Anthony Jones thought we ought to consider *Assassins*, a novel by Nicholas Mosley, son of Sir Oswald, and Elaine Greene suggested to Andrew that he read Andrew Sinclair's *The Breaking of Bumbo*.

I had been asked to write an account of the making of *IHH* for the British Film Institute's Cinema One series. I had written a rough outline and shown it to Andrew, and we had one of the periodic, blazing rows we used to have in those days. As usual, something useful emerged, and we found ourselves once again talking of doing *Comrade Jacob* on our own. I put the thought aside as I relived the grimmest days of *IHH*. I decided we would have to be very masochistic to try that stunt again. But another visit to John Heyman suggested that we might have to. He said it was impossible to set *Comrade Jacob* up as a regular commercial picture, but he felt there would be no problems in finding the kind of money it would take to do the film on our own. He promised us £20,000 in three or four days. Neither of us took this very seriously (I wrote 'Huh' in my diary) for producers, we learned, have to sustain themselves with projects and promises, as the poor addict sustains himself with dope.

The days passed and we heard nothing. Andrew Sinclair rang up; he said he had turned down an offer of £10,000 from Universal and accepted an offer of £5,000 from Granada for us to write a script on *The Breaking of Bumbo*. Andrew and I at last had a paid job, but it was hardly a rewarding experience. And once we had accepted that, all sorts of odd projects poured in – including a war film to be shot in Denmark, for an American producer called Bob Gilson. I went over to discuss the script, which was unreadable. I told Gilson what I thought of it and it turned out he had written it, under a pseudonym. His cheque to cover my air fare bounced, so the experience would have been costly as well as useless, had a mutual friend not intervened to recover the amount.

Our work on *Bumbo* did not please Philip Mackie, who kept assuring us like a tired schoolmaster that we were showing signs of improvement, and he brought in a script editor, Richard Bates, son of the novelist H.E. Bates, who behaved like a very energetic schoolmaster and all but rapped our knuckles. Andrew and I went to various barracks, and army camps, and talked to officers and men and tried to capture the authentic vernacular of army life. For Bumbo was a Guards officer who rebelled at the time of Suez. Mackie insisted that the story be updated, but that was the cause of many of our problems, since without Suez, there was no point to the picture. We quickly realised that Mollo and Brownlow were not Muir and Norden and, what was worse, Mackie and Bates realised it too. We were fired.

Tony Richardson had run into trouble with his editor on *Charge* and asked me to take over. I saw some of the rushes, and some of the cut sequences, and I fell in love with the picture; I had to be part of something so grandly conceived and so beautifully executed. I agreed to work on the picture in a supervisory capacity, on condition I could cut and run as soon as *Comrade Jacob* took to the air. We had heard nothing from Heyman, but there was a rumour that Memorial Enterprises liked the script.

Stanley Kubrick, who had rescued *IHH* by bailing us out with fresh stock, again offered help with this project. He arranged a meeting with his lawyer, Louis Blau, who operated from Los Angeles. He was a heavy-set, hawk-nosed German-American with an Ezra Pound moustache who was clearly capable of pulverising producers. He was full of good sense, and he advised us to insert more pageantry – 'Americans love it' – to give the picture more colour and dash.

I wrote an extra scene in the middle of the script, centring around the Putney Debates, and read a complete transcript of the Debates with some amazement. I still found it hard to cope with the sense of seventeenth-century dialogue, particularly when copied down in shorthand and transcribed verbatim over hundreds of pages. But the ideas and the expression of those ideas profoundly impressed me. This was an aspect of history no one had taught us at school. For good measure, knowing that we could always drop it later, but realising what producers were looking for, I included a sex scene. (When an English producer later quizzed me about this scene, asking me why it was there, I was at once apologetic. 'Oh, we only stuck that in for the American market.' 'But I want more scenes like that!')

The title was once again changed; this time, it was 'Criminals of Want'. It was a fairly dramatic title, taken from the second line of the Internationale, but Andrew and I still referred to the picture as 'Comrade Jacob'.

I cannot recall how I met him, but a student called Martin Small, whose job at a pizza house in Coptic Street enabled him to pop into the British Museum during his free time, had become expert on the pamphlets of Gerrard Winstanley. He told me of the political importance of Winstanley; he had spent weeks in the reading room, copying out his writings. To my regret, I lost touch with Martin Small, for he was a great supporter of the film when it was still only an idea. But he will probably never know how much the film owes to him. For he handed over all his notes, and this proved to be another unexploded bomb, like the Berens book. He disappeared to Wales, no doubt to found a commune. I hope he succeeded and I hope one day he will reappear.

Another young man who knew the importance of Winstanley was a veteran of *IHH*, Pat Kearney, an anarchist who had studied the anarchism of the Digger movement. Winstanley had been established as a founder of the Quakers, the Communist Party and the anarchist movement; Miles was going to carry a heavy burden if he ever played the part!

Inspired by all this enthusiasm, I ploughed through Martin Small's notes, as I had through the Berens book and the Putney Debates. To my eternal shame, I scribbled 'heavy going' in my diary and left it at that.

Oliver Cromwell (Don Backhurst) at the Putney Debates

While it would have been hard to claim for *Comrade Jacob* the slightest degree of topicality, we were surprised by the announcement in *Time* magazine [7 July 1967]: '...the drug scene itself had imposed demands for organisation on the hippies. Foremost among the do-gooders are the Diggers; named for a seventeenth-century society of English agricultural altruists, the latter-day Diggers provide free food, shelter and transportation for down-and-out hippies in San Francisco.'

Our old friend George Ornstein had now joined forces with Charles Bludhorn, head of Gulf and Western, the conglomerate which had engulfed and devoured Paramount Pictures. A meeting was held at the Dorchester Hotel, where Bludhorn was holding court. Young directors were being auditioned – a committee interrogated them, and this new supremo hurled insults as though striving to create a reputation as the new Harry Cohn. His associates, including Ornstein and Michael Flint, squirmed uncomfortably on their sofas. (Michael Flint, an English lawyer, was the only man in the entire picture business who warmed to the subject of Winstanley with genuine enthusiasm.)

Ornstein had read our script and had turned it down some weeks earlier. Knowing this, Bludhorn was short with us. He demanded to hear other ideas. 'Faster.' 'Keep 'em coming.' 'Lousy!' 'What was that? Heydrich? Never heard of him!' 'What else?' 'Terrible.'

Taking a deep breath, I launched into a description of *Comrade Jacob* in the style of a story-reader trying to impress Samuel Goldwyn. One of the lines I used was that the story would prove true communism could never work, because human nature wouldn't let it.

'That sounds good.' Bludhorn turned on Ornstein. 'What's wrong with that?'

Ornstein shifted uncomfortably to the very edge of his sofa.

'To be truthful,' he said, 'and I know Kevin and Andrew would want me to be frank, I just didn't like it. You see, this story may have some validity in terms of the Depression, but to me it didn't have any validity in terms of today. You see, things have changed. We're living in a world of milk and honey. For instance, I've just come back from Romania. Now, the Europa Hotel, Bucharest, the Dorchester it is not. But on each floor there is a glass case and in the glass case there is a bottle of Chanel no. 5. I think that shows that even the communists can afford luxuries, and that life today is very different from the Depression.'

Charles Bludhorn delivered the *coup de grâce*:

'Now, if you'd come along with an idea like your last one – with that kind of impact – why, we'd be right behind you.'

Having been fired by Granada, our morale was not improved by a demand from United Artists that Woodfall return the £10,000 advance they had been given for *IHH*. Ken Troy of the 16mm division had the decency to ring and tell me that the film was one of their most popular, and would prove 'an evergreen'. Woodfall, sensibly, did not return the advance.

I went to see John Heyman to find out the reason for the eight-month silence since he promised us the money, and he thrust a script into my hands called *Hubris*. 'This is yours if you want it. Shooting starts in a month. I'd suggest Schofield and Vanessa Redgrave.' I pointed out that I was on *Charge of the Light Brigade*, and was primarily concerned with *Comrade Jacob*, but I read it anyway. (My reaction at the time: 'Like a Sunday afternoon serial about the Third Reich with Dan and Doris Himmler.') Andrew blazed enthusiastically about a film on the assassination of Reinhard Heydrich, and perhaps to atone for raising our hopes Heyman commissioned a script. He even agreed to pay us, even if he did not enable us to make the film. (It was eventually made by Lewis Gilbert, but not from our script.)

Woodfall warned us that the *Comrade Jacob* option had long since run out, but we (illegally) kept the scripts in circulation. American producer Jules Buck told us: 'Fantastic script – such depth – but it wouldn't make a very good picture.'

Maggie Parker, wife of leading agent Al Parker, who had been kind to me when I was starting out as a film historian, bluntly called the script 'banal'. She said she knew me well enough not to mince her words, and added that we needed a poet to rewrite it.

Andrew and I got down to work on the Heydrich script. This was a much more commercial project than *Comrade Jacob*, and Andrew, being a military historian, had done a great deal of research into this bizarre character, and into the British-inspired plot to kill him. Heydrich was the man placed by Hitler in command of Czechoslovakia – in Cromwellian style he was known as the Protector of Bohemia and Moravia. The operation to assassinate him was cursed with a series of abject catastrophes, and we felt it was as fascinating a study of courage under the worst of conditions as *The Charge of the Light Brigade*.

A surprising coincidence occurred when I was asked to appear on *Late Night Line Up* at the BBC, to talk about my new book *The Parade's Gone By...* I happened to meet Elaine Greene, agent for another guest on the programme, Conor Cruise O'Brien; she proved also to be agent for David Caute. I talked of *Comrade Jacob* with wistful enthusiasm. 'Oh, didn't you know?' she said. 'Jack Gold and John McGrath are buying an option.'

I recalled having sent the script to an agent, Clive Goodwin, agent for McGrath. I did not recall having received it back. Next day, I rang Goodwin, and he apologised profusely.

'I still haven't read the script,' he said, 'and to do so now would be embarrassing.' I thought it could be pretty embarrassing as it was. 'Oh yes, I haven't read it, but you only have my word on that.'

Agents usually assure you energetically that they have read your script, when it's transparently clear that they haven't. So I should have believed Clive Goodwin. Instead, I warned him, with unmitigated arrogance, that we would make the picture, whether his associates did so or not. If necessary we would make it on our own. (We had, at that point, plans to apply to the Bertrand Russell Peace Foundation). How we expected to produce a picture from a novel on which our option had lapsed now bewilders me, but I never had a very strong business sense.

I telephoned John McGrath, who was a friend of David Caute's, and discovered that he and Gold had long admired the book and felt compelled to make a film of it. McGrath was very sympathetic when I explained our position; I have seldom encountered such generosity from a professional. 'I can't start on it at once,' he said. 'If you can set it up in six months, it's yours.'

I bumped into Andrew Sinclair in Old Compton Street. I had first met him through a mutual friend; he had asked me to cut the film-insert sequences for a play he had written, a Dylan Thomas pastiche, *Adventures in the Skin Trade*. I saw the play, and noted in my diary: 'D Hemmings a future star.' D Hemmings was now playing Nolan in *Charge of the Light Brigade*, having become a star almost before I had finished writing that review. Sinclair had always been interested in the progress of *IHH*, and had loaned me rare American books for *The Parade's Gone By...* He commiserated over the fact that we'd been fired from Granada Films, and said he had liked everything about our script bar the end. I knew he was being kind, for we were the first to admit the script did not click, despite all our hard work. He said he was earning such vast sums from screenwriting himself that he would be willing to invest in *Comrade Jacob* if we decided to do it on our own, in *IHH* style. He offered £10,000. We could find a matching sum elsewhere. 'One thing, however,' he said. 'You will have to convince Caute.'

I had met David Caute only once, and I was a trifle nervous about ringing him up after my conversation with his agent. I put off the evil moment, and a couple of nights later I attended a party given by Jules Buck. Big producers spread their invitations far and wide, combining generosity with exhibitionism, and I was not surprised when the hostess did not know who I was or why I had come. But Andrew Sinclair rescued me from further embarrassment and introduced me to a charming girl called Shirley Nassem. I found myself waxing eloquently about Andrew's and my plans, until Shirley gently brought me back to reality. She pointed out that she was a close friend of John's. 'Of who?' John Caute. 'Oh, really? Is he related to David?' 'It's the same man. He uses the name David for his literary work.'

My mind raced over the past few minutes. What vital intelligence would she carry back that might scupper our chances? The very fact that I was talking about it with such conviction, I suppose, because I had no claim to the property any more.

The next day I telephoned Caute. He was not impressed by my announcement that we had at least half the money to make the picture. Icy-voiced, he made it clear that he didn't want Andrew and me to make the film. He wanted it written by John McGrath and directed by Jack Gold. And he asked me to ring McGrath, tell him the position and hand the project back. With the deepest desolation, I did so.

Chapter Four

Producers need projects, and projects need energy and enthusiasm to carry them to fruition. Thus producers need what they call 'young talent'. At this period of our careers, Andrew and I came in for a great deal of romancing from producers. We would be invited to a preliminary meeting, invariably followed by lunch, the discussion drifting on through the afternoon; what might be called an eyeball to highball confrontation. Pleasant as these meetings often were, they were also an infuriating waste of time, particularly since none of them came to anything.

The Swinging London period was still at its height, and Young Directors were all the rage. Producers felt they needed to make contact, just in case we were hot properties like Michael Winner, Peter Collinson or Mike Sarne. We obviously weren't, but producers put on a show for us just the same. Expensive lunches…discreet heart-to-heart talks…had we been blonde and female, the sell could scarcely have been harder. Unfortunately, it was always themselves they were selling. The routine was identical; we would arrive, be kept waiting in order to admire glamorous secretary and high-class furnishings. Then over-hearty welcome, as though he's known you all your life, some rapid-fire intelligence, gleaned from *Variety* about disastrous openings, and washed up careers. And that would lead, via a few pleasantries, to the story of their lives.

I could write a massive volume on the lives of the Producers. None of them were very old, few of them were interesting. And when the weary talk was wrapped up, they would express their interest in 'you boys' as we were invariably called. 'The reason I like you boys is that you're not from television,' was one producer's surprising comment. 'These television fellows know nothing about picture techniques. They screw it all up. But you – you don't piss on the medium.'

One day, I was invited to lunch by a former television producer, now based at Elstree Studios. 'Kevin!' he cried. 'I have a great admiration for your work. I would consider it an honour if you would have lunch with me.'

He named Quo Vadis, a highly expensive restaurant in Soho (beneath the rooms where Karl Marx once lived in poverty). I wondered what 'work of mine' he so admired, but recalled that most producers use this approach. Looking forward, anyway, to the food, I went to Quo Vadis and met the producer. He held up a copy of *Variety*. 'I see your picture is doing fantastic business in New York,' he smiled. His finger pointed to the title *Interlude*. To my acute embarrassment, I realised he had confused my name with that of Kevin Billington, a former television director. 'I'm afraid you've got the wrong man,' I said. 'My name is Kevin Brownlow.' A look came over his face which reminded me of Oliver Hardy. But he recovered with surprising aplomb, and picking up the pieces of his broken day, he said 'Come to lunch anyway.' I was hungry in those days and I did. And no, it led to no offers.

Looking back, I can say confidently that as necessary as they seemed, virtually every encounter of this sort was a dead loss. The majority of a day, borrowed from another project, was squandered, we inevitably had outlines to write as a result of the meeting, and while we sometimes got lunch, we never got paid.

And there was one other experience which resulted from our contact with a producer. John Heyman had commissioned us to write the Heydrich film, and suddenly the film became alarmingly topical; the Russians invaded Czechoslovakia. At first, tourists were barred, and we felt that was the end of our chances of making the film in Prague. But a few weeks later, the barriers were lifted, and Heyman's World Film Productions financed both of us to go over and find out what conditions were like. It was an unforgettable experience, our first view of an occupied country, and I must admit with some shame that we were probably the only two people to derive any pleasure from that particular period of history. Prague was swathed in gloom, as were the people. The museum in Wenceslas Square was pitted with bullet holes, where the Russians had fired over the heads of angry crowds. An incredible subversive newsreel I was shown by a film enthusiast revealed the invasion from the first glimmer of convoy lights to the horrifying sight of Russian soldiers firing first over the heads of the crowd, and then, as they were about to be engulfed, at the legs. We were warned to carry out no photography, as the Russians would confiscate the camera and probably arrest the photographer. But with the voyeuristic armour-plating of the tourist, I fired off footage in all directions: a hospital riddled with bullets…a steamroller with the slogan 'Go Home' painted in English…the burned out radio station. Andrew was a fascinating companion on such trips, because he could see evidence the rest of us would miss. He noticed that the Czechs were still driving around in WWII German army staff cars. When we searched in vain for signs of Russian soldiery, he was the one to spot jeeps and trucks parked unobtrusively down side-streets, identifying them from the white-painted numbers on the back. Following his scent, I was able to risk shots of Russian soldiers sight-seeing, and as I got bolder, he got more and more exhausted and returned to the hotel. I went alone to where we had seen the greatest concentration of troops, and holding my 16mm camera under my arm, I filmed surreptitiously. I would not have made a competent spy. I had hardly turned around after the first scene when a Russian officer arrested me and led me into the dank atmosphere of a deserted house where the troops were billeted. I was interrogated for some time, but since this was my first close encounter with Russian troops I was fascinated, and anyway, they kept interrogating me in Russian. I couldn't understand a word and although I tried a little of my Russian, they couldn't understand me. Luckily, I had a review of *IHH* in Russian from *Iskusstvo Kino* in my wallet – I had been sent it by a friend some time before I left and I'd packed it just in case. It referred to the film's 'revelatory power' and spoke of 'the good opinion of the progressive press'. An officer read it aloud to the troops who had gathered in the room. Then they asked me: 'Andrei Molloy?'

'Nyet,' said I. 'Khevin Brovnlov.'

But they weren't to be fooled. 'Passport!' At last a word I understood. I had no passport but I did have identification. The Barclaycard had just been introduced and I flourished mine. They tried to translate the characters into Cyrillic, gave up and let me go.

We were surprised how friendly the Russians were, but they were not exactly welcomed by the local population and were no doubt delighted and entertained by my diversion. We visited the Barrandov studios, talked with Czech film people, were taken to Heydrich's castle and shown the ruins of Lidice, and were offered every conceivable co-operation. Andrew managed to track uniform collectors to the narrow alleys of Prague's medieval, Caligari-like streets by the simple expedient of watching them negotiating for certain items in shops, and then following them home. Prague at that period was incredibly atmospheric and we were convinced that the Heydrich film would gain immeasurably from being made there.

I managed to get my 16mm film out without being searched and we described everything in detail to John Heyman. But he was adamantly opposed to our working in Prague. 'I am not willing to provide finance which will go straight to the Russians.'

I tried to salvage the trip by offering my 16mm colour footage to an American television newsreel. It was a most salutary experience. Under their withering gaze, I realised the difference between home movies and professional war reporting.

'Jesus,' said the network man when the show was over. 'That stuff's useless. The Austrians sent us fantastic stuff during the invasion – tanks firing, buildings burning. What have you got to match that?'

The Heydrich film was finally put to rest when one of Heyman's associates revealed that he had bought an option to the wrong book; we needed Alan Burgess's *Seven Men At Daybreak*, and he acquired a documentary story of Heydrich by Charles Wighton. In any case, we had discovered so much about the reality of the operation that we couldn't accept Burgess's fictionalised and romanticised account. I wrote in my diary: 'The real story is so depressing, I can't see any commercial producer going for it if told as it happened.' Heyman was generally pessimistic, and said the film industry was going through a very bad stage: 'Everyone's shutting down. Paramount has four pictures, two of them cost 23 million dollars, and they daren't take them off the stage and they daren't not. *Hello Dolly* was made by Fox, and they can't release it because of their contract with David Merrick.'

Andrew Sinclair returned from Los Angeles; he had met Caute and Caute had not liked our script. Sinclair had lined up a CBS producer with a project for us. The subject? A black man in the Guards! We went up to Elstree with our new agent, Anthony Jones, to meet Bryan Forbes. Forbes, an actor, writer and director, had just taken over command of Associated British Picture Corporation, and was regarded as the man who might save the British film industry. We found him surprisingly relaxed for all his heavy responsibility. He had us in stitches with his impressions of Raoul Walsh, for whom he had worked in *Captain Horatio Hornblower*. And he pointed out that he had been doing what we did on *IHH* way back in 1948. He gave us hope; he wanted to announce that he had signed us, and said: 'Assuming I gave you £250,000, what subject above all else would you like to do?'

We described *Comrade Jacob* and he immediately stopped us. '*Comrade Jacob* has already been offered by Jack Gold.' We suggested Heydrich. Not the right time.

Coincidentally, Andrew Sinclair had been approached to write a screenplay. He had been accompanied from America by his friend Jeffrey Selznick, son of David O (*Gone With The Wind*). For grandfathers, Jeffrey had two of the most aggressive producers in the business, one a success, Louis B Mayer, and one a failure, Lewis J Selznick, after whom he was named. Jeffrey seemed a surprisingly docile character to emerge from such a background; he looked as if he would be more at home in an American research foundation. But he thought of himself as an aggressive producer, and endeavoured to act like one. Since this was his first picture, we clashed with him. These clashes were reluctant, on our part, for it all seemed totally unnecessary. But the way the film was planned seemed sheer madness to us. And it was not long before Selznick managed to get us fired – a row over casting – before a frame had been shot. Sinclair took over as director. The film was shelved and never released until a single showing on BBC television revealed the picture to be yet another saga of Swinging London, perhaps the most embarrassing of all, bearing no relation to the sharpness and irony of the novel.

It was galling to be fired twice from the same picture, but the sense of relief was indescribable – like being rescued from the *Titanic*.

Bumbo had one extremely valuable effect on my life. I had attended a society wedding, with Andrew, in order to capture, for use in *Bumbo*, the kind of upper-class dialogue heard on such occasions. At the reception, Andrew introduced me to two red-headed Irish girls. I married one of them, Virginia Keane, in August 1969, and later that year we flew to America and I started work at the American Film Institute's new headquarters in Beverly Hills, California.

Chapter Five

The chances of making *Comrade Jacob*, or indeed, any film at all, were now so remote that a meeting with the National Film Finance Corporation in August 1970 scarcely aroused our interest. The NFFC, set up by Harold Wilson in 1949, was resolutely devoted to commercial profit, and our occasional brushes with the organisation had yielded no more than a pleasant chat over a cup of tea.

John Terry, the head of the NFFC, and since knighted for his services to the industry, welcomed us ebulliently. 'I've read this,' he said, flourishing the script. 'I'm the only one who has, I'm afraid. But since I'm on the church committee of Stoke d'Abernon, I'm in favour of it. The church records bear all this out.'

Terry thought that if we could square it with the union, we might be able to get somewhere. I was more worried about David Caute and the rights. But the sun shone for the first time for months – years – on the possibility of a feature and Andrew and I were in euphoric mood as we walked out of the NFFC's building into Soho Square. Characteristically, we heard no more.

Andrew had started his own publishing business, and was doing very much better with his specialist military books than many regular publishers. He also worked on a series of advertisements for Courvoisier, which had a Napoleonic background. And he acted as technical adviser on the occasional feature film.

I shot a documentary for Sloane Shelton in New York on the poetess Edna St Vincent Millay, and I made for producer Barrie Gavin at the BBC a film about Abel Gance. And I returned to Hollywood at every excuse.

Eric Rhode, a member of the British Film Institute's Production Board, was writing a history of the cinema, and I used to see him occasionally. 'Do put an idea up to the Board,' he said, encouragingly. But I knew that the Board, under its head, Bruce Beresford, was desperately underfunded. It wasn't the kind of organisation one thought of in terms of making features.

In charge of the Institute was Stanley Reed. I had known him for years; I acquired BFI membership when I was around 13, far younger than the lowest stipulated age, but fortunately no one seemed to notice. BFI staff, such as he, had been a great help to a fledgling film historian. And he continued to be. He invited me on to the Governing Board of the Institute – a ghastly experience, but I have always been averse to committees and the deadness of bureaucracy, and I could hardly blame him for that. And one day, he began talking to me in the hall at the Institute about a seventeenth-century Ranter called Lawrence Clarkson. He knew about *Comrade Jacob* and my interest in that period, but he overestimated my expertise. I had no idea what a Ranter was, still less about Clarkson. But it was yet another pebble of knowledge and one which was to prove valuable.

Betty Leese rushed out of the Information Department one day and whispered: 'This is top secret, but Stanley Reed is looking for you. Bruce Beresford is leaving…' The job would not suit me, with my attitude towards committees, but I knew instinctively who should have it. I wrote an urgent recommendation that Stanley Reed consider Mamoun Hassan. Naturally, applications had to be considered and

Mamoun Hassan at the BFI Production Board

people had to be interviewed, but to my intense delight, Mamoun got the job.

Mamoun was also being romanced by producers, and having set his sights on becoming a film director, this job was not exactly what he wanted. But he was having a worse time than we were. He could look around and see clearly that the chances of a feature film in the next year or so were remote, however fulsome the promises. He had made several documentaries, and spent a while in the editing department of the BBC, for whom he made a drama, *Living on the Box*.

A Saudi Arab, born in Jedda, he had been sent to me by director Paul Dickson during his search for a job in the film industry. Trained as an engineer, he was on the point of taking his degree, but threw up his chances in order to become an assistant editor with me. He had the most English of accents when he spoke to me on the phone, and when he walked into the cutting room, I was startled by his Semitic appearance. We went out for a coffee, and as he had heard about *IHH*, instantly became involved in a discussion about the Nazis. His knowledge was so profound that I hired him at once. I knew nothing of his skill as an assistant (he proved to be just as bad as I had been) but his knowledge, his intellect and his way of looking at things proved as valuable as a university course. He was also a great encourager – not for himself, alas – and he taught me a great deal. He and Andrew did not warm to each other.

Mamoun always tried to insist that Andrew was a sleeping partner, and that all the creative contributions were mine. I was delighted that his first-hand knowledge of the making of *Winstanley* reversed his opinion, and he formed an admiration for Andrew that was second to none.

When Mamoun took on the job at the Production Board, he faced an almost insuperable task; he had to make the idea of features acceptable, and he had to attract enough money to make such features possible. Having done that, he had to find the talent to make them.

The first film made under his aegis was not a full feature, but a 48-minute film by Bill Douglas called *My Childhood*. The making of that film was a hair-raising experience, but the result was a masterpiece. Andrew and I were both knocked out by it; it was so moving I found myself sniffling through the reception that followed, when the new policy of the Production Board was announced.

Mamoun asked me to submit a feature idea. He had once, long before *Comrade Jacob*, been passionate about the idea of a film on the Levellers, and he had been very interested in the project when it first appeared. But to him, that was as much of the past as it was to us. He had read another of our scripts, a comedy written for Warner Bros (via Sanford Lieberson) about the early days of Hollywood, based on the interviews I had done with directors like Allan Dwan, Raoul Walsh and Joseph Henabery, involving the Patents Wars, the making of westerns and the rise of the producers. Mamoun thought this was a much better script than *Comrade Jacob*; why didn't we submit that? Because it could not be made anywhere except California. Stalemate. Meanwhile, Virginia kept talking about *Comrade Jacob*, and when I mentioned to Andrew that the Production Board wanted a script from us, he said: 'I still think *Comrade Jacob* is the most feasible.'

Mamoun was inhibited by our friendship. He wanted our project to be put to the committee entirely on its own merits, without any support from him. Therefore, he said, it had to be outstanding. He did not think the *Comrade Jacob* script, as it stood, came into that category. I read it again, and acknowledged it was stodgy, but pointed out that we were not exactly renowned for a slavish interpretation of the script. We might have won the Best British Original Screenplay award from the Writers' Guild for *IHH*, but we wouldn't have got it if they had read the script. We used the script as a guide, but a great many of our best scenes had been created on the spot, often from sheer necessity.

One night, Mamoun came round while I was out, and endured a barrage of bullying from Virginia and her sister Sally about how it had to be *Comrade Jacob*; Andrew and Kevin expressed such Englishness in their films, they said. It would be pointless to try to make the other one. And they expanded upon the merits of the story.

Meanwhile, an evening spent with Andrew's father produced a story about rabbit shooting in the grounds of a French château. The hatch is sprung, the guest takes aim. 'No!' cries the host. That is Francois, and Francois is a pet. We don't know how he got in there.' They try again; the hatch flies open and a rabbit emerges. 'Ah, no!' cries the host, pushing up the barrel of the guest's gun. 'That is Victor. Victor is a pet. We don't know how he got in there.' Bewildered, the guest waits for the hatch to be opened once again. This time, a rabbit hops out with no ears, no tail and a distinct limp. The guest hesitates.

'Go on,' says the host. 'That's Gaston. We always shoot Gaston.' We were like Gaston, said Eugene Mollo. No money from *IHH*. Project after project collapsing. Heydrich called off by the Russian invasion. News that Peter Bogdanovich was making a film about early Hollywood and the Patent Wars. And even the BFI wasn't interested in *Comrade Jacob*.

Nevertheless, Mamoun suggested we put forward a treatment, and the writing of the treatment aroused all the old enthusiasm. I found myself buying a book on Cromwell (Andrew had already lent me Buchan's biography) and another on English farms and cottages for use as a location guide. The BFI wrote to David Caute and he replied: 'Rights are free.' Evidently the Jack Gold-John McGrath version had run into the same opposition as ours. Despite the efforts of producers like Tony Garnett and Otto Plaschkes, they were turned down cold by every company in town. Undeterred, McGrath turned his script into a play and *Comrade Jacob* was presented on the stage at the Gardner Centre, Sussex.

Thanks to a subversive agent, I managed to sneak a look at the McGrath script. I found it fascinating. McGrath used dialogue with remarkable fluency – and it wasn't the dialogue from the book. He had rewritten the entire thing and reconstructed it in his own style. The dialogue was a simplified version of seventeenth century. But all the ideas were there. Everything the film needed to say was included, but expressed entirely with the spoken word. It would probably have made an excellent film, but we knew that this explicit method was the kind of thing with which we could never succeed. It required a first-rate, and thus highly-paid professional cast, and an ability on the part of the director, to sustain long takes. Jack Gold was expert at introducing new setups within a take, his camera nudging aside an extra to create variety within the scene, while the dialogue sustained its own rhythm. Andrew rather liked long takes, too. But being brought up on silent pictures, I liked to cut around within a scene, creating my pace in the editing. And both of us were united against too much dialogue. Unfortunately, modern audiences, accustomed to television, used their ears much more than their eyes, and many people have failed to develop a visual sense. Thus films are expected to contain essential information on the sound track, and some audiences are inclined to miss a point if it is made purely visually. This did not favour our predominantly visual style.

But a film which triumphantly exploited this style was shown at the Academy of Motion Picture Arts and Sciences on my next trip to Hollywood. It was called *The Emigrants* and was directed by Jan Troell...he wrote it, edited it, directed it and even operated the camera in order to achieve precisely the setups he wanted. It was a traumatic experience for me – Troell achieved almost everything I had hoped we would do in *Comrade Jacob*. It was a gigantic epic (I saw a version lasting only half the full six hours) and it was resolutely slow, and uncompromising. Despite its size, it was composed of the minutiae of careful observation and the direction of tiny details.

Although shot in colour, the film was the apotheosis of the 'newsreel' style of reconstruction which we had helped to pioneer with *IHH*, which had been carried on by the Peter Watkins films and which had reached a climax with Pontecorvo's *Battle of Algiers*. Had I not seen Troell's film, *Winstanley* would almost certainly have been made in that style. But now I was both elated and depressed. Film historian David Shepard, who saw it with me, said 'That's the greatest film I've seen since *Intolerance*.' And what happened to the greatest film since *Intolerance*? It was well received in America. But it was shown at one theatre in London, and grossed some pathetic figure like £300. When Virginia saw it, there were two other people in the cinema. The distributors – Warner Bros – withdrew it and did nothing else, ignoring completely the sequel, *The New Land*. And when the Other Cinema asked for *The Emigrants* to show during the run of *Winstanley*, Warners said the print was damaged and refused to supply it. I suggested they took it, damage and all, and that they explained their problems to the audience. Warners then said the print was unprojectable. When the Other Cinema persisted, Warners said they couldn't find it. It had been thrown away. Thus did a high-powered and prosperous distributor care for one of the more difficult films among its offerings.

Two days after seeing *The Emigrants*, a telegram arrived at the American Film Institute addressed to me. It read:
'COME HOME. ALL YOUR PROBLEMS HAVE JUST BEGUN. MAMOUN.'

Chapter Six

The BFI Production Board had been divided about the script. The upshot was that we got the money (Mamoun having persuaded the government greatly to increase their grant) provided we didn't shoot the script as submitted! Fortunately, we had explained that David Caute's condition in assigning us the rights was that he should write the script; he agreed to do so for a nominal sum, giving us the rights for as little as possible, in return for an equal share with us of any possible profits. We were now in March of 1972; the BFI wanted us to start shooting in the summer, and to have the picture cut and dry by the end of the financial year.

David Caute agreed to write the script rapidly. We assembled at his house for a script conference, which went well. He also agreed that the picture should be primarily visual and that the dialogue should be kept to the minimum. We gave him our old script, and listed the scenes in it we were very fond of. And in our first memo, dated 28 March 1972, we added a paragraph about voice-over; at this point we felt that sync shooting would be very difficult on our location – thanks to cars and aeroplanes – and also very expensive, as we would require a sound crew. We wanted to shoot the picture silent, as much as possible, involving sync equipment only for essential dialogue scenes and carrying the rest with commentary. We also anticipated, incorrectly as it turned out, that music would be used a great deal.

'You can play with the elements, because we plan to have a wind machine, and, if necessary, equipment for rain.' How comically that reads now, after we endured so many gales!

That weekend, Andrew and I went down to Larchfield and searched the immediate area for locations – we particularly needed a village. We visited the new Open Museum at Singleton, near Chichester, which was enthralling; a vast meadow on the slopes of a hill, edged by a wood. In this meadow had been erected ancient buildings scheduled for demolition elsewhere, and acquired by the museum, dismantled and re-erected precisely as they would have looked when they were new. There was a fifteenth-century farmhouse, a fourteenth-century cottage and some charcoal burners' huts in the wood. The museum authorities thought we might be able to film there, and this gave us great encouragement.

We shot some 16mm tests at the Devil's Jumps – both colour and black and white – on my Bell and Howell 70DR camera. We had not yet worked out a budget, but we were convinced that the film had to be shot as economically as possible, and that meant 16mm. As I began filming one long shot, I heard the sound of horses' hooves, and a sizeable group of riders cantered through the scene. Useful to know there were so many horses available locally… The tests were humdrum, neither impressive visually nor especially bad. Just dull.

Andrew was convinced that for each area of historical research we needed a consultant. One of the most important of these would be the agricultural adviser, and so we drove to Reading to the Museum of Rural Crafts. The keeper, Andrew Jewell, was adamant that they could offer no help of a practical nature (they were too understaffed) but he made some suggestions, the best being a farm worker called Bill Petch, who came in frequently to carry out research. 'We do not know much of this period,' Andrew Jewell said, discouragingly. He recommended volume IV of the *Agrarian History of Britain*, talked of the kind of cattle we should have, and described the geological change of Bagshot Heath. 'Fascinating,' I wrote in my diary, 'but we'll never get everything done by the summer!'

Andrew Jewell passed us to Ted Collins, who talked in even greater detail about such things as the 'low yield' of 1649, the fact that the rabbit population was not very high and how much land was needed to maintain a commune of 50 people (30 acres). Andrew involved him as consultant, and he drew up a careful dossier on harvesting and land clearance procedures, livestock of the time, and later he inspected our location to ensure the plant life was correct. He warned us that fir trees were not planted on the heath until 1776, and we had an appalling time trying to avoid them. (And, I must confess, one or two small ones fell victim to our cameraman's sense of composition.)

David Robinson, film critic of the *Times*, lived in Coggeshall, Essex, a town recommended by Andrew Jewell for its superb old buildings. (Pasolini used it extensively for his *Canterbury Tales*, but left in the odd television aerial.) David, whom I had known since the 1950s, also had some old farm carts, but confessed that he had let Peter Collinson blow them up for his war film *Long Day's Dying*.

Andrew Jewell also recommended a visit to the Rev. Philip Wright, in Essex. Major the Rev. Philip Wright, MBE had written a number of books on agricultural history, and his title suggested an exceedingly crusty Colonel Blimp. When we arrived, he met us with a vast, bundly dog, He did look a little like a German general, but his personality was the opposite of what we'd expected. His voice was soft, with a Suffolk burr, and he was eager to help, and so enthusiastic that one subject leaped over another in his conversation. He was highly amused that we'd come by taxi. 'Such opulence, these film people!'

Rev. Philip Wright with breast plough

Turned out he thought we'd taken the taxi all the way from London rather than from nearby Chelmsford station.

He took us out to the three wooden huts in which he kept his superb collection of agricultural implements. An old cob and a donkey grazed in the field at the back. When I aimed my camera at his collection of model windmills, he said: 'But they're not arranged for a photograph!'

We wanted a clergyman as adviser as well as to play Parson Platt, and Philip Wright would have been ideal. I asked him if he knew any parson in the Surrey area. 'Oh, I wish I could do it,' he said. 'But you're so far away…'

A few months later, he allowed us to ransack his collection. He was so generous as we carried off his precious implements, some of which were unique, that I felt guilty for an hour afterwards. I hoped fervently none would be broken or lost, but on a film, accidents were inevitable. Philip Wright was the son of a farmer who had been brought up in Suffolk during the First World War. He had a passion for the land, and proved a valuable consultant. One little detail I recall was an ancient rhyme he led us, recited as the seed was scattered: 'One to rot, one to grow – one for the parson and one for the crow.'

This was the honeymoon period of the film – the period when one's illusions were intact, and there had been no real difference of opinion. Your friends said: 'How's the picture going?' with genuine curiosity, instead of avoiding your eye because they've seen it.

Andrew was shouldering most of the burden of pre-production. He acted as production manager, art director, costume designer, property man, set builder, unit driver and historical researcher. He complained that he had far too little time to devote to his current book, a detailed study of German uniforms, the advance for which would enable him to work on the film. I was using a similar device – an advance from an American publisher – but we both found it difficult to concentrate on the chore of writing when there was so much to be done on the film.

Andrew's eagle eye spotted ancient objects visible to no one else. I remember him speeding along a hedge-lined road. I was supposed to be keeping a watch for something or other, but he always proved the observant one. Suddenly, the car screeched to a halt, and noisily backed. He had spotted a shape through a small hole in the hedge, and his mind had fitted that shape into a complete pattern; an ancient farm wagon was lurking behind the hedge. The discovery of one relevant object invariably led to another, and these searches were highly rewarding. One farmyard, far off the beaten track, was littered with the kind of debris we needed for set-dressing and the farmer was only too delighted to get rid of it. Andrew piled up the harness, the yokes and the implements he wanted. Milkmaid's yokes, in fashionable antique shops, sold at that time for £7. Andrew was able to buy the entire heap for £5.

We considered making the film in Wales. We knew we had already found the ideal hill and heath land in Surrey, but we needed more than that. New Radnor had proved an ideal base for *IHH*, thanks to Dick and Pauline Jobson (Dick being the local doctor) and the number of sixteenth- and seventeenth-century buildings in the area was astonishing. Within easy driving distance, we found vast unspoilt parkland at Bredwardine, with huge oak trees, and a beautiful church at Monington with an ideal interior including box pews, and at a place called Malhollam we found (again thanks to Andrew's eagle eye) a derelict schoolhouse and seventeenth-century farm buildings. One of the buildings was occupied, but the owner was such a charming individual that we seriously contemplated using the place for our village. Extra walls were needed and various adaptations, but if we made the film in Wales, we'd be lucky to find anywhere better.

Once we were fully immersed in the seventeenth century, a new world opened up. From a state of resignation that so little evidence remained, we turned to a state of amazement. The journey back from Wales took all day as we crawled from one ancient church to another, from the village of Luntley with its Tudor dovecote, to the town of Weobley, where there were so many black and white timbered buildings that one was equipped with a mock-Tudor birdbath!

At Tewkesbury, we talked to Brigadier Peter Young, wartime commando leader, and now organiser of the Sealed Knot. With a membership close to 2,000, the Sealed Knot specialised in restaging the battles of the Civil War, and we hoped to enlist their support for our battle scene. Peter Young was also a military historian, and Andrew enlisted him as a consultant; we took away sheafs of notes on equipment for troopers, horses, pikemen and musketeers. The following weekend we watched a Sealed Knot battle at Hereford. The scale of it was impressive, but Andrew was dismayed by the costumes; papier-mâché helmets and cloaks of old curtaining were adequate for this kind of pageantry, they might even pass the scrutiny of the lens, but they would never reach his exacting standards. (As Mark Dineley, our old patron from *IHH*, put it: 'There isn't a dustbin lid in England they haven't used.')

The battle was slow, but when the action started, it was fierce. Following one charge, a gunner was struck on the knee by a passing horse. Following another, a man was half-strangled when two pikes lifted him off the ground by the throat. The evening offered further realism; the Sealed Knot took over the town.

The British Army has always had a reputation for hell-raising in garrison towns, and the Sealed Knot provided a spirited imitation. Virginia and I were walking down a side street when a drunken Sealed Knot member knocked the hat off a local resident. A row ensured, culminating in the hallucinatory sight of a man in the costume of the New Model Army kicking the hell out of the poor local. We shot across the road, wondering how on earth we were going to intervene without having our own heads kicked in, when two policemen miraculously appeared and dragged the Roundhead off. The local was shaken but able to walk away. I should like to have seen the reaction that night in the police cells, when the Roundhead arrived. They were probably full of Cavaliers.

During the weekend, we were lucky enough to cast one of the most important parts. Andrew spotted a tall, powerfully built man in Sealed Knot costume crossing the park. 'He'd make a good Everard,' he said. Andrew always muddled Everard, the crazy preacher, with Haydon, the sober soldier. But I took a picture of him anyway. He was carrying a baby, and was accompanied by his wife. The whole family was ideal. Terry Higgins had been a locomotive fireman in the days of steam, and he now worked at a factory in Milton Keynes. He was willing to take part when the picture got going, and so was his wife Muriel. 'And so are you, Don,' he said to his baby.

David Caute suggested we went to his house to discuss the script. He produced one idea, which we thought excellent: 'Wherever you go, odd characters pop out from hedgerows with pamphlets – their solution to the problems of the world.' He called them Merchants of Paradise.

We told him of our progress in location hunting, and produced photographs. When he caught sight of some blowups Andrew had made of a possible village, with cars parked in it, he said: 'You can shoot me down over this, but there is one idea I've had I'd like to put to you.'

'I know,' I joked. 'You want to do it in modern dress.'

'You've got your foot in the door,' he said. And he described an opening in which we see the town as it was in 1972. A woman comes out of a shop with a lot of packages and puts then in the back of her car. Freeze – suddenly it's Mrs Drake in 1649. We return – see a film unit in action. And so the other characters are introduced. Then we go to the burning of the hill.

It struck me as the sort of thing Godard might do. (I did not like Godard.) David Caute said that audiences were becoming increasingly aware of the confidence trick played on them in films – 'All we're trying to do is to hoodwink people that they are seeing something of the seventeenth century. They know they're being hoodwinked. We want them to be aware that we are aware. And we want it to be relevant to

Terry Higgins in Sealed Knot costume, Hereford – as we first saw him

The Higgins family in the film

Terry Higgins, pikeman

today.' Everyone who watches a film about a historical incident, he said, is virtuous. Thus they will all be on the side of the Diggers against the propertied classes. He quoted Kopit's *Indians* which the Americans enjoyed without relating it to Vietnam.

We said that his opening, in our opinion, provided no additional relevance. It would make it all the more difficult for us to recreate the period convincingly afterwards. We mentioned *The Go Between*, and how impressed we had been by it, but how the modern flashes had fractured the flow. He said that he wouldn't include it in the script; he would hold it back until we had done the major shooting. Then perhaps we would try it.

He cheered us immensely by saying that only ten percent of the film was sync dialogue. The rest was voice-over. But we misunderstood each other. That afternoon, I ran him some films. I chose the Robert Youngson *Noah's Ark* reissue, a 1929 part-talkie, which had had all its dialogue removed by Youngson in the 1950s, and a commentary substituted. It was the most extreme example of voice-over I could think of, which demonstrated perfectly the strengths and perils of such an approach. But Caute thought it irrelevant – he said there was a great difference between narrative voice and dialogue. I then realised what he meant. He had constructed the film around people listening, and around voices not connected with the face on the screen. We discussed this problem for a long time. He was not in favour of narration. I mentioned Kubrick's *Clockwork Orange* as an example, and he said the narration in that case had been by the main character. 'Could we not have Gerrard Winstanley?' Caute thought it would be 'too intricate' but agreed to write ten sample pages. For the moment, we left the problem there. 'It may even work,' I noted. 'Who knows?'

Unexpectedly, the BFI decided that this was the moment for a publicity leak. Kenneth Pearson wrote a paragraph in the arts section of the *Sunday Times*. It was a short paragraph, but it managed to cause a great deal of damage. The intention was innocent and helpful. But either Pearson was supplied with the wrong information or he got it wrong himself.

'The Film Production Board of the British Film Institute is about to back a full-length feature picture. It's the first move in its new policy under board director Mamoun Hassan. The film, *The Diggers*, to be directed by Kevin Brownlow, tells the story of a group of seventeenth-century revolutionaries who were finally overwhelmed by the revolution. It's a happy ending for Brownlow. For six years he has touted this tale round Wardour Street. This incident makes Mamoun's main point for him: 'We are not in competition with the industry,' he says. 'We want directors to have tried the traditional sources first.' The film, also financed by the Vivien Leigh Memorial Fund, will take Brownlow a year to make. He needs the four seasons.' (*Sunday Times*, 21 May 1972)

The fact that the title was wrong was neither here nor there, but the announcement left out both David Caute and Andrew Mollo. It gives me no joy, as someone who endlessly campaigns for the film to be recognised as a collaborative art, to be singled out by journalists. It happened again and again – and it still happens. My name was better known, in film circles, and anyway Andrew shunned publicity. On this occasion, the very first public announcement, both victims were furious. I called Mamoun, but he denied responsibility, and said that Pearson had spelled his name 'Mahmoud Hasan'. Caute's agent, Elaine Greene, was herself angry about the piece – particularly upset that we 'touted it round for six years' when we only had an option for six months. I asked Mamoun to leave future publicity to us, but we only had one more ordeal: the press conference to mark the retirement of Sir Michael Balcon as chairman of the Production Board, and to introduce Michael Relph as his successor.

The occasion was a great success, thanks to *My Childhood*, which won enthusiastic praise; I always felt proud to work for an organisation which could produce that picture. Andrew, David Caute and I were interviewed both by the *Times* and the *Guardian*. The *Guardian* (5 July 1972) was straightforward enough; their reporter, Peter Waymark, turned out to have been an old school friend of mine!

He wrote that the BFI had received a substantial increase in its government grant – £40,000 – which would be used to stimulate new talent in British cinema, by helping young directors to set up their films. He was careful to include all three names.

The *Times* reporter was equally careful. He was Stuart Weir, who had been immensely helpful to us in the past and who, we were sorry to hear, was leaving journalism. He wrote an amusing piece, commenting on our odd method of casting people in the street. It was perfectly true, as he related, that I had spotted an ideal Parson Platt on an underground train, and had pursued him along the platform at Piccadilly Circus, only to discover that he was Archdeacon Youens, Chaplain-General to the Army!

'Janet Watts, of the *Guardian*'s Miscellany column, asked for an interview at yesterday's BFI reception and found herself signed up for her "seventeenth-century look". David Caute: "It doesn't mean you look 300 years old."' (Times, 5 July 1972)

That was all it needed. Equity got on to Mamoun the following day, and berated him for permitting such a casting method.

At least we could continue to select our consultants without being impeded. Andrew arranged for a meeting with Madeleine Ginsberg, head of the textile department at the Victoria and Albert Museum. Mrs Ginsberg had a very forthright manner. We chatted pleasantly and helpfully over tea in the V&A canteen until, after a silence, she came out with: 'I am a good and loyal worker, but I work a damn sight better if I'm paid.' There was another silence. We weren't used to this. We depended upon English reticence about money to tide us over the awkward moments. We couldn't afford to pay anyone. But Andrew realised that to secure the best consultants it was essential to pay them. Andrew said he had been turning the matter over; could she give a figure? 'No,' she said. 'That's not fair.' Andrew laughed, 'Don't slam your fist on the table and walk away, but how about £50 plus £5 daily rate?'

'No,' she said. 'That's not on. I'm sorry, I'd like to help, but I feel strongly about this from a professional point of view.'

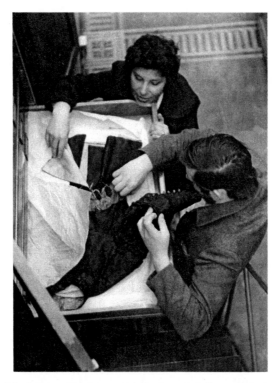

Madeleine Ginsberg with Andrew Mollo at V & A
with original 17th century costume

I felt like delivering a short lecture on Winstanley's ideas, but I left money matters to Andrew. He cannily changed tactics: 'Which is more important to you – to be associated with this project for comparatively little money, or to get properly paid?'

'That,' she said, 'is not a fair question.'

Eventually, a fee was settled, but after the meeting, walking along Knightsbridge, I felt we were going to run into this situation with everyone. 'I'm amazed,' I said, 'that the group of people who could most easily work for nothing – since they are getting paid anyway – demand so much.'

'The world has changed in the last ten years,' replied Andrew. 'Ten years ago, these consultants were dotted around the country. They couldn't get their books published, and no one took any notice of them. Now they are in demand – from publishers, salesrooms, exhibitions – and they have become very commercial.'

And he said he was delighted to have secured the consultants he wanted for a total of £250. Not all wanted payment, of course, but he was convinced that the outlay would save us money in the end.

Mrs Ginsberg turned out to be a very jolly lady, with a caustic wit. She showed us around the V&A's collection of original seventeenth-century costumes, and exuded enthusiasm. Buildings and artefacts can indicate the look of a period, but clothes bring you as close to the human being as you can get. Once the patterns had been copied with precision, and once the costumes had been recreated exactly as they were once worn, hand-stitching and all, the effect when you first saw them on an actor could make you gasp.

Mrs Ginsberg introduced us to Wimbledon College of Art, and the head of their School of Theatre, Michael Pope, agreed that his students could make the costumes for the film as a special project. Andrew would provide the materials, they would do the work. The arrangement sounded ideal.

One consultant approached us, instead of the other way round. Thanks to the *Times* article, I received a letter forwarded from the BFI from Marina Lewycka. She said she was writing a thesis on Winstanley, that she had the kind of understanding of seventeenth-century dialogue that would make her very useful on the film. 'In short,' she said, 'you need me!' The more assertive the approach, the cooler it tends to make me. But Marina was an exceptional person. She looked extremely English, her grave, beautiful features were straight out of a painting, but she had been born in Germany of Ukrainian parents, and although she had no trace of an accent, she had yet to acquire British citizenship. (She has since written the amazingly successful novel *A Short History of the Tractor in Ukrainian*.)

The fact that Marina knew so much about Winstanley made me realise that I knew so little. She referred frequently to Christopher Hill, and singled him out as the only historian who bothered to deal with the history of ordinary people. The others wrote of monarchs and grandees. Winstanley was one of the outstanding figures of his time and it was essential that a film about him be accurate historically, and not fiction-alised. I explained how devoted to the cause of authenticity we were, and she said it wasn't enough to get the costumes and the weapons right...The dialogue had to be correct, and the attitudes behind it. 'No one will understand the seventeenth-century dialogue if we deliver it straight,' I protested.

'People understand Shakespeare,' she said.

A few days later, I came upon a dismissive review of a new book by Christopher Hill, *The World Turned Upside Down*. The review, in the *Sunday Telegraph*, was written by right-wing historian A.L. Rowse:

'It is a pity that he spends so much time in investigating Levellers and Ranters, Antinomians and Grindletonians – for what is the value of what such people thought? What is the intellectual value, especially for students, of studying nonsense? Their lunatic theories would never have worked, either economically or politically. No taxes, no laws, and "all things to be governed by love" indeed! – no sense of humour, for they all fell out with each other like mad. The Levellers' attempt to dig up St George's Hill and hold the land in common melted away like snow in June. Their attempt to democratise the Army and run it from the bottom upwards lasted only a week or two.

'What would Communist Russia say to such lunacy? Exactly what a practical man like Oliver Cromwell said and did – used them for a

Andrew Mollo and Marina Lewycka

moment and then swept them aside with the remark "of whom there is no fear." A whiff of grapeshot at Burford settled their hash.' (*Sunday Telegraph*, 25 Jun 1972)

I can't imagine why I didn't rush out and buy Hill's book, but Marina had lent me volumes on the Puritan revolution, earlier works by Christopher Hill, and a gigantic compendium of the writings of Gerrard Winstanley, by an American called Sabine, published in 1940. While I tackled these books, Virginia looked through the 1906 reprint by Berens, *The Digger Movement*, and kept reading bits out – and now the phrases echoed with sanity and compassion.

David Caute delivered the first part of the script, a sample ten pages, and we found it quite cinematic, and an exhilarating opening, although I felt uncertain about the dialogue; however, we gave him our approval. 'After 12 years away from the seventeenth century', said Caute, 'it's a bit of heaven to get back inside.'

I borrowed a print of *The Parson's Widow* from the Swedish Film Institute, a 1920 film shot in Norway at a museum of old buildings. It was directed by Carl Dreyer and the best recreation of the seventeenth century I had ever seen. David Caute came to see it and he said it was much more relevant than the other films I'd shown him.

It made me acutely aware of our one great omission so far: we had no cameraman. Chris Menges was working with Ken Loach. Peter Suschitzky, who had photographed *IHH*, was working. I tried Dick Bush, who had been given his break by Tony Richardson on *Laughter In The Dark*. Dick Bush had been with the BBC for years. He told me the greatest fun he had ever had on a picture was when he shot *Culloden* for Peter Watkins. He would love to do something like that again. I thought we had him – but it turned out he was going to have a busy summer.

Mamoun felt that one contribution the Production Board could make was in the field of new technicians; we should not hire a cameraman who was already active in features. But, as we had done with Peter Suschitzky, we should take on someone who was obviously competent, but had yet to make it. 'The Production Board,' he said, 'should train technicians.'

I thought hard of hopeful young cameramen, and by one of those coincidences that characterised the whole picture, I received a phone call from Ernest Vincze. He reminded me that he had been Chris

Menges's assistant when we did the tests, that he was fascinated by the story, and he was offering his services free. That was an offer I could hardly refuse. But cinematography was one of my passions, and I was determined that whatever else the film might lack, it would not be outstanding photography. Ernie showed me some of his television work. I can say now what I daren't say then; Ernie's work was above average for television, but it didn't hit me between the eyes. I felt his lighting was rather like that of *A Man for all Seasons* – very glossy and professional, but a trifle artificial. What impressed me was his attitude.

A short talk with Ernie was enough to convince me that we should have him, and Andrew agreed. We were still undecided about whether to shoot in black and white or colour; we dug out the old tests and ran them at the National Film Theatre. Our old tests were gorgeous. I was certain that nothing would be better for the picture than 35mm black and white. Mamoun and I had an argument about it which put me back to square one. The only thing to do was to make a kind of chart of the pros and cons of 16mm and 35mm, of colour and black and white, as much for my own benefit as for everyone else's.

Andrew Mollo, Marina Lewycka, Barry Male & Ernie Vincze

'There is no doubt,' I wrote, 'that under ideal circumstances this picture should be made in 35mm colour. It would look absolutely beautiful. But it is simply not possible.' I listed the reasons: budget (we would need £15,000 extra) and the fact that while we might get an investment over and above the BFI budget, the BFI would not accept it. They were under pressure from the unions; because a number of films wanted to put up very small amounts in order to reap the huge benefits that they felt were at the other end. Therefore, the BFI had undertaken to place a complete moratorium on co-productions for two years.

Andrew wanted colour. He was having the costumes made in their original shades, and he could see in his mind's eye the effect of these soft, oatmeal browns against the forest greens. I agreed that we could still do it in colour, via Super 16 Eastmancolor. This could be blown up and was fairly fast (ASA 64). 'However, it is hard to get away from a kind of colour with which one can create no sense of period. It is rather garish, very much of now, because Eastmancolor 16 is so new. The subtle oatmeal browns you mentioned would come out Hovis colour.' (This situation changed with the arrival of Eastmancolor 7247, with its high resolution and sensitive range).

Ernie was in favour of Super 16. He said that with his special filter, he could provide that warm softness we were anxious for. But Mamoun said that the greatest outlet for BFI films would be in the 35mm market. Why not shoot in 35mm black and white? 'One can obtain absolutely superb results with it,' I wrote, 'without that terrible deadness of 16mm black and white. However, since we are faced with a basic question, crucial to the stylistic success of the film, I will detail the pros and cons'.

Finally, I put forward the argument subjectively: 'What is the point of getting every fork and spoon correct if the camera is going to fuzz the image to the degree that they might as well have come from Woolworths? When this film is finished, colour will be so universal that black and white will be a positive advantage. Naturally, we will lose something – the russet leaves in autumn…the blue smoke curling into the red evening sky…but we will also lose the infuriating prettiness that marred the work of Bo Widerberg, and the films about revolution that show workers apparently living in idyllic country conditions that any stockbroker would throw up his job to share. The points you mentioned in favour of colour – the beauty of the countryside – are the very points that killed the effectiveness of *Adalen 31* and *Joe Hill*. Black and white is not colourless. It can be very colourful. Its rich tones suggest the full spectrum. Would Eisenstein have looked better in colour? (PS Colour = Royalist. B and W = Puritan!)'.

I must admit that when the picture was over, I hoped we could afford to print it on colour stock and tint it, in silent film style. (And the idea crossed my mind of doing the whole thing without sound of any sort except for a full orchestral track!) For the sake of cheapness, we thought up a manoeuvre which would have driven us crazy: all the long shots would be done in 35mm, and all the closeups in 16mm. That we could even have considered it shows how long it had been since we had worked in film. For it would have meant dragging two cameras up and down the hill. And since one of Andrew's first ideas for the visual approach had been 'extreme long shot and extreme closeup', we would have become terribly muddled in trying to cover ourselves.

The black and white dilemma was sharpened when I met Leni Riefenstahl, the great director of *Triumph of the Will* and *Olympia*. She was very sympathetic, for her first directorial effort, *The Blue Light*, had been made 'to repopularise black and white' as the first wave of colour talkies appeared. She wanted the highest possible contrast, and no suitable stock was available. So she had special batches made up – 'it was the nearest thing to infra-red' – and this special stock was called 'R' for Riefenstahl. The softness she achieved in some scenes was inspired by the Lillian Gish films, and she was delighted to see that I had the famous LG lens, specially developed by cameraman Henrik Sartov to photograph Miss Gish. (Unfortunately, Ernie could not adapt the lens for an Arriflex without wrecking it, so we never used it.)

David Samuelson, one of the brothers who own the vast equipment corporation, was a member of the Production Board, and he told me that Super 16 for the kind of film we had in mind was inadequate. The advantage of Super 16, or even regular 16, for us was that Ernie had his own camera. But David Samuelson was convinced his company could give us a deal which would make it worth our while shooting on 35mm. Economics are far greater manipulators of creativity than aesthetic judgment. We had a meeting with David and Michael Samuelson, and the first thing they asked us was how long we wanted the gear for.

We had intended to shoot the picture over the usual eight-week schedule. But it was now abundantly clear that we needed the seasons – we needed to grow our own crops and to see their growth, culminating in the harvest. The seasons, and the weather, played a far more important part in the lives of seventeenth-century people than they do now. So we answered the Samuelsons' question by saying we needed one camera and ancillary equipment for an entire year. Blimps and zoom lenses and other equipment could be borrowed as and when required. It was a difficult meeting, but we got a deal wrapped up; Samuelson's would give us a retired Arriflex B and we could have it and the equipment, subject to availability, for £1,000.

The problem had been solved. *Comrade Jacob* would be made on 35mm black and white, except for the battle scene, which would consume so much stock it would be sensible to shoot it on 16mm. Now all we needed to worry about was the script.

Chapter Seven

It is perfectly clear now that we should never have had a script at all. For it was an insult to an outstanding writer to commission a script, to discuss it and criticise it and finally to accept it – and even begin shooting it – when the final film bore so little relation to what he had written. This would have happened whoever wrote the script, and whatever kind of document he produced. For we are the kind of film-makers who use the script as a spur rather than as a text. But that is no comfort to the writer, particularly when he is depending upon it establishing him as a scriptwriter.

Had I been the writer, I would have been mortally offended by such behaviour. I should undoubtedly have raised a terrible emotional scene. David Caute was annoyed with us, and he probably still is, and all I can say by way of explanation is that he behaved with immense generosity and we took advantage of it.

An artist can only work instinctively. We had forgotten this predilection of ours for abandoning the script, since the last film had been written by us. That script, too, bore little relation to the final result. Our method of filmmaking was a kind of patient consolidation; as we learned, so we moulded the material. And being as ruthless, in a way, as the producers we despised, we accepted the script because we knew it was the only way to get the film made. Nonetheless, some of the best lines in the film were written by David Caute and he gave us some of the best scenes. Without the book, we would never have heard of Winstanley. Without the script, we could never have made the film.

The complete first draft we collected from Caute, after some hilarity over the title. He warned us that there were now some sex scenes in the script involving Platt, and he thought the title should be changed to *The Lustful Vicar* (a film currently showing in Charing Cross Road). Caute liked the title 'Comrade Jacob', but said that he had once considered 'Fire in the Bush'. 'But that's another Charing Cross Road title,' he said. (Collapse of Andrew.)

Caute had departed almost entirely from his book. He seemed to dislike it and to regard it as a youthful folly. His script took me by surprise and, like a difficult piece of music, I didn't know what to think of it for some time. On the way to the script conference, I managed to lose my notes (very interesting!) and when we got there I had to depend on memory.

We went through our combined list of points, and Caute seemed to agree. The sex-and-violence scenes he seemed wedded to; when we suggested a version of the script without such scenes, for diplomatic reasons (for showing to vicars!) he wanted his name removed.

The second draft came through three days later. Accompanying it was a note: 'I hope any further alterations can be restricted to a word here or there. I think there is a danger of trying to pack too much in. Novels always contain more than a film, or play, can properly accommodate. The proper literary basis for a film is a short story.' I returned a short list of requests for elaboration or excision and said: 'The script is very strong.'

Winstanley always claimed that his task was revealed to him in a trance. David Caute's imaginative montage was an outstanding piece of scriptwriting; the production problems were enormous, however, and eventually we discarded all the allegorical elements.

I read the new draft again and again. It was a strong script, but it belonged to a different world. Its very strength gave me nagging anxieties, for my instincts were to make the picture quieter. But creative work cannot be judged like machinery; it can never be 'right' or 'wrong'. It can only be a matter of opinion; very subjective opinion. And Andrew, a severe judge of scripts, as I knew to my cost, liked it.

I asked the girl who typed it, Sue Craig, to let me have her opinion. Whenever she had typed material for me, and I had asked her what she thought, she never hid behind a polite façade, but let me have it, in Mollo style, between the eyes.

'When I first typed it, I was quite impressed. I found it powerful, and the relevance to today strong enough to dispense with the alternative ending (David Caute had written a modern ending along the lines of his modern opening). On second reading, however, I didn't like it as much. I thought the characters lacked depth, but really I am not sure how intentional that was. It's very hard for me to visualise a film in which most of the dialogue is off-screen, and to understand the reasons for doing that. If it's to give distance to the characters, then it's quite justifiable that they should sometimes appear flat and two-dimensional. But I did think that they were perhaps too stereotyped.'

Nick Rowling and Terry Higgins

Marina Lewycka thought it was good; she objected to the treatment of Mrs Platt and she drew attention to some inauthentic dialogue. She said that apart from little differences of style – i.e. obliged and obleeged – there was no distinction in accent between the gentry and the lower classes. Sir Walter Raleigh spoke with a broad Devonshire dialect.

Apart from Mrs Platt, her one objection to the script was a scene in which Winstanley lost his temper with Platt. 'The most moving thing about Winstanley for me is his reasonableness,' she said. 'He felt that by appealing to reason, he could convert anybody without the need for force.'

Marina's boyfriend was Nick Rowling, who was to play a role in the film, as well as becoming one of its consultants. He was an expert in architectural history; although he was a teacher, he looked like a student in a revolutionary picture. Well-built and handsome, wearing spectacles, he combined enthusiasm and knowledge with a sense of humour. One of the first stories he told us we shot for the film, but it proved to be a cutting room casualty. He used it as an example of the lack of communication at that period. Before Marston Moor, a King's Messenger discovered a peasant hoeing. 'Get away, man, get away! King and Parliament are doing battle!'

'Oh,' said the peasant. 'Don't they get on then?'

Nick Rowling saved us weeks of unnecessary work by taking us to the Royal Commission for Historic Monuments, where photographs are preserved of every old building in the British Isles. Pictures taken at the turn of the century revealed familiar black and white Tudor buildings in a town like Weobley to have been completely covered with stucco. We guessed that this was the way they were originally, but Nick explained that in the eighteenth century, anything old was hastily modernised with Georgian facades, or by obscuring the timbers with stucco. It wasn't until authoress Marie Corelli (*The Sorrows of Satan*) began a campaign to reveal the Elizabethan timbers in Stratford-upon-Avon, in the early 1900s, that the impressive frames came to light. Many ancient timbers are obscured by plaster to this day.

Nick escorted us on a location trip, based on a study of photographs of Kent. Andrew spotted a timber yard in the village of Loose, and in that yard he saw some ancient timbers. He and Nick counted four or five ancient houses lying there. A boy scrambled into the yard and proudly told us that his dad had torn the buildings down. Nick, not a tactful person, told him that his dad was someone he didn't want to meet. The boy misunderstood and raced for his dad.

He proved to be an ideal Digger, bushy black beard, powerfully built, with an authentic Kentish accent (the basis for Cockney), a rough, tough man who suddenly waxed eloquent as he talked about reconstruction. He explained he was using the timbers to restore his 400-year-old house. Having studied all types of Kent chimney, he was using correct Tudor bricks, two inches thick. He amazed Andrew and Nick, who said later that he knew far more about the subject than they did. I was baffled by all the technical terms, but impressed by the man – especially when he demonstrated how to split a log in four with one blow. His name was Roy Hood, and he explained how the council had laid the cobbles around his house. Awful, he said. He had pictures taken to show the proper way of laying cobbles, while he was laying a section correctly. The council ordered him to take them up. He managed to defeat that move, and now he had persuaded the council to lay them properly. I tried hard to persuade Roy Hood and his family to take part in the film, but they were too busy. They remain in my mind, however, as a symbol for the astonishing enterprise that existed, all over the country, unpublicised and largely self-financed, and which we were lucky enough to experience through the film.

One of the spectacular achievements of this pre-production period was the demolition of an Essex barn and its rebuilding at Larchfield. I wasn't involved in this, because a day or so before Andrew and Nick set off, I was seized with a violent pain in my back – I had collapsed, appropriately enough, right outside the entrance to the British Film Institute – and was laid up. In retrospect, I am relieved I missed it. The barn was thatched, and in order to demolish it, Andrew, Nick and their team disturbed a colony of fleas. The way they described it was pure Laurel and Hardy. Having seen the barn, an open affair, the thatched roof supported by massive ship's timbers, I was convinced that the job of demolishing it was hard enough – the idea of transporting the timbers to Larchfield, well nigh impossible. To assist Andrew and Nick, Miles Halliwell produced some schoolboys, but with the manpower available, the job was the equivalent of transporting the stones to Stonehenge. In two days, the timbers, numbered and photographed, had been driven to Larchfield, ready to be converted into Winstanley's barn. And by using primitive technology, and a lot of sweat, the timbers were hauled into position, and a thatcher rethatched the roof. By that time, I was well enough to tack a few weatherboards to the side, and feel involved again.

Larchfield, under strict conditions, had been offered to Andrew by his father as our base, and so the idea of shooting in Wales was abandoned. Driving through hundreds of miles of England, we found a great many seventeenth-century buildings, but they had passed through what we rapidly learned was the great Age of Titivation – and most of them resembled Ye Olde Tea Shoppes with their spotless white walls and blackened timbers.

Larchfield's wood became our back lot where the commune would be built, protected from the public gaze by a screen of trees. And once the decision to shoot in Surrey was made (Larchfield was between Churt and Tilford), a surprising series of people turned up…a black-smith, overjoyed at the idea of reproducing such old implements as the breast plough…volunteer labour from Frensham Heights School ('one of them turned up with a hawk', Andrew told me)…a mushroom farmer

Edgar and John Stokes help to dismantle barn in Essex

Reassembled it becomes Winstanley's house

who gave us a field at the foot of our hill for nothing, so that we could grow our own crops…and a stable with plenty of horses.

But when it came to renting the correct type of saddle, we found only one man had them – George Mossman, near Dunstable, Beds. He was pleasant but intractable. He could not have cared less about our financial problems; he was in the business of hiring horses, and we couldn't have the saddles without the horses. The same applied to coaches and wagons. This was tragic. His farm was littered with old carts which would have been ideal; he even had some rare breeds of cattle and sheep. The saddles had been made up for *Anne of a Thousand Days*, and he had only six of them. Unfortunately, horses cost £5 a day, plus transportation – £12 there and back. A coach with two horses was £20 a day, and the coachman – obligatory – was £15 a day. Plus transportation. But Mossman made one concession; if we could find a suitable part of his farm, we could shoot right there. He saw me looking longingly at his longhorn cows. '£3 a head,' he said.

Andrew visited Joe Henson of the Rare Breeds Survival Trust, in the Cotswolds, and won his support. He contacted Russell Robinson, Master of Armouries at the Tower of London, who offered the loan of original seventeenth-century armour for our battle scene. He arranged for a factory in Northampton to manufacture peasant shoes on the lines of the single model extant in Northampton Shoe Museum. The costumes were on schedule at Wimbledon College. To give them the aged, worn look, Andrew handed them out to the volunteers building the commune – an afternoon in the sweltering heat added 20 years to the age of a costume…With all this activity, it wasn't surprising that Andrew felt that we could start in the summer. Trouble was, it already was the summer, and we had a cast to collect.

Ernie Vincze with Arriflex B

Chapter Eight

Postponement was inevitable, for casting had not been rewarding. Three months of (part-time) pre-production had been consumed, we had ploughed through casting directories, and the photographs held by agents, yet we hadn't found the right people. Anxious not to displease Equity, we were casting in the approved manner – or trying to. But inevitably, we were falling back into our old ways. Casting in the street was much more successful. Once you get involved in a film of a certain period, your eye picks out perfect characters wherever you go. We found an ideal trooper, with long blond hair (we were grateful to current hairstyles) on a station platform, at Chelmsford. And Andrew found Captain Gladman on the Piccadilly line. Having recently studied the engravings of Jacques Callot, Andrew had a certain face in mind – and he saw that face on the tube. 'I'm convinced he thought I was trying to pick him up,' said Andrew. 'He was very tall, extraordinarily dressed with a vast lion medallion round his neck. He had long hair and a face right out of Callot.' He talked to this strange figure, who retreated to the other end of the carriage. Then he slowly returned, and told Andrew he was a former child actor, turned stunt man, and was now a newsreel cameraman for Australian television. He was very bewildered when I met him at Andrew's flat, but there was no doubt of his suitability. His name was Dawson France.

Dawson France as Gladman

Having worked for Woodfall, Andrew and I knew the value of Miriam Brickman, London's most imaginative casting director. We asked if she could help us on this film, warning her of our poverty-stricken budget. She agreed, or at least I thought she agreed, but apart from allowing us to look through her photographs, she never came through with any names. She explained later that she felt we would find the people we wanted outside the casting directories. And of course she was right. But if Equity had created the fuss we expected, such reasoning would not have helped us much. I'm afraid the appearance of a client without money in the exorbitantly-paid world of casting directors and agents disturbed their equilibrium. Miriam Brickman allowed us to use her office once or twice. But the other casting directors were not so generous.

Recommended to two other ladies, I paid a surprise visit, having mounted their endless stairs, and entered their office out of breath. I was startled at the hostility with which they greeted me, and I gradually realised they thought I was an actor. I explained why I had come, and their whole manner changed. They fell over themselves, produced a chair, smiled sweetly and said: 'I'm so sorry.' For a moment, I realised what poor, struggling actors have to go through.

We held some casting sessions. Some of the agents had been surprisingly brusque; as soon as they heard that we were paying the Equity minimum, they terminated the conversation. One went as far as to slam the phone down. At the first session, comparatively few of the actors called bothered to turn up. Those that did listened to our explanations about weekend shooting and minuscule budgets with equanimity. We were encouraged, for these actors were quite close to the kind of faces and voices we wanted.

We called another casting session. This time, I ran into further resistance; the agents were the same as before, representing different actors. 'What kind of thing is this?' snapped one. 'I mean, I sent one of my actors over to one of those minuscule budget things, and he didn't know what was going on. They were working at weekends or something like that.'

'I would have thought with the business in the state that it is, actors would be glad of a chance to supplement their income at weekends,' I said.

'Well, John Barron it was, had to come from the Isle of Wight – had to leave his family and so on. I must know these things so I can put it to the actor. A hundred pound a day actor getting offered ten pounds – is it one of those things?'

'You sound so suspicious!'

'I'm not being suspicious...I just want to know the position.'

'It is one of those things. In fact, it's the same one. But John Barron did not come.'

'Oh yes, it was cancelled. Well, it was John Barrett...'

'It's the same thing and we're paying as little as we can get away with.'

The agent had the grace to laugh, but he wouldn't send any more actors, so we cancelled the session.

Postponement of the whole picture was inevitable, not only because of the actor situation, but because Miles Halliwell was going on holiday, the students at Wimbledon were going on holiday, most firms from which we needed services were going on holiday – even the actors' agents were going on holiday. Mamoun talked to the BFI's Deputy Director and the *Comrade Jacob* schedule was postponed.

Andrew, who liked deadlines and furious activity, was absolutely fed up with the anti-climax, as was Ernie Vincze. Andrew was further depressed by the fact that Wimbledon had spent £286, and Michael Pope had been forced, through promotion, to opt out of the whole project.

The only alternative was to withdraw his materials and patterns, and the few costumes already made, and set to work himself. And this is where his wife Carmen saved the day. Being an expert seamstress, she took charge. Virginia was roped in, together with every friend we could muster, to sew voluminous seventeenth-century shirts. I was left with the menial task of sewing buttons on jackets – but I know how long that took, and I can only gasp at the time Carmen had to invest in those superb costumes. The grinding effort was well worth it, for virtually everyone who has seen the film comments on the costumes.

It was an immensely encouraging sight to see the costumes stacked on racks at Larchfield a few weeks later, ready for Ernie's tests. Carmen, Virginia, Miles, his wife Alison and an assortment of children, including the Mollos', Alexander and Nicholas, appeared in these tests. I should say 'cavorted' for there was little sense of purpose, just an amiable camaraderie, with the kids bundling about, the bonfire going, and a faint sense of the commune construction coming together. We shot short rolls of 16mm colour and 35mm black and white. Miles looked superb, but Andrew and Carmen felt his costume was all wrong, and they decided to remake it.

'What a fascinating experience,' I wrote in my diary for 24 August 1972, 'to see the tests. The colour is lifeless, dull and only comes alive in the murky closeups lit by the fire. But when the 35mm comes on we all nearly fall out of our seats. All except Ernie, who remains rather unhappy and wishes a) the Eastmancolor was graded and b) the Super 16 had been blown up. But Andrew and Carmen were completely won round. Giddy with delight, I insist Mamoun comes up and sees them – he doesn't think our discovery is so spectacular. He knew it all the time. And he chats about his problems. "I don't care about other people's pictures," he groaned in mock-seriousness. "What about MINE!"'

Chapter Nine

Research is immensely enjoyable, until you become ensnared in bureaucracy. We needed photographic reproductions of the title pages of Winstanley's pamphlets to make up as props. The pamphlets were preserved at Jesus College, Oxford – who were efficient and helpful – and the British Library, London, whose custodians behaved like guardians of the Berlin Wall. I went to apply for a reader's ticket, to be met with a notice 'No More Tickets. Too Many Readers.' Try again. Success. Reserve pamphlets by phone. 'Ready at 11am.' Arrive eagerly at Reserved Books. Suspicion aroused by notice 'Rapid Orders Take 3 Days'. Boy takes name, examines ticket, disappears. For hours. Returns, clutching 1814 volume on British Empire. Start again. Tackle forms.

'How do I look up reference numbers?'

'I don't actually know.'

Find out. Fill in seven forms. Deliver. Clerk peers over glasses. 'I'm glad you saw me. I'm afraid you've wasted your time.' Requires carbons. Do them again. Deliver, seething. No seats. Wait. Still no seats. Books arrive. No books without seats, says clerk. Come back tomorrow.

Next day, I can have two out of seven. Rest with readers Goldschmidt, Black, etc. I wonder at this sudden interest in Winstanley. Can I have the two? No. To examine those go to North Library. Get lost in corridors. Where is North Library? This is North Library. Examines list; returns, holding one volume. 'Reader's ticket, please.' I produce ticket. 'Wrong one. You must have TEMP written on it.'

'Could I just look at the title page?'

'I'm sorry, I can't let you touch the book without the right ticket.'

Explain that I have read pamphlet; now just need to look at title page to see if suitable for photograph.

'I don't make the rules. I suggest you see the supervisor.' To supervisor. Not there. Wait. Long wait. Finally, get supervisor's signature. Return; find seat. Receive volume. Open at title page. Ideal – except for the words MUSEUM BRITANNICUM stamped across it. March out, smouldering at the vandalism of archivists.

The privilege of examining an original Winstanley pamphlet was undoubtedly worth all that hassle, and as the film progressed I had to

THE
Law of Freedom
IN A
PLATFORM:
Or, True
Magistracy Restored.

Humbly presented to Oliver Cromwell,
General of the Common-wealth's Army in
England, Scotland, and Ireland. And to all
English-men my brethren whether in Church-
fellowship, or not in Church-fellowship, both
sorts walking as they conceive according to
the Order of the Gospel: and from them to
all the Nations in the World.

Wherein is Declared, What is Kingly Government, and what is Commonwealth's Government.

By Gerrard Winstanley.

In thee, O England, is the Law arising up to shine,
If thou receive and practise it, the crown it will be
thine.
If thou reject, and still remain a froward Son to be,
Another Land will it receive, and take the crown from
thee. Revel. 11.15, Dan. 7.27.

return to the dreaded Reading Room again and again. Winstanley's writings were bound with other pamphlets of the period; some of them were dated by the man who had collected them and a bookplate inside the main cover stated 'Gift of George III'. A letter to Lord Fairfax had been printed in 1810 as an example of a 'curious or amusing' pamphlet. The Museum also preserved the broadsheets – the newspapers of the time, which, in their descriptions of the Diggers, appeared to have the same regard for accuracy as the newspapers of today.

Realising that casting would now depend on voluntary support, we duplicated an enrolment form: 'We need people willing to appear who are prepared for the hard work, the long hours, the tough conditions (we shoot whatever the weather) and the inevitable waiting around. Because we need the seasons, shooting will be sporadic. A film like this depends entirely on the goodwill and initiative of those involved with it…Those who run the industry tell us that it is impossible to make this film for the budget we have. If you join us, you will be helping to prove them wrong.' We had a good response to this, many replies resulting from a paragraph by Tony Rose in *Movie Maker*, the successor to *Amateur Cine World*, which had been of such help during *IHH*.

We had one professional actor still to see, Jerome Willis. His attitude was immensely encouraging. He had played the part of Fairfax before, in a BBC play called *The Cruel Necessity*, about the death of Charles I. He had also played in James MacTaggart's BBC play *Comrade Jacob*, which we had not heard about. (We wrote at once to the BBC, but they had wiped the tape.) The play had been staged in an experimental style – 'I played Captain Gladman, and sat on a stepladder, pretending it was a horse' – and the whole thing had been shot in the studio. Jerome Willis thought it had been very successful, and he was fascinated by the story. (Other members of the cast had been Sheila Allen (Mrs Platt), Andrew Keir (Winstanley) and John Woodnutt (Platt). Not only did Jerome Willis agree to play the part of General Fairfax for the Equity minimum, but he put us on to an extraordinary location, Chastleton House, near Moreton-in-the-Marsh, Gloucestershire, which the BBC had used for *The Duchess of Malfi*. We had been to Chastleton in our location sweep, but the exterior of Chastleton House (1603) was of Cotswold stone, wrong architecturally for the Surrey area. But Jerome described the interior, with its original furniture. We drove up again and found the place ideal for virtually all the interiors in the picture.

Chastleton House (1603)

Hearing that the Sealed Knot were to hold their next battle at Crow's Hall, Debenham, we decided – with their agreement – to take advantage of it. The battle would have to be shot very carefully; the Sealed Knot in their regular costumes, would be used for extreme long shots. We would then take a small group, re-equip them with the original Tower of London armour, and shoot the closeups. One immediate problem Andrew had to add to all his others was the length of pikes. The Sealed Knot used 8ft pikes. The New Model Army used 16ft pikes, and although they used to chop a couple of feet off the end, they were still twice as long (and half the thickness) of the Sealed Knot variety. He had 150 14ft pikes made up. But how would we transport 150 14ft pikes? Borrowing a Land Rover, and acquiring a trailer, Andrew constructed a Dexion framework and lashed the pikes to that. They rattled deafeningly against the metal roof of the Land Rover, and occasionally the load shifted but the system worked.

Crow's Hall was a superb old building, roughly of our period, surrounded by a moat. It was owned by Vic Knowland, whose son Nick, by coincidence, was a cameraman. For the benefit of the Sealed Knot,

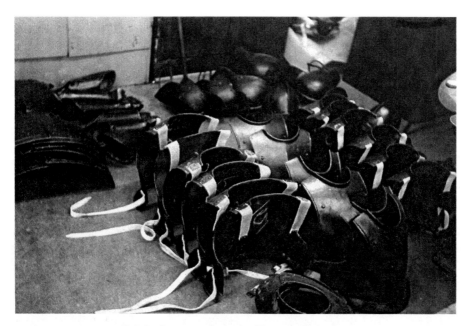
Original armour from the Tower of London

the Knowlands had built an extra wing – out of hardboard – which the army could set on fire and blow up.

The Sealed Knot talked about their past battles like veterans of the Thirty Years War. One of the officers was extremely sniffy about the film. Hearing me mention the word guns, he said: 'I think you probably mean muskets, don't you?' Imagining we were equipped with fake weaponry, he said: 'I'm not touching one of the fibre-glass things from Bapty's.' And he rattled off technical questions with terms like 'split trail'. Andrew wasn't around and the interrogation annoyed me. Finally, he followed me into a shed, where he saw the original armour laid out, along with pikemen's morions, lobster-tail helmets, buff coats and original swords and matchlocks. It looked as if we'd ransacked the contents of a museum. The officer stared, a glazed expression creeping into his eyes. And then his tone changed and he said: 'If you'd given us more notice, we could have done this properly.'

As soon as Ernie arrived, we went to select a location. We decided to do the closeups on the first day of the weekend, and the long shots on the Sunday morning, when the Sealed Knot would be all be assembled and we could take advantage of their great number. The inspiration for

the battle scene was Orson Welles's battle in *Chimes at Midnight*; not that we could possibly afford to stage ours on the same enormous scale. But the intricate cutting of that masterly sequence had given us an idea. Andrew and I had often talked of the feasibility of doing a large battle on a small scale. We felt it could be done so long as the audience didn't feel cheated; long shots were essential, to establish the numbers, but once the long shot had been absorbed, then we might get away with six men in a field. I had sent Ernie a memo about the way we wanted to shoot the battle:

Because things will undoubtedly be chaotic (and probably wet as well) I thought I'd jot some notes down about this battle scene.

- There should be no zooms in or out throughout the picture, but you might find it necessary to crash in during the fighting to pick out some useful detail.

- Movement of the camera should be avoided until the battle reaches its height, when anything goes 'à la *Chimes at Midnight*'. The buildup should be shot with every closeup static.

- The sequence will be shot either in very long shot or in extreme closeup. The closeups should be shot with a long lens to reduce the

depth of field and throw the background. In a closeup of the barrel of a musket, the rim of the barrel should be crisp, the rest should fall off in a blur.

   - All scenes of movement by men or animals should be undercranked at 20fps.

   - Tracking shots will have to be shot from the Land Rover.

   - Andrew had the idea, which seems feasible, of using the long focus lens to squeeze perspective, and keeping the horses upfield of the pikes by a couple of yards. They can then seem to charge in.

Slowly pikemen and musketeers arrived for the closeup shooting. The straps of the armour seemed too new, and I sent Virginia to the costume store to tell Andrew we needed something to darken them. She returned, beaming, with Andrew's remedy: a cardboard box full of mud.

   The closeup shooting was not the most exciting way of launching the picture, but it went smoothly enough – until an original matchlock was fired, and a fire started inside the barrel. Very few of the Sealed Knot would have anything to do with us, and we had to keep manoeuvring our men to avoid seeing the empty field in the background. Terry Higgins, as a pikeman, looked absolutely superb.

A few more Sealed Knots joined us when the horses arrived. (£40 for the afternoon!) The troopers were members of another organisation, the Medieval Society, chosen because they regarded themselves as stunt men, capable of falling off horses and fighting from the saddle. The horsemen charged the pikemen and slashed the heads off quite a few of the pikes, to Andrew's alarm. For the first and only time on the film, I felt a second camera might be useful, and used my Bell and Howell 70DR. I didn't look where I was standing and came within an inch of being trampled. I abandoned my role as second cameraman forthwith. The horses, recent arrivals from Ireland, were only riding school horses, but they took to battle with apparent delight. We decided they were homesick for gunfire (the Troubles were in full flood). The horses were fitted with the right saddles, in most cases, but not the right bits. The old S-bit of the seventeenth century was regarded as a cruel device, and we decided not to inflict the sole example we had been able to find on any of these horses. They had enough to put up with.

We had a lot to put up with, too. Eric Mival, who had been an assistant director on *IHH*, told us that he intended to make a film about the making of *Comrade Jacob*. We had warned him that he wouldn't get any help from us – the idea of a camera peering over your shoulder when you're trying to work is intolerable – and he would have to make do with what he could get. He had teamed up with Patrick Lui, from Hong Kong, and had fired off several rolls of colour film on our activities so far.

Ernie revealed that he had been shot in the stomach by the wadding of a blank charge, and showed us the circular wound.

Another had hit him in the face. On both occasions, he kept turning and never mentioned anything to us. Russell Robinson said he was enjoying himself. He said that he had been thrilled to see the armour he had looked at for years suddenly come alive. He thought the characters looked superb, the costumes and accoutrements faultless. He said the musketeers looked exactly like characters from a Thirty Years War painting.

That night, the village of Dedham was crammed with Sealed Knots, and it was impossible to get anything to eat.

Next morning, Crow's Hall was surrounded by mist, and the Sealed Knots, some of them suffering from hangovers, slept late. It was October, early autumn, and one couldn't blame them for preferring their snug tents to the morning chill. However, we had a job to do, and we made sure an announcement was broadcast over the loudspeaker. Colo-

Andrew Mollo

nel Hastings-Read, in charge of the battle, put us on to our liaison, Philip Stearns.

Philip Stearns was reluctant to round up soldiers for us. 'There has been a little resentment…hanging around yesterday…' We walked round the camp ourselves and tried to recruit people. We met with little success until we encountered Charles Kightly, who had just arrived without a costume. Could he borrow one of ours for the battle that afternoon? We lent him a costume and explained our plight, and he said he ran an outfit called the Roundhead Association. He would produce his men, even if the Sealed Knot failed to turn up.

The location was in the next field. Ernie and I set up the camera position and waited. More and more men turned up until the skyline was thick with them. Andrew equipped them with his long pikes and yelled across to us through his bullhorn: 'They are going to pray!' We had talked the previous night of having them singing hymns, but the idea of a prayer was better. So pray they did and because the Round-head Association often did this, it looked perfectly natural.

One SK officer, very portly, with the careful enunciation of a clothes-shop assistant, told me that his men refused to come because of lack of action. He then suggested the swordsmen could have run out to engage cavalry. The idea sounded all right to me, and since we were about to do a tracking shot, behind horses, I said: 'Let's do it.' He lit up like a child and rushed away to get his highly-trained swordsmen. During each take, however, he seemed to be the only one doing anything, and his behaviour was operatic. Andrew finally got livid with him when he kept interrupting him with such suggestions as this: 'A lady bursts through ranks, to be set upon by Royalists…she delivers a body blow but is carried off screaming.'

Charles Kightly was very effective in dealing with his troops, but he finally told us: 'Pubs are open and they're getting restive.' I asked him for 20 minutes more, and we shot the last tracking shot. I risked a shot on my camera on the 10mm wide-angle lens, walking as close as I dared to the hooves of the rear horse, while Ernie shot from the roof of the Land Rover (both shots ended up in the film). I grabbed a bullhorn and told the Roundhead Association, and the Sealed Knot, how good they had been and they emitted a mighty roar, lowered their pikes and charged down the hill, which was very alarming, as I was caught in the middle.

Rushes were shown at Filmatic Labs and the first thing that came on the screen was upside down and negative. 'Lucky we got a V-gate,' said Ken Nelson, the lab man. 'Someone's laced up your original negative.' When the print came on we were amazed at the quality Ernie had given the closeups. But our delight soon evaporated. I had felt awful all day waiting for the rushes. I knew that too much would be expected of them because of the exhilarating weekend. The horse stuff started out well, but gradually it got duller and duller. Ernie kept everything tight and disciplined at the beginning, but as we had to work faster and faster, the inserts became looser and looser. When a trooper fired a pistol, instead of seeing just the barrel, you saw the rider and some of the horse as well – and the fact that he was virtually alone in an empty field.

The feeling of doom in the pit of my stomach increased. The stuff of the horses charging was no good; too loose. At the end, Andrew said: 'Perhaps what we were trying to do is impossible. Perhaps one can't get the feeling of masses of horsemen charging. We can use bits…but I'm not even sure we got what we went for. I'm not even sure we've got an establishing shot.'

So reality returned. Andrew said he had a splitting headache and we returned to the car. 'Depressed?' he asked, as I clambered in with the cans. I was more depressed than I cared to admit.

I called Mamoun at the BFI and asked for cutting facilities at the Production Board in Lower Marsh, Waterloo; at least I could get rid of the no good material. 'Come over at once,' he said. I laced the rushes on to a Picsync and wound the NGs on to a separate roll. Mamoun peered over my shoulder, anxiously. As he saw Ernie's opening close-ups, he said: 'Kurosawa!', which is the greatest compliment a shot can receive from him. When he saw the shots of the pikemen, he said: 'It has a feeling of its period unique in the British cinema.' I told him the stuff was lousy and it was too soon to be writing reviews. Nonetheless, I was immensely encouraged. Derek Hill had this ability to raise one from the deepest gloom on *IHH*; I wondered if Mamoun would be *Comrade Jacob*'s Derek Hill.

With the NGs out of the way, the rushes looked a great deal healthier. Andrew rang to say he hadn't been feeling well at rushes, and wanted to know if I was still depressed. (I am the pessimist of the team and he is the incurable optimist.) I told him we needed another session to cope with the inserts, but I mentioned Mamoun's reaction, and he

Nick Rowling on horse

seemed pleased. Later, we ran the rushes to Russell Robinson and our morale rose higher. He said: 'It's nice to watch a film and not have to criticise anything. It all looked absolutely real.'

Before the insert session, Miles Halliwell asked us over to Frensham Heights School to introduce *IHH*. It shocked us to realise that none of the pupils had been born when we started that picture! The 16mm print looked dismal, and the picture went over without any noticeable degree of enthusiasm until Miles appeared, as a Nazi lecturer, when the audience cheered him to the echo. Andrew couldn't stand seeing the film again and left; I stuck it out in order to operate the sound controls. After a discussion, a blonde girl, wearing a silver-studded leather jacket and a toy revolver in her belt, bounded up and inquired: 'Where d'you get the guns?'

Frensham Heights had supplied most of the volunteers to work on the commune. Among the most helpful were David McLean-

Execution of Private Arnold, Corkbush Field, Ware

Thorne and Mike Hackman; regrettably, both left before the picture got properly under way. For the next session, Miles brought along members of the staff together with a few friends.

During *IHH*, my stomach used to rebel just before sessions, and I put the attacks down to nerves. Those attacks had long since ceased, so I was horrified when we began to shoot the inserts for the battle at Larchfield, and I was once more overcome. This was a simple session, I told myself; I wasn't in the least nervous. What the hell could it be? The violent stomach pains forced me to hand the direction over to Andrew and retreat to bed. I was examined by a local doctor who thought it might be appendicitis, but didn't know for certain. (The pain recurred and it was.) Terry Higgins came upstairs when shooting was over and said in the army, only sergeants who lived on beer and whisky got gastric stomachs. 'I was in the medical corps,' he said, 'and I'm telling you, a cup of tea and a fag is your cure.'

Andrew directs battle scene

Filming main battle

I was well enough to return next day. The stunt men from the Medieval Society had balked at falling off horses, so we put Andrew in trooper's costume and pushed him off a fence with a pike. (All the falling horsemen in the battle are Andrew, as are almost all the battling troopers.) He had been injured the day before when the sharp end of a pike (made of fibre glass and as rigid as metal) jabbed him violently just above the eye. An inch lower and he'd have lost the eye. Since the blood was so much more realistic than makeup, he kept on shooting.

The rushes were just what we hoped. If anyone wanted to know if Andrew could direct without me, the evidence was there; his material was terrific, Ernie had understood the vital necessity of keeping close, and we had done what we'd always wanted to do – shoot a battle with six men in a field.

Unfortunately, it had been four and a half years since I had edited anything – since *Charge*. I was very much out of practice, and found it hard and frustrating to slash into the mass of footage. I lacked courage and decisiveness, and just contented myself with winding backwards and forwards in the viewer, adding a bit here and a bit there.

A few days later, I ran a rough cut which I felt was still too long and lacking in punch. Andrew thought it okay. Mamoun said nothing about the battle, but talked at length of Bill Douglas's new film *My Ain Folk*. The Production Board seemed to be producing more feature films than any British studios. And they were all very promising: *A Private Enterprise*, about Indians in England, by Peter Smith, *Requiem for a Village*, by David Gladwell, a short dramatic film called *Home and Away*, about a Scottish boy at prep school, by Michael Alexander, *Moon Over The Alley*, a musical set in Notting Hill Gate, by Chuck Despins, and an experimental picture which took even longer to make than ours, *Central Bazaar*, by Steve Dwoskin. Animated shorts and the occasional documentary were also in production. It was an extraordinarily creative and exciting period.

By the end of 1972, when we originally planned to have completed the shooting, we had only the battle sequence to show. I borrowed a Muray viewer from the BFI, and set up a cutting room at home, worrying the sequence until it began to work. However, as I wrote in my diary: '*Chimes at Midnight* it ain't.' Pat Kearney had given me that sequence from Welles's film on 16mm and I ran it silent to study the cutting; it was majestic. Run silent, our sequence seemed limp. To gyp it up, for a screening to Ernie, I played a record of the *Battle on the Ice* from *Alexander Nevsky* by Prokofiev. The sequence suddenly took wings. 'Wow!' said Ernie. I silently thanked Prokofiev, and from that time on, we were stuck with that music. We felt such a direct reference to Eisenstein and the Russians was wrong, but no matter how we tried we could never shake it off. Eventually, the sequence was cut to the music and the decision cost us several hundred pounds.

Chapter Ten

The New Year began with a visit by Peter Harvey, and had I realised how much he would contribute to the film, I'd have regarded his visit as a fine omen. Recommended by Mamoun, after working on the Bill Douglas films, he struck us, the moment we saw him, as someone ideal to play in the film rather than working on it. Tall, with shaggy hair and beard, he had a face which belonged under a broad-rimmed hat. I had just been to Holland and seen the seventeenth-century paintings in the Boymans and the Rijksmuseum, and my head was full of their images. But to act was not what Peter had come for. He was offering his services as a sound recordist, and since he seemed a dedicated and enthusiastic character, we were only too glad to have him. No sooner had we made the decision than the BFI whipped him off on to Peter Smith's film, but then most of our recording would consist of guide tracks, since Larch-field lay beneath a busy flight path to London Airport. We made certain of Peter Harvey for all sync shooting.

The new schedule, spreading sessions over weekends, and the odd full week, until winter, dismayed Ernie; he had to keep working on television documentaries, and these would inevitably fracture some of our dates. Ernie wasn't the only person worried by the amount of work facing us.

Thanks to the battle sequence, we were growing accustomed to some of the faces appearing in it. The camera transforms the human face; when a face is blown up several times larger than life you react to it much more strongly than normal. Phil Oliver, a former Welsh miner, now a teacher of music at Frensham Heights, would, we felt, make a striking Everard. Neither Andrew nor I noticed him when he helped us with the battle. Yet on the screen, you couldn't take your eyes from him. George Hawkins, too, had a sensitive, somewhat weather-beaten face, ideal for Coulton, one of the leading members of the commune.

David Caute had written in the book that Mistress Platt was a sad-looking creature: 'Her face seemed to suggest the shape of a pear, narrow at the forehead, broad in the cheeks, while the skin, dry and pallid, apparently deprived of sun and air, was drawn taut across her large nose and into deep, bluish caverns under the eyes.' (p50)

One afternoon, Carmen, Andrew and I were discussing the problem with Alison Halliwell, Miles's wife. 'Trouble is,' I said, 'she has to be an ugly old harridan – not old exactly, but fairly repulsive. And it's oddly hard to find such people.' Carmen was thinking hard. I saw her looking sharply at Alison. Regrettably, Alison was much too attractive, although her age – late thirties – was right. We turned the problem over again and again. Finally, Carmen declared; 'Well, I think Alison would be perfect.'

It wasn't the most tactful thing to say after my description, but Carmen was right. Abandon the idea of the ugly woman – it would be hard to find someone willing to give up their free time to parade their wretched looks! – and settle for Alison. Again, the camera transformed her face in the tests and proved that she had a period look we'd never guessed at. So that was another vital part filled.

Parson Platt was a tougher role to fill. Platt was a Presbyterian fanatic, a kind of Reverend Ian Paisley, and such men believed that free and tolerant discussion was sinful and that a society which tolerated improper beliefs would draw down upon its head the wrath of God. To find the kind of face that suggested those views, I wrote to Tony Richardson.

'What good news that you have got *Comrade Jacob* going,' he replied. 'I do hope it will be a huge success.' He listed a dozen possible actors – Richard Pasco, Frank Finlay, John Neville, John Woodvine – and added 'I would have thought you might easily get Eric Porter. Certainly I should not give up without trying.' (5 January 1972)

Like virtually everyone who saw the series, I had been impressed by Porter's performance as Soames in *The Forsyte Saga*. I wrote to him, explaining the project. Porter replied that if he remembered rightly, Andrew Mollo was the historical adviser on *Nicholas and Alexandra*, so he knew one half of the team. (It was actually Andrew's older brother John.) He asked for a script. And he added that payment – or lack of it – was a drawback, although not necessarily an insurmountable one. Far more of a drawback was the extended schedule. We sent the script and were somewhat dismayed by his reaction. 'I am sorry to say that neither the part nor the film appeals to me sufficiently to want to do it.' I asked him to elaborate, and he had the prescience to anticipate some of the less favourable reviews we received when the picture was complete:

Alison Halliwell as Mistress Platt

'I don't think it's enough to say: here is a group of indisputably worthy people trying to live according to different lights; to see them prevented from doing so by bigotry, prejudice and stupidity, and expecting an audience to fill in the human and humane gaps that must result from so starkly a black and white situation. It smacks of propagandism which will only preach to the converted and certainly fail to convert the uncommitted. I would have said that a closer focus on a more intimate area (by which I mean the whole situation and events worked through and seen through the lives, actions and reactions of one family group) would have resulted in a more sympathetic engagement of an observer's interest. One clearly sees the parallel of the modern breakaway communes, but if one were creating a film about those, the larger political issues, although relevant, would hardly be placed in such prominence.' (4 February 1972)

David Bramley as Parson Platt

Many people who have seen *Winstanley* would warmly respond to Porter's opinion. I am quite sure even now that he was right; one need only think of John Ford's masterpiece *The Grapes of Wrath*. But again 'right' and 'wrong' have no place in the discussion of art. We were moving intuitively towards a certain kind of picture, and while we were anxious that it should be neither dull nor repetitive, we had no idea what it would look like.

When I think of Eric Porter in the title role now, I laugh; not because he would have been unsuitable, but because as a highly-paid star, he would have been subjected to such abominable treatment. Another actor was keen on the part; I thought the actor was suitable, Andrew was undecided. Then Miles introduced him to David Bramley, the editor of a trade magazine for the heating industry, who lived locally and who had done some amateur acting. Andrew told me Bramley was dead right as far as he was concerned. I was extremely sceptical, but agreed to meet the man. As soon as I set eyes on him, I knew we had Platt. I was worried about his capacity for learning lines,

Phil Oliver as Everard

let alone delivering them, but David Bramley reassured me. I was also concerned at his lack of riding experience. Bramley promptly took riding lessons; his horse threw him and he broke a rib. We shot scenes with him in violent gales and pouring rain on a lonely heath, far from shelter, and even farther from location caterers, makeup men, hairdressers, and caravans. He was equal to all this, and turned in a performance outstanding by any standards.

Because of the postponement, we sent a circular to everyone who had so far sent us addresses, explaining why we had not yet called upon them:

'Although we hope that you will be able to attend sessions as often as possible, we will ask you only when we need you. There is a lot of standing around inseparable from filmmaking and there is no point in creating more than we have to. But there are also some extremely exciting moments – often accidental – which spell the difference between just another picture and something unusual. They invariably occur because the people who attend the shooting have a real sense of involvement – and enthusiasm. However hard this picture will be, that one element of enthusiasm could make all the difference to the final result.'

Many of the people who had volunteered were never called at all. I have heard that this caused a certain amount of disappointment. I have never accustomed myself to the idea that people enjoy filmmaking, and thought I was doing people a favour by passing over their names. In any case, the cast we assembled in Surrey proved so reliable and so steadfast that further additions became unnecessary. (On *IHH*, we often had totally fresh faces for every session.)

We contacted agents for the actors Richardson recommended – still imagining we could mix amateurs and professionals – and tried a new tack, asking them if we could see their clients in a play, or a film on TV in the near future. That method worked; no, we couldn't…which proved that they were free! But as soon as the agents heard the deadly words 'Equity minimum', they drew back. And Richard Pasco's agent said his client could not appear with non-Equity members.

One of the primary requirements for this film, which embraced all the seasons, was snow. Early in February, I was woken by a phone call from Andrew: 'Wakey, wakey, rise and shine – there's snow.' He was down in Larchfield; we were due to shoot a couple of days later, but we alerted Ernie, packed up and raced down the A3. 'Pull out the deckchairs,' said Andrew as we arrived. 'We're having a heatwave.' The lawn at Larchfield was covered with snow but trees had deflected it from the barn and the settlement. We were to be cursed with a succession of mild winters and no sign of snow in Surrey until the film was finished.

Bob Davies was our stills photographer. Andrew and I had known him since the days of *IHH*, when he used to process our stills. Before then, he had been stills photographer at Ealing Studios, and he offered his services to us in this capacity. Having never seen his work, we were apprehensive of its quality, but his skill was outstanding, and he produced many superb pictures.

Charles Ware filled in whenever Bob was unable to come, but since he was supposed to be an assistant director, his time was strictly limited. A former student of Reading University, Charlie Ware was devoted to his job, and he was able to do a great deal for the film. It turned out that he and his parents lived in the next village to Churt – Tilford – and he came to our rescue many times, with everything from transport and accommodation to the loan of a cat...and when the occasion demanded it, medical aid (his mother was a doctor).

Charles Rees, brought into the industry by Mamoun Hassan in the days of Samaritan Films, was also an assistant director. One of the most dedicated of film enthusiasts, he was also very talented. He was my assistant editor on *Charge* and when I left for America, Tony Richardson entrusted his next feature to Charles, who was then only 23. He cut a number of features and then threw it all up and worked for a while on a building site. He cut several Production Board films and was planning his own production with Ian Sellar when he agreed to help us on *Winstanley*.

Charles Rees

Chapter Eleven

The session we regarded as the first – the battle scene being a diversion – was held on Friday 16 February 1972, at dawn. Ernie operated our Arriflex. Miles and Phil Oliver (Everard) appeared and we used the barn and the commune for the first time.

It was a very minor session, but no sooner had the day begun than an accident occurred. Andrew, wounded in the battle, had already pulled a muscle in his leg. As he reached to pull a tarpaulin from the top of a shed, his 150 pikes crashed on to his leg, and he spent the rest of the weekend hobbling around like an arthritic. As the light gradually penetrated the wood, we laid mist with a smoke grenade contained, rather unromantically, in a saucepan, Andrew limped round the wood, trying to make the smoke spread convincingly, while I shouted: 'Run this way – now that way – back the way you came! Quickly!'

'I can't!' he yelled.

By 8.45am we had finished the scenes of Winstanley outside the barn and Everard walking into the mist, and Miles dashed off to school at Frensham Heights. Phil Oliver wasn't needed there until 10.00, and he hung around talking of his youth in the pits, how he left the mines and set himself up in the electricity business. 'I was making a lot of money and becoming a bastard – so I dropped out, five years later than I should.'

I was on the phone when Andrew brought in a young man who had just arrived from Edinburgh. 'I'm Ian,' he said. Charles Rees had told him about the film. He had worked on the two Bill Douglas pictures, and had travelled down from Scotland by coach, catching a local bus as near as he could and walking the rest of the way. He was dressed for a mild summer day, with no gloves and a thin leather jacket. Later, we worked on weatherboarding the barn and he told me he was fascinated by films; he was fond of Kurosawa and Fellini, and was taking steps towards making his own film, hopefully through the BFI. Ian Sellar was quiet, smiled a lot and generated a gentle passivity. He was also a very hard, uncomplaining worker, and a first-rate assistant.

The weekend was to be devoted to the scenes of the Diggers burning and clearing the land. I waited anxiously for the cast to arrive,

Bill Petch

and was delighted when a car, packed with people, crunched up the frost-covered drive. But it was Eric Mival's crew, making the film-about-the film – all five of them. Next was a shortish man of about 60, the very personification of a Digger, except for his close-cropped hair. He had a humorous, weather-beaten face, and as he walked towards me he laughed – a sort of Mr Magoo laugh – which I shall remember as the trademark of all the sessions. He introduced himself as Bill Petch, the farm-worker who had been recommended to us by the Museum at Reading. Bill was an absolute delight, and all of us looked forward to seeing him at sessions. He knew agricultural practices back to the year dot, and better than knowing them, he could demonstrate them. His advice was invaluable (he did all sorts of other research, such as locating further pamphlets) and he became an important character in the film, I wish we could have made more of his part, bringing out Bill's special qualities, but they would have been difficult to capture in such a context. Bill worked on a farm in Hampshire, and was occasionally slightly late because he had to feed the bullocks before setting out on his long drive.

Andrew and I used to meet people whose enthusiasm shone from their eyes as they talked of filming, and how anxious they were to help. We would give them a pickup point, assigning them a precious seat in one of our few vehicles – and they would delay the whole operation by failing to turn up. So we gave our drivers instructions to wait just 15 minutes and then leave. It was one of these people – airlines called them No-Shows – who delayed us this weekend, keeping Charles Rees hanging around Waterloo station. Charles had borrowed his mother's red Mini – a car which saved us from disaster time and again (as did Charles himself) – and he brought down instead a National Film School

The Mival team – making a picture about making a picture

student. This fellow watched the crazy muddle of making pictures with a bland expression, never saying anything, just hovering on the horizon like Nemesis. What with Eric Mival and this student I felt we were over-exposed.

There was a slow beginning, as we set up the camera and waited for things to gel. As usual, I couldn't think of anything to shoot, and discovered that a storyboard, which I had prepared the night before, was too perfunctory. Andrew limped up to the commune – which had been cleared, but was otherwise untouched – and sat on a tree stump, 'breaking down' costumes with paint. It was at this point that we realised fully the superlative value of the walkie-talkies, without which this session would have been far harder and much more fraught. Andrew, who in the old days usually switched such instruments off – 'to save the battery' – now enjoyed sitting on his stump issuing orders to Carmen and Virginia at the other end.

When all the cast had been assembled, we began laying smoke, and creating attractive effects against the hard winter light. The Mival crowd were as busy as beavers, but they were shooting with lightweight 16mm. We moved slowly on 35mm, and I wondered if this was due to Ernie's lack of familiarity with the gauge. He had no assistant, and had to lug the camera and tripod on his shoulder, to and from the commune, up and down the hill, with no complaints. When I tried, the tripod bit savagely into my shoulder and I could hardly make it to the top.

We had bought a pickup truck to transport the cast, and that afternoon we clambered aboard and bounced over to our field, where the land had to be prepared for our crops. The Diggers began work with mattocks, clearing the heather and burning it. It all looked great to the naked eye, but we wouldn't know for certain until we saw the rushes. The first full day reminded us of the atmosphere of *IHH*, and we were exhilarated.

Next morning, Virginia, who had taken charge of catering on the film, made breakfast for everybody at 6am (discovering that porridge and eggs and bacon was surprisingly time consuming) and by 7.30am we were on the hill. It was icy cold for the poor actors in their open shirts and sacking coats. Andrew and I wore the Spanish army great-coats he had brought back from *Dr Zhivago*, so we scarcely felt the cold. Despite the weather, a group of Sunday morning strollers gathered to watch. The performances seemed a bit odd, both to Andrew and me. The Diggers were facing a camera and having to speak lines for the first time, and some of them had no idea how to give a look or deliver a line. The camera was enough to make them self-conscious, but they also had to put up with bystanders and a microphone (Wm Diver recorded all our guide tracks). I tried my best to take the mystique out of it. Andrew helped Phil Oliver by suggesting he ran up and down so that he could pant convincingly. He also suggested that the delivery of one of the lines should be cynical. It worked. But I wasn't sure about how far to go. I felt that if we shot on and on, just to get the delivery right, we would have the same situation we sometimes had on *IHH*: a collection of identical takes and a waste of film since it all had to be post-synched. (Post-synchronising is a process by which voices are added after shooting – the layman calls it 'dubbing'.)

Back at Larchfield for lunch, we all ate in silence. Everyone was hung over from a party Alison and Miles had given us the night before, frozen stiff from the hill and rather shaken by the evidence that being natural wasn't easy.

The atmosphere quickly improved. Phil showed that he could use the breast-plough; apparently they use them in Wales to this day for small and awkward fields. We shot a spontaneous scene around the fire in the twilight which promised to be amusing. The light went before we were absolutely ready, but Ernie said we had shot 14 rolls. 5,600ft! Nearly an hour!

Shaken by this inordinate amount of footage we had consumed on relatively short sequences, I felt alarmed about the rushes. There was no justification for such concern. The scenes looked great to the eye, they were on 35mm and they were shot by Ernie who had already proved his ability. A large audience gathered at the rushes theatre in Dean Street. The very first shot was incredibly depressing – printed at least four points too light. We had chosen Studio Film Labs to do our work because of their high reputation and because they had successfully printed all our tests. We could hardly blame the lab for the lacklustre look of the material. I sank lower and lower as shot after shot came up, devoid of vitality and meaning. Where it should have been stark, it was empty. Where it should have been harsh, it was flat. Where it should have been simple, it was boring. I nearly wept when I saw that carefully planned silhouettes were hopeless. Closeups appeared to have been dropped on to the centre of frame, washed out and lifeless. There was a ghastly sense of anti-climax. I was grateful that my mind could not cope with figures and that I could not calculate the cost of 14 wasted rolls.

Andrew, Ernie, Ian and I went to a coffee bar for a post-mortem. Andrew tried to keep our spirits up, but the old problems confronted us; do we go back to 16mm? Colour? 'Is it my compositions?' asked Ernie. We tried to talk it out, but it was hard to be frank. Ernie was sure the stuff would look better properly graded – 'this is a one-light print'. I was sure it would – slightly – but at that moment I was wondering if we could replace Ernie. For I was sure it was him. Oh, I had checked each setup through the finder, and Andrew had checked some, too. But ultimately, you have to trust your cameraman. If you don't, you may as well shoot the picture yourself.

I rounded up Mamoun and the original tests and we went to Studio Film Labs. Alf Dosset, one of their veterans (who had printed *Napoleon*), passed down the corridor and overheard my tale of woe. 'We must help the old ones,' he muttered, adding quickly 'I don't mean age…' The lab agreed to reprint some of the scenes darker. We had them project our tests and part of the rushes and the difference was staggering. One was pale, washed out – the other full of richness and contrast. Afterwards, Mamoun wondered whether Ernie had been playing safe, because it was 35mm. I called in on Andrew to explain all this. He wasn't so downcast, but we veered back to the idea of 16mm because in the battle, Ernie had achieved the quality we wanted.

The next day, half-hoping I'd find I'd been dreaming, we took a look at Studio Film Lab's reprints. A bit better but not much. SFL said they would try again on high contrast. Another show was marred by wretched projection at Illustra; a cheap projection lens made the dawn shot lighter than ever, and ruined the focus. But the widescreen made a difference to the composition. Mamoun seemed relieved, but criticised the fact that the Diggers didn't do anything very much. Over lunch, Alison Halliwell was harsher. She said a) the Diggers walked like sheep; b) their hats flew off; and c) there were too many men on the job. When Andrew arrived we related this and he became angry, said something unprintable about such self-criticism and warned that we would end up with nothing if we carried on like that.

At the Production Board, Mamoun showed me shots from Bill Douglas's *My Ain Folk*, processed at Hendersons. The difference was fantastic. 'What did you shoot it on?' I asked Bill.

'FP4.'

'Why?'

'Because I saw Ernie's test for *Comrade Jacob*.' I began to see that perhaps the problem lay with the laboratory. I grabbed some trims and shot over to Studio Film Labs.

'You want that soot and whitewash?' said the grader. He and the lab's technical man studied the printing stock and identified it as Gevaert. They showed me their reprint – better, but when I got it into the cutting room, I discovered that the 3Ms stock was so feeble that a mere touch with Sellotape was enough to remove the emulsion. This made me so angry I decided then and there to abandon Studio Film Labs and to take the picture to Hendersons. In any case, Hendersons were cheaper, although SFL's managing director had agreed to match their charges in our case. I regretted having to make the move because SFL had done all the printing on my 35mm reconstruction of *Napoleon* and it had been superb. But the life had certainly gone from their black and white now and temporary or not, we couldn't afford to waste a frame.

The labs were not the only culprits. We had teething problems with Samuelson too – literally; a magazine cog was missing a tooth, which caused the film to rip…another magazine was too tight, and that, too, caused the film to tear…the lens hood didn't fit the front of the Arriflex, the retaining tongue in one of the lens sockets was missing…and the zoom lens, which we picked up specially, was missing its support bars so that we couldn't use it at all.

The zoom lens contained part of the clue to the mystery. Ernie, in common with most contemporary cameramen, was trained from his earliest days with a zoom lens. He was not expert with standard lenses, and admitted to me later when using standard lenses that he would find a setup which was fair, and compromise on it because of the time it took moving the camera around. This was one of the reasons for the loose compositions. Another reason was that he had been working on TV jobs for four months and the style we had all agreed upon had merged in his mind with the style required for television. The stock was another clue; it was Mark V (Ilford) faster and less crisp than FP4 (Ilford). (Although the last three reels of the film were shot on Mark V and Hendersons were able to process it with the proper contrast.) But above all, the problem lay with the lab.

We reshot some of the sequence with a zoom lens and eagerly awaited Hendersons magical treatment. Mamoun called early. 'Hendersons rang yesterday to say that your negative was under-exposed.' I realised what must have happened; in order to increase the contrast, Ernie had rated some of the material at 250 ASA. They must have developed it normally. I rushed in to Lower Marsh, to find the roll black as a stormcloud. I could hardly see anything. Taking a deep breath, I called the Henderson grader, Cecil Fennell. I decided to be as cool as possible.

'I believe you had some problems printing the rushes for *Comrade Jacob*.'

'I had no problem. No, we've done all that was required of us.'

'And you didn't encounter any problems?'

'No.'

'That's strange. Someone telephoned the BFI about them. Who graded them?'

'No. I had a lot of trouble grading them, I don't mind telling you. I might have mentioned this in passing.'

'Could you tell me perhaps what kind of development the material was given?'

'Yes, we gave it our normal six and a half minute development.'

'That would explain it, because the cameraman requested you on the camera sheets to rate it at 250 ASA. The rushes are so dark you can't see them.'

'Oh, it looks as if we've fallen down at this end. It was so under-exposed, this negative, I thought you wanted a night effect.'

Some of the material had been developed properly, and that material was splendid – clear, crisp, as rich in contrast as anything Bill Douglas had shown me. Ernie was away; I wrote him that when he got back, he would see something. 'But I must say the burning is superbly shot. The compositions you decided upon for the grabbed shots were absolutely magnificent. If the whole picture (at least in exteriors) can have that look, we'll have no problems. The lesson is underlined; we must create good liaison with the labs.'

Ernie was aboard the Ark Royal, shooting a short entitled *The Iron Village*. We fixed our shooting at Chastleton for his return, decided to have nothing developed until Hendersons had made careful tests. Andrew was alarmed at the shortage of time before the Chastleton session, when Carmen and he had to produce several extremely complicated and elaborate costumes.

Various volunteers had been pressed into action. One was a French girl, Françoise Pelling, the wife of the local curate. When she announced that parish ladies were only too keen to help, she was given a vast batch of sewing and stitching to hand out to them. She found the ladies were anything but keen, however, and she had to give up housework and slave away day and night, to fulfil what she thought was our schedule. And when I called her to offer another huge batch from Carmen she nearly fainted. What we needed was not midnight toilers, however heroic, but people who could offer steady continuity. They were hard to find. Eventually, a girl called Barbara Paynter, who had worked with costumiers, joined Carmen and proved a great help.

Assembling old books and pamphlets meant tramping from shop to shop and trying to persuade the owners to rent their valuable merchandise. One or two would hire books without argument – Peter Murray Hill of Sloane Street was helpful in this respect – but other stores kicked up a terrible fuss. One explained that he had rented a prayer book, valued at £140, and it had been sprayed with paint for an Emu commercial.

Charles Ware, assistant on the picture, organised the printing school at Reading University to make exact reproductions of the pamphlets The New Law of Righteousness, and luckily their work was first class. Virginia spent her time hunting for dogs of the correct breed following a talk with the Kennel Club. We arranged for a breeder of Papillons, Mrs Clarke, to bring some of her dogs to Chastleton.

An outbreak of IRA car bomb explosions across central London, combined with a rail strike, made these searches hazardous as well as frustrating. There was also a sense that we were letting the history of our own time slip by, as we buried ourselves in the seventeenth century.

As the Chastleton session approached, a session spread over a week, and involving virtually all our interiors, Miles Halliwell grew apprehensive about his performance. For the first time we would be recording sync sound. The last two sessions had shown that he had nothing to worry about, so I sent him details of what we planned to shoot, and added: 'Miles, don't be concerned about the acting. There really is a world of difference between this picture and *Anne of a Thousand Days*. Naturalism is everything; the self-consciousness you complained of feeling registers as a splendid detachment, so you have nothing to worry about. I shall provide the minimum of direction (I'll probably be in bed!) and you just play the scene as you feel it – and it'll be great. Conviction is all; don't try and do anything that is out of character for you. Take your guidance from an excellent performance in a film you may have seen about the German occupation; a young lecturer, played by…'

I was confident of Miles. But almost everyone else would be tackling sync dialogue for the first time, and it would take a lot more than a letter of reassurance to get good performances out of them!

Chapter Twelve

Andrew had returned the Land Rover, and we were now the proud owners of a Ford truck. The morning we were due to leave for Chastleton, the Ford drew up outside my flat, and I saw at once that it was absolutely full. On to the back had been packed all the props, costumes and furniture we should need for the week's shooting. 'What about Samuelson's?' I groaned. We had to pick up a blimped camera this time, as well as taking our wild Arriflex. And a blimped camera, together with its ancillary equipment, took up an incredible amount of room.

'Oh, we'll manage,' said Andrew, with his usual offhand optimism. I visualised two gruelling trips from London to Gloucestershire. We unloaded some of our old furniture at Samuelson's, including a reproduction seventeenth-century cradle. The transport department were most intrigued – especially one expectant father. An Irish foreman judged the space Andrew had made in the truck and reckoned we could do it. And to my utter astonishment, we did – cradle and all. We had an excellent drive, passing an antique shop to whose sign some wit had added an extra Gothic 'D', so that it read 'OLD FORGED ANTIQUES'.

My literary agent, Michael Sissons, had invited us to use a cottage he was renting, and we found it was virtually across the road from Chastleton House. An ideal place, remarkably comfortable, with enough room for nearly all of us (the actors had booked into hotels). It was a contrast to the freezing Nissen hut we had on *IHH*.

Chastleton House was not run by the National Trust, but by a descendant of the original owners; Alan Clutton-Brock, formerly Keeper of the Ashmolean, was quite elderly, but he resolutely kept up the guided tours from which he derived the revenue to maintain the house. He was not exactly in awe of the public, and he would judge from their degree of interest whether to walk straight through the hall, pointing merely to the Jacobean ceiling, or to go into greater detail. He told us that when he heard a car stopping at the gates, he would look out the window and say: 'Bloody people.' If the car drove away, he would say: 'Bloody insensitive.' We agreed that the tours could continue while we were shooting, and we paid £200 for the use of the house.

Being built of stone, the house was as cold as a deep-freeze, and you had to wear an overcoat to survive in the old rooms. What was so exciting from our point of view was that virtually every room was exactly as it had been when the house was built. The Clutton-Brocks had an apartment of their own, but the Great Hall, with its vast fireplace and intricately carved screen, was perfect just as it stood; all we had to do was take some ornaments from the wall and move out some furniture. One of the bedrooms had the original tapestries on the wall, the original bed (extremely fragile) and the original canopy and counterpane. The only drawback was the delicate and old-fashioned electrical system, and we solved that by paying the Midland Electricity Board to give us a direct link to the mains. The other, much more minor, problem was the windows; the old leaded lights had been blown out, we were told, by the great storm of 1770 (which wrecked the Eddystone Light) and the panes that replaced them were too large for the seventeenth century. While Andrew prepared the set, I cut up yards of black gaffer tape and restored the leaded lights. So long as you didn't look too closely, you couldn't tell the difference.

Virginia brought Peter Harvey in her car, and during the leisurely evening we learned more about his background. He had been a student at the Royal College of Art Film School. He became a sound recordist because he had to, en route to a location in Bristol; he learned to use a Nagra on the way down. Another fellow became the cameraman in the same way. He was as interested in photography as he was in recording, and had photographed *Scarecrow*, a Production Board film made in Ireland by John Sharrad. Peter's other great passion was for the telephone; his girlfriend was Nita Bird, Mamoun's assistant at the Production Board, and at the end of the day's shooting he used to make long-distance calls to London. I suspected he might be a front-office spy, with Nita checking everything he said against our budget. But when I got to know them both, the idea became hilarious. The telephone was his way of letting off steam, and he was so amiable, enthusiastic and hard-working that one could hardly object – particularly when he paid for the calls. 'His favourite director is Jiri Menzel [director of *Closely Observed Trains*],' I wrote. 'So he can't be all bad.'

Shooting was due to start on 17 March, St Patrick's Day. A sprig of shamrock brought me no luck. Ernie, due back from the Ark Royal on the 16th, failed to turn up. You cannot make a picture without a cameraman. We moved into a bedroom at Chastleton and rehearsed endlessly with Alison and David Bramley.

By midday, I was getting frantic. This was long before the era of mobile phones. We had called his home in Parson's Green, London; no answer. Françoise Pelling arrived with her son, Damien, cast as one of Platt's children, and Carmen and Ian had brought Phillipa Johnson, cast as the other. We picked up Ruth Woollett, chosen by a local vicar to play the midwife, and she was excellent. Because we were shooting sync, Ernie had judged it sensible for us to employ an assistant cameraman. Barry Male, with his jet-black fringe and beard, looked extremely forbidding, but he had an easy personality and quickly came to the rescue. We waited for Ernie until 3pm and then gave up. Barry set up the camera and we began shooting, abandoning Mark V and rating the FP4 once again at 250 ASA since there was so little light. In between worrying what Hendersons would do to this lot, I worried about Ernie. If there is one thing I am good at, it's worrying.

About 6pm, as we were moving setups, Ernie arrived. The brakes on his vast and ancient Humber had failed and he had driven very slowly. 'Why, oh why didn't you call us?' I lamented, suspecting that he had

Alison Halliwell and Ernie Vincze

driven via South Shields. Ernie was staring, shocked at the camera. I apologised for starting without him, but we had no choice. He began to learn of the problems of making independent films with people who weren't being paid. 'David Bramley, who only needed one day off, now wants three, and we have to finish with him as fast as possible…Miles can only come for one day, so his main scene must be shot on Sunday…Dawson France can only come for a short time, so we'll shoot his scene by candlelight, and since Alison has to look after the kids, we'd better do her disillusion scene tonight, by firelight.'

We set up for that scene: a closeup of Alison, tears in her eyes, confessing to Parson Platt that she had been wrong in her opinion of the Diggers. The sole source of illumination was a firelighter, which was held as close to her face as possible, balanced on a shovel. Alison was inhibited and hesitant and I used all my powers of persuasion to wring a performance out of her. 'Hang on a minute,' said Andrew, giving her a slug of gin. Alison coughed, grinned and did the scene perfectly. So much for the Auteur Theory, I thought.

We were behind schedule, but morale was restored now we had the cameraman with us. But everyone has their little foibles. If Peter Harvey's was the telephone, Ernie's was punctuality. He was always slightly late. Even when racing to see his own rushes, one had to allow for Ernie Standard Time. As someone who is far too early for everything, I find unpunctuality infuriating. Andrew never wears a watch, but has an inbuilt sense of time. Ernie hadn't. It was as well he had one fault, for he was impeccable in every other respect. He wore clothes which looked as though they'd just been bought. In the heaviest downpour, or the wildest gale, he looked like a fashion plate. He was neat in everything he did, and was painstaking in his work.

Ernie had been about 14 during the Hungarian Uprising of 1956, and he spent the time in a department store, making petrol bombs to drop on tanks. 'Russian soldiers used to desert all the time, and they would be brought to the store, and we would take clothes off the rack and give them to them.' He said his involvement, at that age, had nothing to do with politics. 'I would have been making petrol bombs whoever was in those tanks – it was the event.' He had left Hungary much later, and not for political reasons. He just felt he would have more opportunity in England. He often took his wife, Lynn, and their son, Christopher, back to Hungary, a country he was very fond of.

Since working for television, he had been involved in one of the most beautiful documentaries I could remember; *The Last of the Cuiva*, made for Granada's Disappearing World, and directed by Brian Moser. It was the story of a vanishing tribe of South American Indians. Curiously enough, this tribe, like the Diggers, believed in sharing, and they lived a communal life. Ernie's camerawork was inspired and had he shown me that as an example of his work, my confidence would have been higher. But I didn't see it until we were well into the film, and were already accustomed to his outstanding qualities. At this point, I had only seen some rushes, badly printed by one lab and all but ruined by another.

Andrew and I were devoted to the use of natural light, and we pleaded with Ernie to avoid artificial light wherever possible. For the scene at the end of the film, when Winstanley brings his papers to Platt, we used part of Chastleton's dining room. It was essential to have a fire, but the chimney was blocked and smoke drifted into the room. Ernie and Barry set up the heavy blimped camera, and I left them to it. When I returned, the room looked as impressive as a painting. Winstanley's slight figure confronted the heavier shape of Platt; the smoke provided a fantastic atmosphere. Winstanley's face was thrown into deep shadow by his hat, so you couldn't see his features. The figures were outlined by just the right degree of natural daylight, and I was relieved that Ernie hadn't used his quartz lights. But suddenly there was a click and the scene vanished. Outside, the daylight was too dim to penetrate. Ernie scrambled on to a window-sill and adjusted one of his concealed lamps.

Dawson France arrived and Andrew fitted him in his Gladman costume. He looked stunning. But word came that he had been carrying on just like Gladman himself. Nicky Mollo, aged three, went up to play with him in the cottage and he said: 'Piss off, you little bastard.' He complained to the other members of the cast how inefficient and amateur we were, calling him, bringing him all this way, and then not using him for hours. (This was true, but he wasn't on the phone so we couldn't warn him we were behind schedule.) Andrew felt a direct confrontation was required. He led both Dawson and me into an empty room and pulverised poor Dawson with a catalogue of his complaints. 'There is no point going on if you feel like this, and you might as well get back in the car right away.'

'I didn't say that,' protested Dawson. 'I didn't mean that – no, no.'

We calmed him down and brought him to the set. While Ernie lit him, he asked questions like 'Is it T stops or f stops?' to show that he, too, was a cameraman. When I tried to cheer him up by saying that we would shoot extra scenes with him if his character worked, he said: 'Save it for those who like it, Kevin.'

'Do you dislike it?'

'I can take it or leave it.'

The scene showed Platt and Gladman at dinner, drunk, with a disapproving Mrs Platt. We asked Dawson's girlfriend Jane if she would play the servant, and she agreed. But Dawson shouted: 'Now don't let them force you into it!' and she was so shy she gave way. Alan Clutton-Brock's daughter, Eleanor, played the part instead. David Bramley had been tanking up so that he would sound authentically drunk, and when the scene got under way Dawson proved outstandingly good. When we shot his closeups, and he repeated and even improved on his performance, I was so delighted that I shook his hand and congratulated him. That is not the best thing to do when other actors are present, because it implies they are less worthy. But Dawson had created such an atmosphere and caused so much anxiety – almost certainly because of his own nervousness – that relief overwhelmed discretion. And we knocked back a few ourselves and had an absolutely hilarious evening.

Chastleton was a magical place. The next morning, the landscape was swathed in mist, and through the mist were the vague shapes of horses, munching the grass around a folly. The scene was too good to resist and we shot far too much film. Alan Clutton-Brock let us into the house shortly afterwards. 'Those are thoroughbreds,' he said. 'Arabs. No good for your film. And the folly over there wasn't built until the eighteenth century.' I silently cursed his folly and ours.

With David Bramley gone, and all his scenes shot, we ground to a halt. I was at a loss to know how to keep the unit occupied, and invented a scene from a Dutch painting of Alison, lit by the sun streaming through the diamond panes of a tall window. An American couple next to our cottage had a three-week-old baby, and he lay in the cradle, making gurgling noises while we waited for the sun to make the right effect. As it crept towards the window, Ernie brought up all the lights he had in order to expose at f11. We tried it with two cameras, with lights and without, and at varying exposures. It was very self-indulgent, so I resisted, to my later chagrin, a closeup of the baby. It was quite a show, with cast and crew standing in line, watching, and the sun playing the most effective role it had played so far. Such time and effort for a solitary and not very important shot!

After lunch, we staged the meeting of Winstanley and the Drakes in the Great Hall. Mrs Clarke arrived with her Papillons, four tiny, fluffy dogs who did a comedy routine whenever they spotted anyone new; they raced up, barking and snapping. It was like being attacked by a swarm of butterflies. But Mrs Clarke

warned us that she had had to have stitches after one of them bit her. The scene was difficult. We rehearsed with Miles and Philip Stearns, cast as Francis Drake (a relative of the seafarer, and landowner in Surrey) and Billie Skrine as his wife. Billie had just married an uncle of Virginia's, and it was while photographing their wedding that I realised how good she would be in this part. She had never acted before, of course, and agreed to it from family loyalty rather than enthusiasm for the film. I anticipated enormous trouble with her, for she had a lot of complicated seventeenth-century dialogue to remember. But she sailed through the part without a second's hesitation. Miles and Philip Stearns, however, were a different matter. It quickly became apparent that neither of them had learned their lines properly. Furthermore, Philip was unable to submerge his American accent. We tried the scene again and again and never achieved an entire take. I lost my temper. It seemed so unreasonable that we should take all this trouble to stage the scene – and Carmen's costumes for the Drakes were works of art – while they couldn't be bothered to learn their lines. This was grossly unfair, of course, for untrained people often imagine they are word-perfect when they are anything but. However, a little tension on the set is sometimes a good idea. Fortunately, Philip Stearns looked marvellous and eventually came through with the scene from start to finish. But while he suppressed his Boston inflexions, the odd vowel betrayed his origins and eventually we had to post-sync his voice (David Markham did the job).

What gave the scene additional suspense was the sun. Unless the sun was in exactly the right place, we couldn't shoot, for the hall was much too large to light with a few quartz lights. And once the long shots had been achieved, we had to race through the closeups before the sun moved, giving us matching problems. Ernie shot extra footage on this scene for Hendersons to use as tests, before they touched another frame of our rushes.

As soon as the Chastleton session was over, I visited Hendersons, a laboratory at Norwood Junction. The manager, Bob Henderson, was helpful enough, but I was intensely suspicious of Cecil Fennell, the grader. I handed him over the tests, with careful instructions, but kept all the rushes at home. We had shot a great deal of the film in one short week, and no careless handling was going to ruin it.

The tests came in to Lower Marsh. We had asked for sections of the same shot to be developed at eight and a half minutes, at nine and at 10 and a half. On the Moviola the eight and a half minute scene looked best but once on the screen it appeared grey and lifeless compared to the 10 and a half minute one. This was rich, with deep, velvet blacks and creamy whites; quite magnificent.

When I called Hendersons, Cecil Fennell had gone on holiday and no one else knew anything. I said I wanted to run the test to the person who would be dealing with all our rushes.

'The person you will be dealing with is Cecil Fennell.'

'And he's on holiday.'

'Just leave the stuff with instructions.'

'The last time we did that the stuff was ruined. I don't want to take the same risk again. All I want is for the test to be seen by the person who'll be handling the job. It's essential to establish some sort of relationship – or the same mistake will happen again.'

'We sent you a test this morning.'

'You did.'

'Did you see it?'

'Yes,' I sighed.

'Which one did you like?'

'The one developed at 10 and a half minutes.'

'That wouldn't be very convenient for us.'

'Then I'll go to another lab,' I snapped. 'Either the stuff is processed properly or it's not worth doing it at all.'

The manager, Bob Henderson, came on the line. He said no one could see any difference between the tests, and if we insisted on 10 and a half minutes 'it would bring our machines to a halt. You'd get arcing and chemical deterioration and all sorts of things. We just couldn't manage that for 10 and a half minutes a roll. Your rushes would take three days to develop!'

After all, he said, he was getting us out of a hole because we were underlit. I put a stop to that particular slander, and agreed to await Cecil Fennell's return from holiday. A fortnight of intolerable suspense followed. God, how I hated laboratories at that moment!

Don Higgins with Arriflex

Chapter Thirteen

A film which made a profound impression on Andrew and me was a German silent of 1923 directed by Arthur von Gerlach, *Zur Chronik von Grieshuus* (which is old German for *Chronicles of the Grey House.*) Dick Jobson showed us his 9.5mm print in Wales. The recreation of the seventeenth century was achieved with vast exterior sets, so well aged they seemed to have resisted the elements for years; the interiors were subdued and smoky (another reason for our smoky room scene) and the exteriors, rugged and windswept, were notable for their gnarled trees and threatening skies. One scene, shot on Lüneberg Heath, had obviously been filmed in the teeth of a gale. We ran the picture for the cast on the evening before one of the Larchfield sessions.

The session gave us a headache in advance. Andrew, Ernie and I talked and talked of ways of shooting the scene in which Platt meets Winstanley on the open common; it seemed contrived. Why would Platt and Winstanley meet so conveniently, simply to exchange arguments? It was no fault of the writer; the task of giving the scene conviction lay with the directors. We thought of a quasi-western approach, the two men advancing like gunfighters (!). We considered a more accidental meeting. The more we discussed it, the more 'set up' it appeared; Winstanley enters from one side of frame, Platt from the other, they talk, they part. Absolutely lifeless. Fortunately, both Andrew and I are great believers in the felicitous effect of accident. In this case, however, we needed a miracle. We abandoned the problem for the night and went to bed.

Next morning, I was woken by a rushing sound outside the window. I assumed it was rain, but when I poked my head out, I saw the fir trees being pounded by the wind. Oddly enough, the *Grieshuus* connection did not immediately strike me. One of the lines in the scene was 'Unusual weather for the time of year' referring to the beneficent sun and warmth, unexpected in early spring. We faced not only a high wind but leaden clouds and rain. I can hardly believe my stupidity, but I rang David Bramley and Miles Halliwell and postponed the shooting until later when the weather forecast promised brighter conditions.

I realised my mistake when Ernie, Andrew and I surveyed the area from the top of the hill. The vegetation, battered by the gale, provided a marvellous foreground for the magical lighting effect on the heath. It was pure *Grieshuus*. Luckily, Miles and David were soon on their way.

We placed them down below us, poised at a point where two paths formed a crossroads (highly symbolic). We braced ourselves against the gale, waiting for a particular lighting effect – the shadow of a cloud rolling over the heath, allowing the bright sunlight to fall on the two characters. It was like a military operation. We kept in touch with the actors via walkie-talkie. Far in the distance, a spot of sun hit a distant town. A heavy wet cloud hovered overhead. The actors waited patiently; Carmen had produced a massive coat for David Bramley (she had made it in a single day) and he was grateful for the warmth it provided. Poor Miles had to shiver in his insubstantial Winstanley costume. Virginia called over the air that there was a dog down there we could use. 'Too late!' we cried. Closer and closer swept the light, but then it stopped, and veered off in the wrong direction. Further waiting. The wind had now reached force 7 and was so violent as to all but sweep us off our feet. One layer of clouds scudded across the sky at high speed. Now the other layer was synchronised; the light filtered across the wood we had fixed as the starting signal for the shot. 'Turn

Platt and Winstanley meet in the gale

over!' Andrew had told David Bramley to raise his arms when he felt himself in a pool of light, to link with our next cut. And this he did, as a bar of light swept from the wood across the open heath, like a vast blind being lowered. Sunlight flooded the area and – whoopee! – we had it in one take.

Down below, we shot the closeups and midshots in true *Grieshuus* conditions. We experienced not just high wind and bright sun, but black clouds, rain, hail and thunder and lightning – all in one afternoon. The rain didn't register on film – it seldom does, unless specially lit – but the hailstorm was a useful alternative. Ernie took several shots at different focal lengths, hoping it would prove useful. (It did.) When the storm eased, Ernie set off like a truffle hound, looking for extra setups. He called me over to inspect a long shot of Platt and Winstanley. I peered through the finder. 'It looks foreign to me – I'm sure it will look fine on the screen, but I can't tell.' Andrew looked through and said he liked it and Ernie playfully pushed me into the heather.

'That was just like *Chronicles of the Greenhouse*!' said David Bramley, as we tramped over the common towards Larchfield. The gale had certainly saved the sequence. Perhaps Winstanley was using his celestial influence on our behalf? Even so, the line 'Unusual weather for the time of year' makes me wince every time I hear it. Unusual it was – but not in the right sense.

While Ernie was available, we paid a visit to Hendersons. On the way, he said – a little too wryly, I thought – 'We shot the scene very straightforwardly after all our elaborate planning. That seems to be the story of this film.'

I agreed – not until we saw the rushes could we be sure that the simple approach would be vindicated.

Bob Henderson received us in his office, with offers of tea. He quickly came to the point; ten and a half minutes was impossible; the machines would stop. Seven or eight would be fine. I suggested we ran the test with Cecil Fennell, and he took us into the screening room. There wasn't much difference between the first two attempts, but the 10 and a half minute development was superb. Then we ran the Studio Film Labs test, which Ernie had shot in the commune. That, too, looked superb. The Henderson people were obviously impressed by it. I suggested we could give SFL all our forced material, since they had no objection to such work, and Henderson consented in a very grudging way.

Naturally, they didn't want to turn away business, and that's what I was depending on.

Back in the office, Bob Henderson said: 'Well, I don't think there should be too much difficulty. Ten and a half ought to be all right – it's a small quantity, isn't it?'

'Twelve thousand feet.'

'Twelve thousand feet?' (Gulp) 'Yes – I thought it was going to be the whole production, but twelve thousand feet...'

'A thousand feet will take an hour,' said Cecil, flatly.

'Yes,' said Henderson. 'Twelve hours – well, I think that should be possible, don't you think so, Cec?'

Cec seemed reluctant to make an opinion. Ernie asked them whether the regular rating of FP4 was 80 ASA. Cecil Fennell's reply shattered us.

'I don't know anything about this ASA business. I didn't understand it on the first sheets you sent me. It doesn't mean a thing to me. I don't know what you're talking about. Before we did *My Ain Folk* we'd never done rushes before. [The lab did mostly the printing of show copies.] I have to feel my way.'

My instinct was to run as far away as possible. To my surprise, Ernie gently explained what ASA stood for, and to my horror, he left another couple of rolls of rushes.

He told me afterwards that he was very impressed with Cecil Fennell's honesty; he was the first lab man he'd ever encountered who admitted that he didn't know it all.

An amusing postscript to this encounter occurred when we rang up Ilford to receive the manufacturer's carefully considered advice about the development of material forced by two stops. 'Suck it and see,' they said.

The mere sight of those 29 glistening cans, staring balefully at me every morning as I stepped over them, was highly distressing. Perhaps chemical decomposition was taking place as they lay there? Waiting for Hendersons to admit them was like waiting for an operation.

The telephone rang and I fell over the cans in my anxiety to reach it. 'Your rushes are through,' said Mamoun. 'They're sensational. Come on over.' It would be a day when the Underground was experiencing 'staff shortages and delay'. By the time I raced up the stairs at Lower Marsh, the rushes had had several command performances.

(Illogically, I hate anyone seeing rushes before I do.) 'My spirits are lifted for the first time,' said Mamoun. I laced the roll up in the Moviola; when the first shot appeared, it was Ernie's long shot that had appeared so 'foreign'. It was so superior to what I'd expected, I hardly recognised it. The texture of the material was what struck me; utterly different to the television-style grading of Studio Film Labs. It reminded me of top quality processing of the silent era. (And this was confirmed when I asked Cecil Fennell when the laboratory began: 'Nothing's later than 1922 in this place,' he said, 'including the staff.') The shots of the hailstorm registered as furious rain, and Ernie had fired off several useful stock shots of waving foliage – all of which ended up in the climactic gale sequence at the end of the film.

'If only the picture could look like this,' I muttered, as the rushes clattered through.

'It does,' said Mamoun.

Andrew was equally heartened by these two rolls, and we now felt it safe to put the Chastleton rushes in for processing. And we hastily lined up the next session.

This required a wood – not a spindly Forestry Commission wood, with regularly spaced pines, but an ancient wood, with sturdy trees, preferably gnarled like *Grieshuus*. We found most things easily enough in Surrey, but an ancient wood eluded us. David Bramley, who lived in Midhurst, recommended Close Walk Woods on St Anne's Hill, where Queen Elizabeth had once held a vast alfresco banquet. We drove over, but Lord Cowdray was busily chopping it down for a housing estate. We found some vast, incredibly old oaks on the edge of Cowdray Park, but there were pitifully few and most of them skirted a car park. One possible location, an avenue behind Benbow Ponds, was marked 'PRIVATE'. David Bramley called Lord Cowdray's estate manager and said 'I suppose we wouldn't be able to shoot there?' and was told, bluntly: 'No.' At the last likely spot, still on the Cowdray Estate, the best setups were ruined by a newly-built public lavatory.

Alison saved the weekend by taking us to Waggoner's Wells, where waggoners once pulled off the highway to refuel their horses at the vast ponds. It was a place of incredible beauty – huge trees like Arthur Rackham illustrations spread as far as the eye could see – but it was infested with trippers. Nevertheless, what choice had we?

The scene was the first appearance of the Haydon family. Terry Higgins had been glimpsed in the battle scene. Now he appeared with his wife and child wandering through the forest towards St George's Hill. The script provided for Haydon to fall asleep in the woods, and for the battle and the Putney Debates to follow as a flashback. But we had shot the battle in a style utterly at odds with the rest of the film, and the only place for it was in a prologue. Furthermore, the addition of Haydon's family changed the character of the scene. Whether our approach would work depended very much upon the look of the characters. If they so much as hinted that they were wearing costume, the audience would lose its sense of conviction.

So I was alarmed when Andrew, exhausted from driving around the county in search of woods, said he wouldn't prepare the costumes the night before, but would run them up in the morning. Run them up in the morning?! After years of working with Andrew, I never ceased to be surprised, but this was one surprise that I was certain would turn out a shock. While we were organising the equipment, I peered in to a back room at Larchfield, and there he was, cranking away at a sewing machine, running up sacking cloaks.

We got to Waggoner's Wells, and Andrew produced these peculiar looking garments, which Terry and Muriel regarded suspiciously. No sooner were they inside them than the sacking changed their whole countenance. It was astonishing to see them shed their twentieth-century aspect and re-emerge as characters out of Dürer. These were, in my opinion, Andrew's finest creations – and they were run up in a few minutes in the back room…

The session went smoothly. I had drawn a storyboard once Andrew and I had decided how the scene should go, and found the technique invaluable. On the left hand side of a sheet of paper was an outline of the shot, and on the right was everything about that shot I had to remember. Despite this, we had the inevitable problem of trippers wandering into shot. We stationed assistants to hold them back, but a small crowd attracts a larger. 'Are you doing Robin Hood?' asked a passer-by. 'He looks more like Robinson Crusoe,' said another, eyeing Terry's wicked-looking knife. Terry flourished it, muttering: 'Robinson and Cleaver.'

Virginia was ill that day, and our catering department was reduced to bread and cheese. It was cold and we badly needed the soup

Muriel and Don Higgins

that characterised her usual meals. Food is essential for morale – we learned that on *IHH* – when we neglected to provide any – and the worst crisis can be alleviated by hot coffee. Virginia proved so successful at providing basic food at low cost that the BFI employed her on several of their other films.

The Haydon family was supposed to shelter from the rain. Although it was snowing everywhere else, and England was undergoing the lowest April temperatures for 37 years, Waggoners' Wells remained dry and we resorted to the exclusive *Comrade Jacob* rain machine – a watering can. Terry and Muriel (clutching Don) scurried for a hole in the bank as the first drops fell. But when we moved for closeups, Don's eyes kept wandering to the camera. And as soon as a character stares at the camera, you become aware of it. So Ian Sellar and Charlie Ware jumped up and down waving rhododendron bushes to attract Don's attention, while Andrew stood on the bank above and emptied the watering can. The expressions of the passers-by as they caught sight of this bizarre scene should themselves have been filmed. We were in hysterics by the time it was over.

Back in London, I called Hendersons and Cecil Fennell said: 'I've got some bad news. One of your 29 rolls stopped in the developer.'

'Oh my God,' I said, ageing ten years. 'Was it due to forcing? Was it because of the long developing time?'

'No. I don't think it was that.'

The slate number he read over to me corresponded with the Drake long shots in Chastleton's Great Hall, and most of the closeups of Billie Skrine. There could hardly be a more difficult scene to reshoot, since Billie Skrine had come all the way from Ireland, and the Great Hall was the centre of the Chastleton tours. Not to mention the sunlight effect we had spent so long waiting for. Whereas this was a crushing blow, it was not all. Cecil Fennell rang back to say several takes were fogged. The damage list grew longer and longer...slates 104-1, 105-1, 105-2, 122-1, 122-2, 123-1, 125-2...

What turned the knife in the wound was a call from Bob Henderson. 'I understand you're having trouble,' he said. 'Well, my advice is to print up all the NGs.'

NG (meaning No Good) is the abbreviation marked on camera sheets so that the labs remove the scene and you don't get stuck with unnecessary printing charges. Henderson felt we should print all the NGs in case one of them might substitute for a ruined scene. It was a sensible idea and I agreed.

'They amount to 2,100ft out of 11,300ft,' he said. 'Cecil would have to spend time sorting them out and he has a lot of people on his neck.'

'I thought it might be more economical for you to print right through,' said I.

'It would be, if you're prepared to pay for the 2,100ft.'

'I thought that if we saved you time cutting them out, you might divide the cost with us. Obviously on our tiny budget we can't afford to pay for an additional 2,000ft.'

'I can't give you any reduction. We're doing your stuff at 10 and a half minutes as it is, and we're having a terrible time with our other customers – having to put things back – I understand you want a print tomorrow.'

'We're not in a hurry for our print,' I said, hastily. 'What I said to Cecil was that if any print was available, we would drive down and look at it this afternoon. Otherwise we'll see it when it's delivered to Lower Marsh. We have waited this long. We can go through the agony of waiting a few more days. If it would help you.'

'It would help us, yes. We can get you your print by Tuesday and I can have the NGs cut out so you don't have to pay for an extra 2,000ft.'

Henderson didn't know how much 2,000ft would cost. Suddenly, he said: 'And another thing – what are we going to do about that 400ft that stopped in the developer?'

I thought for a moment he was going to offer compensation.

'What *are* we going to do?'

'Well, that developer has completely stopped. I've got other customers on my back and I don't like it. I told you that 10 and a half minutes would be too much for my machines.'

'Cecil told me that that was not what caused it. He said the developer didn't know exactly, but thought it might have been a slight nick in the side of the film. That 400ft roll contained key scenes – absolutely irreplaceable, and very expensive to stage. It is very depressing...'

'It is very depressing for us,' he said, 'with all our customers held up.'

Hendersons weren't finished with us yet. Following another session, I popped into Lower Marsh to deliver rushes. No one was there except Cedric Pheasant, the Production Board's technical officer, who was checking a sound track. 'Cecil thinks you can cut round all your fogged takes,' he said.

'*All* the fogged takes?'

'Yes, Cecil told you about them yesterday.'

'We were shooting yesterday. No one spoke to us.'

'Didn't you talk to Mamoun? We wanted to establish which magazine was causing the trouble and stop further shooting until we had. Over there – there's a complete list on my door.'

Taped to his door was not one sheet, but two, carefully annotated with dozens of ruined takes, all with P (Print) against them.

It turned out that Mamoun didn't know about the extent of the fogging, either.

He had checked on our negative insurance cover with the BFI lawyers and read me the following memo:

Negative insurance; there is a standard market wording which covers loss or damage to negative film during the production period from any cause except, of course, war risk – and the following processing risks:

a) fogging

b) use of faulty materials

c) damage arising from development

d) breakdown of developing machinery.

Someone obviously had us in mind.

I phoned Cecil Fennell and arranged to go down at once. He had 2,500ft we could see. Andrew being tied up, Virginia drove me down and I dashed up the stairs to Hendersons with Virginia in hot pursuit. The receptionist knew at once that we were the anxious parents. She raced out for Dr Fennell. To my amazement, he came in with a smile.

'We've one roll laced up,' he said, leading us down a dingy corridor into an even dingier theatre. I noticed the calendar on the wall said FRIDAY THE 13TH and underneath there was a quote: 'I know and love the good, yet ah! the worst pursue.' (Petrarch)

I was shivering with fright when Cecil gave a thumbs-up sign to the projectionist and the lights went clunk. Deep blackness. The sprockets chattered angrily, protesting at having to run this green (i.e. brand-new) film. Then up came a low angle of Philip Stearns. It was so sharp and black and white, it burned its way off the screen. Even Virginia gasped at the quality. It was perfect. And as we squirmed in delight, the image became stained and mottled.

'Did I mention this one?' came Cecil's voice from somewhere behind us.

'Er...no,' I said.

'Yes, you've got fogging on this one.'

The fogging was like no fogging induced by light. This was straightforward chemical fogging. Several more takes showed it was possible to cut around the low-angle. But a new defect showed up – as though the unit had been standing around Philip Stearns and pelting him with snowballs. They appeared every few frames for one frame at a time. It looked as though Cecil had spread our negative on the floor and invited a herd of caribou to picnic on it.

Cecil thought it must be a stock defect.

We passed to the bedroom scene. It was hard to judge Barry Male's initial take, for the image appeared to be under severe heat. It rippled and wobbled as the 'fogging' began again.

'Did I give you that one?' said Cecil.

'Er…no,' said I.

'Ah well, you've got fogging on this one.'

The shot of the smoky room caused us to cry out in delight; Virginia thought there was too much smoke, but I thought it perfect; it was impossible to believe it wasn't filmed by natural light.

The 2,500ft contained enough triumphs and disasters to suggest that the other 9,500ft would be quite an experience. Cecil had an idea what the blotches might be. He led us into his sacred domain, the negative examination room. I will admit the floor was polished. But the very fact that we were allowed in alarmed me. Cecil's desk was covered with ancient film-cement bottles, bits of film, razor blades, paper clips, old corks and a velvet pad upon which the negative rested. He put a roll on the flatplates and began to wind. He didn't even put gloves on. The film reflected a small light above his head, and I noticed considerable scratching.

'Er – that looks to me – correct me if I'm wrong – as though there is some scratching there.'

'Yes,' said Cecil, who was honest to a fault. 'There do seem to be some fine cell scratches, but you don't notice them, do you?'

I had to agree that with all the blotches and fogging, I'd clean forgotten to look out for scratching. Cecil picked up a magnifier and examined the negative closely.

'Hallo,' he said. 'This looks…this isn't water, it's oil.'

'Oil,' said I, quivering on the edge of breakdown. 'How could that be?'

He showed us. He had put the roll on a measurer, forgetting that a mechanic had had it in pieces that afternoon. He put his finger on it and his fingertip was coated with oil.

'Can you get it off?' I stammered.

'No trouble at all,' he said cheerily. 'It's clean oil.'

Virginia and I were quite hysterical with laughter as we came out. I felt a sense of relief that the rushes looked so marvellous, but a sense of resignation that we were in the hands of such an eccentric outfit.

'You'll just have to realise that to get that standard of processing, you'll have to lose a certain amount of film,' said Virginia.

And of course she was right. The difference between the Hendersons material and that from Studio Film Labs was the difference between Vermeer and Warhol. As I wrote to Ernie 'We will get another consignment on Tuesday. Some of it will be fogged. Some of it blotched. Some of it ruined. But the rest of it should be photographically the finest black and white the cinema has seen for a very long time.'

The rest of the material lived up to the initial promise. The fogging affected some vital shots, but it was impossible to ignore the richness and beauty of Ernie's work when it wasn't fogged. As the bedroom scenes came up, Andrew remarked on the lovely black and white. When the midwife appeared, he remarked on the beautiful lighting. After a few more shots he was so relieved he said 'Well, no one can say the hand-stitching doesn't show.' There was hardly an indifferent shot in the whole 29 rolls. Ernie had grasped our hopes and realised them with superb lighting and flawless setups. Unhappily, he was away on an assignment in Minorca, and could not partake of this experience.

'I really regret you were not there,' I wrote to Ernie. 'For very seldom in one's career does one have such a moment. Just once – when something one has dreamed of takes shape before one's eyes, and nail-biting nervousness ebbs away, to be replaced by relief and then exhilaration. You may be disappointed when you finally see the stuff. I am sure we'll come down to earth when the sound goes on, for I doubt if the performances will match the visuals. But as silent rushes, sitting there for two and a half hours, the stuff looked considerably better than I had dared to hope. As you know, I am a fairly harsh judge of photography, and was pretty suicidal when we had seen the first lot – as developed in weak minestrone by Studio Film Labs. So this rave review is unsolicited and genuine!'

When the show was over, each member of the cast and crew departed with smiles, the exhilaration affecting each of them because of their vital contribution.

Chapter Fourteen

By April 1973, we had photographed one third of the film. A few new titles had been suggested to replace *Comrade Jacob*: 'Such Men Are Dangerous', 'Brink of Utopia', 'The Diggers of Weybridge', 'Stand Up Now!', 'Fresh Air of Freedom', 'Divine Blessing and Manure'... None of them survived for very long, although Andrew stood out for 'The Diggers of Weybridge' until the very last.

We had a long interval between sessions, as Ernie went off to a lengthy assignment. A new member of the crew joined us as editor, Sarah Ellis. She wasn't exactly new. I had first met Sarah when I attended the Edinburgh Film Festival in 1964, and she had been one of the guides. She impressed me enormously, and when I realised she wanted to break into the film industry, I invited her to work (unpaid!) as assistant editor on a short film I was working on for the BFI. She worked with me and Charles Rees on *Charge of the Light Brigade*. She had been the best assistant imaginable, for besides being efficient and systematic, her enchanting personality had kept up our morale through crisis after crisis. Since *Charge*, she had edited documentaries and worked with her husband, editor Mike Ellis, on the sound editing of Sam Peckinpah's *Straw Dogs*. *Comrade Jacob* was to be her first feature.

On her first day in the cutting room, she learned the special nature of what her problems were likely to be; Cecil Fennell phoned. 'I'm afraid there's been a disaster.'

He had been cleaning oil from our negative by hand, it was taking too long so he had put it on a machine, which promptly mangled a complete take. 70-1 was no more – an effect shot of the pattern cast by the leaded lights on the sunlit floor, as the midwife scurried across. Not important, but when was this war of attrition against our material going to stop?

The next time Sarah came in, she was told the master of one of the sound tapes had been ruined – by the BFI this time. Mournfully, we began the dreary task of logging the rushes, for while Sarah was officially the editor, such was the paucity of our finances that she had to be her own assistant.

Andrew and Nick Rowling work on village

Down at Larchfield, another honeymoon period – helping to build the first stage of the commune. Andrew was anxious to build the huts the way they would have been originally, with wattle and daub. A certain licence was necessary, however, and a little cement was substituted for cow dung, to everyone's relief. Andrew had enlisted the help of George Barrett, a thatcher from Alton, in Hampshire. Together, they made thatched sections which made neater (but not too neat) roofs for the huts. Being very impractical, I wasn't much more help in all this than Nicky and Alexander, but I found it immensely enjoyable – freed from the responsibility of the picture, experiencing hard work in the open air, for a distinct purpose.

One evening, a huge truck arrived, and inside was a horse. Andrew had bought it for the film, and immediately called it Jacob. It was hard to see it in the half-light, but it was later revealed to be an ideal animal for the Diggers – a thin, brown, sad-looking animal, with lice, worms and thrush. Andrew led him to the barn, and hammered up some planks so he wouldn't clamber over a half-finished wall and vanish. But we found next morning that he had eaten great hunks of straw from the thatch.

While we were slopping around with wattle and daub, we heard from London that Philip Jenkinson had introduced *It Happened Here* on BBC2, and had scarcely mentioned Andrew's name. Philip was probably trying to be friendly, since he knew me but not Andrew; however, such incidents were galling and potentially divisive, and created a lot of unnecessary bad feeling from Andrew's immediate family. Andrew always shrugged such things off by saying: 'I'm used to it. I couldn't care less. But my father and my friends find it odd.' This keeps happening to partnerships in the cinema – another victim of

that period being Paul Humfress of *Sebastiane*, whose name is always missing from this 'Derek Jarman Film', despite the fact that he co-directed it. It comes back to mere convenience, but for a man whose future employment may depend on such a mention, it is cold comfort to know that some journalist finds the absence of his name 'convenient'.

Rain is a terrible dissuader for potential extras. We learned this on *IHH*, and expected the downpour on Saturday 5 May to deter all but the

Ernie Vincze with Philip Oliver as Everard

Lunch break

L-r – the Higgins family, the Gower family,
Andrew Mollo, Marina Lewycka, Kevin Brownlow

most committed. Certainly, people arrived sporadically, and there were plenty of phone calls: 'Are you filming in this weather?' We had to have a vast amount of villagers and a sizeable number of Diggers, this being the scene where the Diggers are ambushed in the wood. But the numbers increased faster than we could cope with. Miles called to say that his group would not be arriving until 1.30pm – and we had called everyone for 9.30am! There are few things harder for a director to face than a large crowd of people standing in the rain with nothing to do. You realise the ungodly time they must have got up and you appreciate all too well that they are giving up their weekend – but there is absolutely nothing that can be done until everyone is in costume. And that takes time. Barbara Paynter was in charge of dressing the crowd; we gave her one of the walkie-talkies and Andrew and I joined Ernie on the common. We did a couple of odd scenes while the crowd of onlookers grew larger and larger. I was feeling as I sometimes did on *IHH* – oppressed by all the people, I kept trying to push them into the scene. Andrew pushed them out again. 'Too many people' was one of his watchwords. I thought the poor extras would be miserable, wet and hostile, as they

Tom Haydon (Terry Higgins) and Coulton (George Hawkins)

sometimes were on *IHH*, but apparently they weren't at all. (It took me the whole production to realise that the cast actually enjoyed their experience.)

At noon we moved to the ambush scene – and people were still arriving. Inevitably, some of them weren't used. The scene was a tough one; Andrew's and my liaison was bad. I would start to give directions, and he'd talk over the top – or he'd issue instructions to someone, not hearing mine. Nothing seemed to gel. But the fight was convincing.

Jacob, our horse, ignored the fight and didn't

Mistress Platt confronts the Diggers

Villagers ambush the Diggers

Filming an attack

The aftermath: Winstanley (Miles Halliwell) and Everard
(Philip Oliver) survey the damage

turn a hair at the screams and thumps around him. But when the
villagers tried to push the cart, loaded with Diggers, Jacob became
mulish and refused to budge. I tried to direct a closeup of his 'terrified'
reaction to the ambush, but although we screamed and jumped in front
of his nose, he scarcely raised an eyelid. I fired a starting pistol and his
ears flickered. Jacob was the Robert Mitchum type.

Before the crowd dispersed, I asked someone to take the names
of the participants. That's what I got – the names...and no addresses.
Moral: say everything you mean.

Miles arrived with his group of extras from Frensham Heights –
too late. Apparently they'd been choosing a new headmaster. But even
more frustrating, Phil Oliver told us a) he was going to India, and b) he
had to get back to school and could only give me ten minutes. It was
an intricate and emotional scene – a reunion between two old soldiers,
Everard and Haydon, as Haydon and his family arrive at the commune.
To their credit, Phil Oliver and Terry Higgins did a good job. But it
lacked the extra something that such a scene demanded, and never
quite worked when we cut it together. The film needed the scene, but
we never had a chance of reshooting it before Phil left the country, the

seasons changed, and the commune altered out of all recognition. It was thus that the script was turned over and over, like the Diggers' soil, some of it bearing fruit, and some of it lying fallow, as we struggled with our difficult aesthetic climate.

A location in Sussex; the church at Itchingfield, one of the last with a medieval timbered section at the base of the tower (So unusual is it that no one ever recognises it in the film as a church). The most impressive piece of civil engineering I witnessed in the film was accomplished here by Andrew with the help of Jeff Cornish and Don Skinner (two of our most irrepressible Diggers, who were to *Comrade Jacob* what the Gardner brothers had been to *IHH*). I had asked the vicar's wife if there was any way we could get a cart into the churchyard.

Rebecca Halliwell &
George Hawkins

Imprisoned in the church

The Diggers are released

No, she said. The gate wasn't wide enough. So the cart, on the truck, was backed up to hedge level with the top of the fence surrounding the churchyard. Planks enabled it to reach the thin metal fence. The four men behind the fence were in imminent danger of being crushed. The whole operation seemed crazy to me, but being utterly impractical, I clung to one of the wheels and hoped. The wheels were then rotated, the planks pulled further out, and they became the ramp down to the churchyard – with us rushing to the other side. It worked without a hitch.

The scene showed the Diggers being released from their imprisonment in the church by a Justice of the Peace. Keith Ramsay, another master at Frensham Heights, took this part. He had agreed some time earlier, and the matter had slipped his mind. He was therefore alarmed when he arrived home to find a note from a neighbour: 'Although you have done serious wrong in trespassing on another's land – common land owned by Francis Drake, esquire – the methods taken against you have not been in accordance with the law and consequently I have no alternative but to release you.'

Scanning the note quickly, Keith Ramsay said it had given him quite a turn. 'I haven't been trespassing,' he said to himself. 'And I don't know any Francis Drake.' These were the lines I'd dictated over the phone in his absence to the next-door neighbour.

During a lull, as Ernie changed magazines, Jacob got fed up with the cart, bucked violently and broke the shafts.

Mamoun telephoned us at Larchfield, and said that the BFI Production Board had attended a meeting with the film industry union,

Alexander Mollo and Don Higgins

Harvest (Sarah Ellis)

ACTT (Association of Cinematograph, Television and Allied Technicians). They had received complaints from members that we apparently had a budget of £70,000 and a guaranteed release through MGM-EMI. And production companies were complaining that we were in competition with them; they said: 'Brownlow and Mollo were making *Comrade Jacob*, which should have been made commercially.' It was, in a way, comforting to have one's worst prejudices about the industry confirmed from such an unimpeachable source.

We ran some of the rushes to David Caute, who had just been married; on honeymoon in Holland he had taken a tour of the Dutch museums and art galleries. He was thrilled by Ernie's work, and said he was 'immensely cheered'. I warned him that we were having to make changes in the script, but he did not seem over concerned. Mamoun was tougher. He pitilessly criticised some of the performances. He liked the long shots, but thought the use of closeups as well made them ordinary. He developed an idea of using key lines as subtitles; this did not prove necessary for the main body of the film, but we did use subtitles in the prologue. Fortunately, Mamoun was passionately wedded to the idea of non-interference, and only gave us his views if we asked for them. As such, he made the ideal producer and a staggering contrast to the men we'd met before. Alas, he was probably unique in film history.

Ginni Little with stills photographer
Bob Davies

Chapter Fifteen

Spring brought a new aspect to the common; the trees displayed a freshly-washed fluffiness, and even in black and white this colour change was noticeable. We staged scenes where Gladman and the troops visit the hill.

Dawson France, who played Gladman, was not on the telephone, which made him one of the more awkward members of the cast. But Charles Rees took over the burden of transporting him. And this was more heroic than it sounds, for Charles was planning his own picture, and was on the point of shooting tests on Dartmoor. This very weekend, he decided he would simply pass through Larchfield en route to his location when he found himself trapped by our desperate demands. Once again, he and his mother's Mini saved the weekend.

The local horses, just when we needed them most, were suffering from an epidemic known as horse cough, and we had to import six from Goody's of Reading at the huge cost of £75. They had the cough, too, but their owner was happy to exploit the poor animals.

A near tragedy; Terry Higgins, camping in the garden at Larchfield, asked me to get the key of his van from Muriel. I couldn't find her, and popped into the kitchen to ask Carmen if she had seen her. My query caused Carmen to look in my direction and at that exact moment, through the back door, she saw Donald, the Higgins' infant son, fall silently into the fishpond. Without a word, Carmen streaked past me and hauled out the dripping and gasping child. Don emitted a roar, which showed he was all right, and soon he had forgotten the whole incident. But it was the grimmest moment we had on the picture.

Ernie was so overworked, having to give up his free weekends to the film, that it was hardly surprising that he arrived for the weekend later than usual, having slept through two alarms. He had been working until after midnight the night before. I was very sorry both for him and his wife Lynn, who now hardly saw anything but a blue streak as her husband arrived, changed gear and departed.

We needed expert riders to play troopers, but we didn't find them. We knew that Jack Osborn, a friend of Virginia's, had been in the Life Guards, but none of us realised that that had been in World War II. He hadn't been on the back of a horse since 1945. Yet he was about the only man who managed to stay aloft. Charles Rees, who hadn't ridden since he was nine, was de-horsed twice when his saddle cinch was not tied tightly enough. And Nick Rowling was hurled on to the heather in a Grand National fall. That wasn't the end of the mishaps; Phil Oliver came hurtling down the hill and crashed with all his weight on to the sandy surface. It was a sensational fall – no stunt man could have done better – and we quickly wrote it in. But he was very shaken, although he didn't admit until much later that he was in great pain; he asked for the hill to be cleared of trippers for his closeups.

All the morning, trippers and friends of friends and vast hordes of school children had appeared on the hill. The school kids fired bright questions in a surprisingly aggressive way: 'What year's this set in?' 'Why's he got modern shoes, then?' 'Who's the producer?' 'What's it cost?'

Phil's closeups were pretty gruelling, and time was running out. To avoid another setup of Miles, we gave Miles's line to Phil. At the end of the hilltop scene, Miles came up to me and said, gently, 'This isn't a case of jealousy, but why did you give that line to Everard?' He explained convincingly why he thought it essential he – Winstanley – would say it; of course he was right. So we quickly shot a closeup, in a totally different location, and no one has ever spotted the difference.

The rushes were very sobering. The crowd of Diggers on the hill looked exactly like extras from a Pinewood historical film, and Andrew held forth about this – about their costumes, their faces, how each one had to be very carefully dressed. It was no good aiming for a large crowd per se if they ended up looking like this. Fortunately, I had shot enough cover, so that Sarah could eliminate the shots that looked too posed. Ernie's work, however, was excellent, but we were taking it for granted that it would be. Even Hendersons were settling down and automatically reprinting scenes they thought inferior from their point of view. It was just the direction that was at fault.

I tried harder the next time: the long shots of the villagers beating up the Diggers in the field, seen from the top of our hill. The broken walkie-talkie caused communication problems. It was impossible to yell across the two hills and Andrew got shirty when I interrupted him setting the scene from close quarters. 'Give me time to talk to the extras,' he yelled. The cast all looked at each other and said: 'Extras?!'

Then I was seized by doubts – obviously the scene would work in long shot, but wasn't it criminal to go off without covering it properly and shooting closer shots? After all, cover had saved us on the Gladman scene. Andrew was adamant that it wasn't necessary, and I weakened a little when I realised what it would do to our schedule. In any case, we had worked the villagers until they couldn't move, and they sat on the hill and panted. We switched to an easier scene – Everard charging off down the hill. One idea Mamoun had suggested was that we should shoot this through agitated leaves. But it wasn't as easy as it sounds. First of all, there wasn't a breath of wind. William Diver, our indefatigable guide-track recorder, climbed the tree and tried to shake both branches with his feet, but merely caused us to shake with laughter. Then he slipped, and abandoned the stunt.

For the scene in which the villagers wrecked the commune, we needed chickens. Dr Ted Collins stressed we should have game fowl, and Andrew located a farmer who bred such rarities. In fact, he offered us the loan of the fowl free. Alison drove me over, and the man gave me instructions on the care of the birds. 'Would you like us to clip their wings?' I was convinced this would somehow impair their authenticity and said no thanks.

It was the wrong decision. Because Andrew didn't hear all the points direct from the man who gave us the chickens, he didn't take them in second-hand. He left the chickens untethered, but secure in one of the huts. When Mrs Lodge (one of our staunchest Diggers) heard this, she said they must have their wings clipped. She went into the hut to do the job, while Mr Lodge stood guard at the entrance. The cock went shooting past Mr Lodge's right shoulder and the hen went shooting past his left. Their disappearance led to a dragnet being staged that evening. Andrew, realising he might have to do battle with what amounted to a fighting cock, protected himself with trooper's breastplate and gauntlets, and he and Terry set off for neighbouring houses, where the cock could be heard crowing. Despite their hunt, neither bird was seen again, although a few days later a neighbour called at the house and flourished a handful of feathers: 'If this is the tail of your cock, he's been eaten by a fox.'

The surviving chickens acted well for the camera when the villagers invaded the commune. Andrew's technique of building the huts properly instead of mocking up skeletal sets was triumphantly vindicated when the villagers tried to knock a hut down with a battering ram. One thump with this heavy log and a film set would have crumbled. But this stout wall of wattle and daub (and a little cement) resisted the assault, until we got worried at the amount of footage the attack was consuming. Then we set the villagers to tearing the hut down with their bare hands.

I felt like tearing Hendersons down with my bare hands when Cecil Fennell called at 8.30 the following morning. 'Some bad news, old boy,' he said. 'It saves putting it in a letter. Some is our fault and some isn't. I have assembled five rolls; roll L has had a stop in the developer – man writing with horse nudging him.' (This was a charming scene of Winstanley working on his pamphlets in the barn, while Jacob came across and peered over his shoulder.) 'Roll N, two shots of mansions in distance and peasant meeting man with a stick' (Winstanley approaching Drake's house). 'Twice on second shot there is a terrific shower of white spots embedded in the emulsion at the critical moment when the men meet. Our theory is that this is caused by the ink used for edge numbers.'

The shot of Winstanley and the horse had been a great achievement, for actually Miles couldn't stand animals, and his apparent

Winstanley nuzzled by Jacob – a scene lost in the lab

162

fondness for Jacob had been masterly acting, and Ernie, a city boy, could put up with anything in life except horse manure. The bad news took the edge off our satisfaction at shooting some more difficult scenes, and we cleared up Larchfield – camouflaging trampled flowers and Jacob's hoof marks – with a sense of disappointment.

Chapter Sixteen

The New Diggers had their headquarters in Kentish Town. Phil Oliver showed me a report of their activities in *Time Out*, and I thought it was worth meeting their organiser Sid Rawle.

Rawle was squatting in a Victorian house, the last survivor in a demolished street. He emerged in a cloak, yawning profoundly (he'd been working until 4.30am). He was in his late twenties, and wore his red hair long, with a full beard. He talked straightforwardly, with a slight West Country burr, seldom resorting to the vernacular adopted by the alternative society, but always illustrating his points with graphic stories. His conversation was interrupted by children, one of whom kept running into his arms for a hug. He seemed to get on well with children.

He told me that his group had started in 1967 as the Hyde Park Diggers. 'I didn't know about Gerrard Winstanley – I was copying the San Francisco Diggers. It took us a few months to discover the San Francisco Diggers were taking off the British Diggers. Do I follow Winstanley's ideals? I would be Winstanley's idea of a Ranter. I am definitely not a Puritan. I am surprised that he sussed out everything, yet supported the male chauvinist syndrome. The Ranters were really Diggers, but they were against marriage and into the free love thing, which I admire.'

Sid Rawle proved to be one of the few people in the country with experience of the kind of commune we were dealing with in the film. John Lennon had given them the island of Donanish, Co Wicklow, Eire. I asked him how he had managed for food.

'In the second year it was all right because we grew our own crops. In the first year, so many people came and went; it was easy to rob them. By that I mean, say you had someone coming for the night. I'd say, how about a donation? If he was travelling about Ireland, he was liable to have £30 at least on him. Well, if he gave us £5, it would feed two people for a week. The usual reaction was "Far out! Can we stay forever?" Those usually left two weeks later. The commune varied from two people in the worst winter months to 20 in the summer.'

'How did you run the commune? Was it really communal?'

Miles Halliwell and Sid Rawle

'By dictatorship. Me. Benevolent dictatorship – but I'm used to being in charge of people. I was a shop steward at 18. There were lots of bids to take over. "Let's have a proper commune." I'd withdraw to my hut for a day or two and eventually someone would come in and say: "Sid, he's worse than you were. Come back."'

'What would you want to see in a film about a commune?'

'I would want to see some anger and falling out with one another as they try to live together. Humour – that is very important. I remember once I was in the cook tent having a bath in an iron tub. Outside, two people were digging in the garden, two chicks were sunbathing and this army sergeant, who was living with us, comes in army boots, shirt undone, socks hanging down. He had been tinkering with the engine of a boat. He salutes, says: "I wish to report that I feel we have a viable alternative to the straight society, sir!" I can't explain, but at the time, it was very, very funny.'

'Were you alarmed that the villagers might come? Were you pacifists?'

'We were pacifists all right, but let them come! If they'd come to tear down our houses, we would have kicked them off the island, and we had a double-barrelled shotgun to get them back in the boats.'

'I can never comprehend how Winstanley was able to keep his Diggers, who were mostly ex-soldiers, standing by while their houses were wrecked.'

'It's a bit the superiority thing – a reluctance to attack ordinary people. "They know not what they do." But you know, a real madman can come along and create hell with a group of people.'

'Did you share everything?'

'Most people shared most things. If you had a guitar, no one thought it would be communal unless you said so. People didn't hoard food, but they did hoard cigarettes and tit-bits. No one cared, because the minute they broke them out, everyone had a share. The important thing to stress is the dream – if you live in a commune, you're always dreaming of the day when this will be happening, that will be happening. But idyllic? Huh! In the winter, with the rain pouring down, it was hell.'

Sid Rawle expressed great interest in the film, and I promised to let him know when we were showing a rough cut. I was longing to have his reaction. A few days later, Sarah brought in the *Ham and High* with the headline 'Rampaging Squatters put Council under Siege.' Sid Rawle and 150 squatters had poured into a council meeting, challenged the proceedings and in a Cromwellian gesture, Rawle had flung aside the mace. The police broke up the occasion…

It was now June, and we were delighted to be back at Chastleton House, shooting the Fairfax scenes during one of Jerome Willis's infrequent breaks from his television assignments. The place was idyllic at this time of year. The tall banks were a riot of buttercups and cow-parsley. The front garden at Chastleton was full of colour and daisies covered the lawns.

Mamoun came to watch us shoot, with his wife Moya and children Sherief and Anies. The Hassans had recently bought a house in the Oxfordshire village of Deddington, and we instantly took advantage of the fact by billeting several actors on them. We were doing one of those simple scenes that take hours to light, and hours to shoot – and are discarded from the film in seconds. We shot a couple of takes and Mamoun left. Ernie told me later that he had received the greatest non-compliment of his life. 'Congratulations on the standard of the rushes. They're so much better than the first lot.'

'But when they're reprinted,' Ernie smiled, 'they might be okay.'

'It's nothing to do with the labs,' said Mamoun. 'It's you.'

Sunday's shooting depended upon Phil Oliver. It was the crucial scene in which Winstanley and Everard visit Fairfax, and refuse to remove their hats. Phil had gone to a pit reunion in south Wales, so I was very apprehensive. Miles had arrived the day before, and been given treatment appropriate to the star of the film – he had slept on the floor. The first words I heard that Sunday morning were from Miles, as he peered out into the early morning sunlight: 'No Phil Oliver.'

Jerome Willis, on the other hand, proved himself a true profes- sional. We fixed an 8am start and he was the only member of the cast on time. The group staying at Mamoun's must have got a huge break- fast because they turned up 45 minutes late. But there was no point worrying about unpunctuality – there was still no Phil. Jerome was fitted into a replica of the original costume worn by Fairfax – Carmen and Andrew had surpassed themselves – and he and Barrie Shaw (Col Rich) went through their lines. Jerome indicated that he was not one to learn lines parrot fashion, in case he learned them in too set a manner. Still no sign of Phil.

As each member of the crew arrived, Andrew and I discussed what we could do in the event of Phil not coming. It amounted to virtually nothing. The day revolved around Everard, Winstanley and Fairfax.

I went back to the cottage, and as I emerged through the garden gate, Phil Oliver's yellow Volkswagen van was parked on the bank. At least it looked like Phil Oliver's. But there was no one in it. I found him in the cottage. He had driven up from south Wales after 'one helluva night'. 'It's just 9.30,' he said. 'That's the time you told me to come.'

I was ashamed to admit I'd forgotten. Phil's arrival acted as a wave of new energy, and the Fairfax scenes flowed without problem. Although he was working with amateurs, Jerome never pulled rank on them. He was calm and patient throughout the day, and in the long lighting pauses he talked enthusiastically of the seventeenth century. He had studied Fairfax, and suggested giving him his northern accent. But the regional accent business had already defeated us.

Jerome Willis as Fairfax

Miles may have looked perfect for Winstanley, but he had an upper-class, public school accent. Winstanley had been a merchant before his bankruptcy, and would have spoken with the accent of Lancashire. We gave serious consideration to post-synching Miles. David Bramley had already adopted the accent of Parson Platt's place of birth – Wiltshire – and we initially intended making everyone speak correctly. But you cannot impose accents. Miles's attempts at North Country were pure Workers' Playtime. His natural delivery, on the other hand, conveyed a sincerity which would have been erased by another voice. So, with Winstanley speaking standard English, the class situation required Fairfax, the Drakes and Col. Rich to speak with upper-class accents, too.

Since the previous Chastleton scene, Miles had greatly improved his memorising of lines. He surpassed himself in the Fairfax scenes, where he had to deliver several long paragraphs. But we gave him a hard time. Had we thought about it, we could have avoided it. But it was something that never occurred to us.

The opening long shot showed Fairfax and Rich entering their headquarters. Our two men, sitting on a bench, rise and approach them. Fairfax and Rich turn. Winstanley and Everard have their backs to camera. The scene had been lit with great care, and efficiency demanded that we completed all shots favouring Fairfax before relighting for the reverse. By the time we came to do the all-important closeups of Winstanley, he had delivered his lines so often he was growing stale…and he began to fluff. Luckily, his performance in the long shots had been so strong we barely needed the closeups. But this was a valuable lesson we should have remembered from *IHH*, when we consistently left Pauline's closeups to the end of the day.

Filmmaking, at best, is a Chinese puzzle of interlocking difficulties, some of which can only be solved by miracles. And a miracle to us may not seem a miracle to anyone else. Once the Chastleton shooting was in the can, we faced the huge Fairfax-visiting-the-commune session, for which large numbers of animals, as well as people, were needed. It was further complicated by dates; Jerome Willis was free for the next two weekends, but not free again for months. Ernie was free next weekend, but was off on another assignment immediately afterwards. So we had to consolidate two fairly leisurely weekends into one hectic one.

Ernie then told us the date for his job, with Granada TV, had been brought forward. He would not be free next weekend. Once the mechanism of a session has been put into action, it is incredibly hard to stop it. A small session is easier to cancel because fewer people are involved. But a weekend of this scale required dozens of letters, sent out well in advance, and scores of telephone calls. Once past a certain date, it was impossible to cancel, for not everyone was on the phone. Later, when Andrew was ill, we had to cancel one session and despite the most assiduous cross-checking and assurances that everyone had been told, eight people still turned up at Larchfield.

There was no chance of stopping this one. We were horrified at the loss of Ernie, and the thought of changing the style of photography midstream. But it was a choice of doing the Fairfax session without Ernie, or doing it without Fairfax. Ernie's point was a strong one; he had already cancelled a Granada job at our behest. 'Granada will not employ me if I fail them this time. They were so pissed off the last time.' He would only be employed if he retained his reputation for reliability with the big TV companies. Reluctantly, we asked Barrie Male, Ernie's occasional assistant, but he was off to Greece. Our sound recordist Peter Harvey had been a cameraman; with Ernie's unhappy agreement we settled on him. A further series of setbacks turned the few days before the session into a nightmare. The atmosphere at Larchfield grew very strained. But then the phone rang, and Ernie announced: 'My job has fallen through.' We had our miracle. Our spirits soared.

Arrival of General Lord Fairfax

Chapter Seventeen

For Fairfax's visit, the commune had to look busy. It was summer; more huts had to be built, together with enclosures for the animals. What kind of animals would the Diggers have had? Pigs, certainly – but not the sort of pigs common today. We had to find the right breed of pig and for this the Rare Breeds Trust proved valuable. We were given the whereabouts of some Gloucester Old Spots at a school, Rotherfield Hall, Jarvis Brook, Crowborough in Sussex. The headmaster was sympathetic to our project, and offered to lend us the pigs for nothing. But he put in a plea for their gentle treatment: 'They are much loved by the children.' Transport from Crowborough took the edge off this generous offer; it cost us £30. We had no room in the budget for this unexpected charge, but rationalised it with the thought that £30 a week for 14 weeks had been put aside for each of us as a salary and we had never touched it.

The first shots we had to shoot on the Saturday morning were distant scenes of Fairfax and his retinue approaching the hill. Here was where a low budget was a distinct disadvantage; the great Lord General would hardly be escorted by a handful of horsemen. We needed a large troop of cavalry. Remembering that Tony Richardson had used the Household Cavalry for certain scenes in *Charge*, we gave passing consideration to them. Apparently, during the summer, they camped not too far away. But then Andrew came up with a simpler solution. In extreme long shot, you can't tell who's riding the horses; why not use the local pony club? And that's what we did. Helen Clarke, in charge of a local stable, rounded up all the girls of reasonable height, and Andrew rented buff coats and plastic helmets for each of them. He doubled Fairfax and Charles Rees doubled Gladman, and David Bramley rode his own. We had no idea how many girls would volunteer and I had put out a call for more riders.

One of these expert riders had appeared briefly in *IHH*, and now belonged to a group he called The Horse Film and Pageant Society.

He came down to Farnham station with a colleague, and telephoned through to Larchfield. Terry Higgins drove off to pick him up. What happened next was related in a furious letter I received a few days later: 'We were taken to the stables, where Andrew Mollo greeted us and told us there were no uniforms or mounts left! Even after it had been arranged that we ride for you. We were then shuttled around and offered some filthy rags to wear as "Diggers". Not quite the job we were offered and accepted I feel. Then, after seeing a group of kids on ponies, and a few others who were obviously scared stiff of sitting in the middle, whom our services were waived for, we were dropped off to the station without such a thing as a word of thanks or goodbye from Andrew.' He then charged us £14 for the loss of his day's work. I wrote back, saying how sorry we were that he had arrived when it was too late:

'I notice your heading refers to your group as a film society. You cannot have had much experience with filmmaking, or you would know that it is an exceedingly unpredictable undertaking, which demands the maximum of generosity from all who participate in it. Otherwise the experience becomes unpleasant in the extreme. So far, on *Comrade Jacob*, we have had the most remarkable people taking part, and working on the crew. There were several others who arrived for the express purpose of riding, but were found unsuitable for some reason or other. Had they been bitter, nursing a grudge, or too proud, you might have had some company on the way back to London. But these men were not the kind that would be defeated by a minor setback. Instead of deserting, like the French in 1940, they picked up those "filthy rags", tramped across the common and joined the main unit on the hilltop, where they were enrolled as Diggers. The riders were being filmed in such long shot that you couldn't tell who was on the back of the horses. The men in the filthy rags were the ones getting all the closeups. I enclose your train fare.'

The angry letter reminded me of those days on *IHH* and provided a striking contrast to the attitude of the cast and crew on *Comrade Jacob*.

Since most of the Saturday was to be expended on extreme long shots, the walkie-talkies were more important than ever. We carefully tested them, and when Ernie and I drove to the hill, Andrew's voice came over loud and clear from the stables. Ernie packed the *Guardian* with his camera gear. 'It's not that I'm not interested,' he grinned, 'I know we'll be sitting around a lot.' He was right.

We reached the top of the hill and set up. I tested the walkie-talkie again, and it merely hissed and crackled. Nothing came through from the other end. I remembered the surrender scene on *IHH*, when Andrew had switched the machine off 'to save the battery' and I was sure the same thing had happened again. I had a .22 starting pistol in the pocket of my greatcoat and I fired it to attract his attention. It made a sound like a hiccup carried on the wind. Eventually, two horsemen, Charles Rees and Nick Nascht, galloped towards us and stopped at the base of the hill. I ran down and gave Charles a fresh battery. 'Tell Andrew to switch on his walkie-talkie and tell us what's going on. If it doesn't work, send a rider to the hill with information.' Off they went, and I clambered back up the hill. Ernie was deep in his paper. We waited for what seemed hours, when suddenly the radio sprang to life. Two words came through. 'Kevin, will...' and that was all. Alison went round by car and reported on her return that Andrew had had a bad fall from his horse. Wearing his armour, he had crashed on to concrete and had damaged the walkie-talkie. However, he was back in the saddle again. When they were ready, they would wave their standard – when we were ready, we were to wave something white (Ernie's *Guardian*!). We sat for a very long time staring at the gap in the trees, where we could just see the immobile horses. Andrew was obviously still dressing extras. At last the standard waved. I waved the *Guardian*. The camera turned. The column appeared and the sight was most impressive. It did, indeed, look like a large troop of cavalry. The buff coats and red sashes against the heather made me wish for once that we had colour. Just then, two elderly ladies appeared on the path and hovered, right on the edge of frame. The cavalry halted, there was the sound of shouting, and the elderly ladies sought cover behind a bush. The column moved off again. 'I'm keeping close,' said Ernie. 'I can see civilians.'

'Not too close,' I warned. 'Remember that the riders are mostly schoolgirls.'

'Oh yes,' muttered Ernie. 'It looked so good I forgot.' He pulled back on the zoom, the civilians vanished and the riders spread out across the common. The dust rose in a cloud. It looked most effective.

We tried one more take. Jeff Cornish joined us. His pal, Don Skinner, had got lost. As the cavalry moved forward again, we saw he was still lost. Don's car appeared on the path directly behind the horses.

Following pages:
Andrew Mollo Terry Higgins Kevin Brownlow Jerome Willis Miles Halliwell
Virginia Brownlow (seated)   Ernie Vincze (cameraman)

175

How could we attract his attention? Jeff then revealed that he had the loudest voice in the country. He rent the air with his yell: 'Stop and move the car!' It sped away like a scalded cat.

The takes were slow, because manoeuvring horses consumes a great deal of time. When the long shots were over, our impetus had gone. David Caute and his wife Martha appeared on the hill. I was glad to see them, but their presence put me off. Perhaps because of the feeling of being supervised, perhaps because I was reluctant to shoot anything that Caute hadn't written, the few inserts we had left frittered to a conclusion. Enthusiasm evaporated; we felt as if the school inspector was paying the class a visit. Caute himself was intrigued by the operation of making films. He said to someone later: 'I know they've changed the script a lot, but it's a bit much casting Jacob as a horse!' It turned out that David Caute had attended Frensham Heights during the war, and that evening Miles invited us to a folk concert at the school. David Caute and Andrew between them stopped the show in its tracks when the singers sang a number about Ronald Biggs, the train robber: 'a hero – for your crimes were against property, not against other men'. Caute exploded: 'That was the most dishonest song I've ever heard,' and he and Andrew enquired about the fireman, injured in the Great Train Robbery, who was still in hospital. 'Yes,' agreed the singers, 'that's the only flaw in the folk myth.' The discussion grew more intense and the singers said they'd take the matter up later, but could they continue? They then sang about Dick Turpin and Robin Hood!

One of the leading actors for tomorrow's session had still not arrived – Dawson France (Gladman) – nor had we heard from him. But the Gloucester Old Spot pigs turned up in a huge truck while we were at Frensham Heights. Mr Chambers, the driver, was shown the hut in which we planned to keep them for the night. 'Oh no,' he said. 'They'll get out of those huts in a second, and they'll walk so far you'll never catch them. You'll need a guard all night. We'll look after them and deliver them at 8am.' This was very considerate of him. When he returned next morning, I was startled by the size of the animals. And even more startled by the appalling shrieks and squeals they emitted. Mr Chambers instructed us to stand either side of the trucks with large boards; he then hauled the unruly animals out by the tails, swivelled them round, and we gingerly escorted them towards the commune with our boards. We felt the power of the animals when they decided to try a different route. Once in the hut, a board was placed over the entrance, with stakes holding it down, and the pigs were given a special guard – Jeff Cornish. We returned to our breakfast of fried bacon, feeling it tactful not to take Jeff his breakfast.

The pigs, Cordelia and Hotspur, behaved well (they lived until 1981), snuffling round the commune as though they'd been born in it, until we went to shoot some inserts on the hill and they were pushed into one of the huts. The entrance was blocked with the board, held firm by stakes. The pigs huffed and snorted until they got fed up with the indignity of imprisonment – then jammed their noses under the board and sent it flying. Out they came, like bulls into an arena, charging through the nearest gap – between an extra's legs. The poor fellow was carried along on the back of the boar until the animal hurled him off into the undergrowth. The other extras had a fine song and dance chasing the huge pigs around the lawn, and were suitably in awe of them for the rest of the session.

When we returned from the hill, Jerome Willis said: 'This looks like Brighton beach.' Diggers were playing football, sunbathing and drinking homemade lemonade provided by Nick Rowling. We still had no word from Dawson – and he never turned up. (In the editing, however, we realised that a man on a horse against the sky looks much the same however many times you shoot him; we restored Gladman to the sequence by using an outtake from the previous session.)

We had always hoped that Fairfax's tour of inspection would be reminiscent of a visit by the Duke of Edinburgh. The choice of Jerome proved particularly fortunate; everyone had seen him on television, and they responded to his presence with just the right degree of deference. We secured reactions from the Diggers by having Fairfax fire questions at them. Bill Petch guarded the pigs, and kept them sweet-tempered by tickling their stomachs until they lay down. He came up with a splendid ad lib. Fairfax asked him: 'Where did you get the pigs from?' And he replied: 'You shouldn't ask an old soldier where he gets his pigs from, Sir.'

Sid Rawle, the New Digger, watched from the sidelines. When I asked him his opinion of the session, he replied, ambiguously, that he was thinking. Despite, or because of, the initial tension and suspense, this session struck both Andrew and me as the most successful so far.

Perhaps because we shot an extra take for Cecil on every scene, Hendersons reported no mishaps. In fact, Cecil was so relaxed about our rushes that he was able to comment: 'You've got gorgeous porkers there. Who made those huts? Very handy, I must say.'

The marathon two-hour rushes session was held at a Wardour Street viewing theatre, and was marred by sub-standard projection. The arc on one machine was incorrectly balanced, so that the light dropped from one roll to another, and both projectors were equipped with cheap lenses, which smeared Hendersons rich blacks to an all-over Studio Film Labs grey. The small erosions of quality achieved by the slap-happy projectionist were astonishing, but they reached a climax when he insisted on projecting out of focus. We offended the man mortally by asking again and again for the focus to be adjusted, and whenever we were forced to use his theatre on future occasions, he adopted a flounce of smouldering outrage which suggested that he was the in-jured party. After rushes, we adjourned, as was our habit, to the last old-fashioned Soho teashop, Valori's, and blew vast sums on huge sticky cakes.

Setback invariably follows success. We received an anxious letter from David Caute:

'My worries concern the relationship of the film to the script. I am alarmed at the extent that the script is being discarded...Of course the Director is and should be the prime creative element in the making of a film. The writer however is peculiarly concerned with language. He is not happy when words attributed to several characters are given to one or two (as in the Drake house sequence) and what you write about Fairfax's arrival on the hill does not fill me with joy. I wonder what questions Fairfax (Duke of Edinburgh) fired at the Diggers in your scene; what words did he use? With the writer far away and the pages of the script turning at the edges, it is all too easy to imagine that improvisation on the spot is the solution. But whether in the theatre or on film, the result is usually crass and not something the writer would put his signature to.

'The script tells a story which illustrates the conjunction of political and economic radicalism with a historically distinctive form of religious mysticism, with a strong sense of the supernatural, of "voices" from another sphere. If this latter aspect is neglected, then it will certainly do violence to my intention. A passion for documentary and historical accuracy of detail is splendid, but it does not in itself make for an interesting film. I am all for depicting it "like it was" but if this becomes a final aim and end on set the results may prove disappointing.' (17 June 1973)

Andrew and I were as disturbed by this letter as David Caute was alarmed about the film. We could hardly deny we were changing the script, and yet to have the carpet pulled from under our feet at this crucial stage was an appalling thought.

We decided to answer him as straightforwardly as we could. 'Your anxiety about the allegorical sequences and our improvisation and invention requires a rather involved answer,' I wrote, incorporating several of Andrew's themes:

'I realised as soon as we started shooting that our style is not to follow closely what is written in the script. This came as a surprise to me; I had forgotten, with the ten-year gap, that we use the script to set the direction of the sequence. Once all the elements are there, we try to inject a spark to produce something spontaneous, for without that spontaneity, the picture – if made by us – would become mechanical.

'The script acts like a party manifesto; it sets out the aims in broad terms, but does not explain how they are to be achieved.

'While you were writing the screenplay we had no idea how we would treat the abstract area of the story. The documentary approach and historical accuracy of the detail is as much a stylistic device as playing Shakespeare in modern clothes, or using step ladders for horses. Complete accuracy of character, dialogue and details does not easily intercut with masked figures and other allegorical devices. Even a stylised camera angle, we have now discovered, sticks out like a sore thumb.

'When we discussed these scenes with you at the script stages, we were in complete agreement that they should be included. But we didn't have the style of the rest of the film at that point. Now these scenes seem out of place. Just to put them in for the sake of our previous commitment would be the wrong way, we feel, of going about it. We have to persuade ourselves that we can do them. If at the rough cut stage this element is lacking, to the detriment of the overall effect, we will shoot the allegorical scenes and attempt to cut them in.

'Spontaneous dialogue is not a faith with us, but when we achieved a complete atmosphere, as we did in Fairfax's visit to the commune, it works very well. If we are doing violence to your intention, it is certainly not our intention. We can only work by intuition and experience, like any other artists, and, as we live with the film, so our ideas must change.' (21 June 1973)

I ended the letter by saying that of all people, we wanted him to be pleased with the result, because without the book, the film would never have occurred to anyone. But we knew that, of all people, he would not be pleased.

Chapter Eighteen

An outstanding moment in any film is the first rough cut show. In our case, the picture was only half there. We booked the expensive De Lane Lea theatre because of the superb projection, and ordered enough time just to show the picture. That was a sensible gesture towards economy, but we reckoned without the notorious lack of punctuality of some of the cast and crew. One should always ask people 15 minutes early. Even if you don't get into the theatre at once, it saves paying for wasted time. We had to abandon the opening reel, which gave an unbalanced effect to the rough cut. But the reactions afterwards were better than expected.

Terry Higgins wanted more blood and thunder. Andrew looked like a pleased cat and simply said: 'There are a lot of little things,' and when pressed said that he didn't like the face of one of the extra girls – 'too modern' – and she'd have to go. This was the equivalent of an Academy Award, considering he saw 50 minutes. Marina Lewycka was delighted, and her complaint was equally obtuse: 'When Everard gets to the top of the hill, he looks at a forest wreathed in mist. It's full of fir trees. You must find a deciduous forest.' Nick Rowling said it would be a historical film to be seen again and again and thought it might become *the* film on the period. He said he at last understood Andrew's obsession with detail. He had thought it a substitute for ideas, but now realised it put over ideas in a very rich way.

All the same, the rough cut showed that in the second part the emphasis had to change. We were at a loss to know how to achieve this. Mamoun felt the Ranters might provide the polemical difference we needed. David Caute had briefly referred to Ranters in the script. Mamoun suggested we developed the idea, and do more research. 'Your Ranter should be someone of supreme arrogance,' said Mamoun. 'He knows he is absolutely right and everyone else is a fool. Yet he has a kind of fearlessness. You need someone very good looking, with grace, who behaves appallingly.'

Research into the Ranters led to Christopher Hill's recently published *The World Turned Upside Down*, which contained a superbly-researched and highly entertaining account of what a contemporary described as 'these profane people, who blaspheme, curse, whore and openly rejoice in their wickedness'. For the Ranters, there was no afterlife; they lived entirely for the present, believing that 'to the pure all is pure'. A group of them descended on St George's Hill, offering support for Winstanley, but bringing the commune into disrepute with their outrageous behaviour. The situation became so bad that Winstanley had to defend himself with a pamphlet, *A Vindication of the Diggers*, in which he pointed out that while they called themselves Diggers, the Ranters were a very different breed, and he listed their failings.

Frequent references to Lawrence Clarkson, an ex-soldier known as 'Captain of the Rant', whom Stanley Reed had mentioned, led me to the British Museum once more, to examine Clarkson's pamphlet *The Lost Sheep Found* (1650). Following the usual confusion and delay, Virginia had to take over the research and she found that Clarkson had visited St George's Hill, probably with the group that stayed there, and he dealt with the experiment in a scathing paragraph: 'For I made it appear to Gerrard Winstanley there was a self-love and vain glory nursed in his heart, that if possible by digging to have gained people to him, by which his name might become great among the poor Commonalty of the Nation' (p27). Clarkson made a cruel charge which history, fortunately, has not confirmed. 'Afterwards in him appeared a most shameful retreat from St George's Hill, with a spirit of pretended universality, to become a real Tithe-gatherer of propriety.'

The similarities of the Ranters to the squatters and hippies of the 1970s were almost too obvious. Worse still, Ken Russell was written all over them. The difficulty would be to present these people as revolutionaries, without making them seem like extras from *The Devils*.

Christopher Hill, we were told, was planning a new book on Winstanley. I made renewed efforts to contact him, and was rewarded with a letter from France. He was not writing a new book on Winstanley, but editing a selection of his writings. I had asked him if he knew why, during the period of the commune, the Diggers moved from one part of St George's Hill to another. 'Reading between the lines,' he wrote, 'the Diggers clearly had trouble from a group of Ranter-hippies, who latched on to them, and the move may have had as part of its object to shake them off. But this is mere hypothesis; I couldn't produce a shred of evidence.'

So here was confirmation that we should develop the Ranter sequence. But who should play the part? We thought of various fringe theatre groups, made a list of the craziest of our acquaintances, and then I remembered that Sid Rawle had always regarded himself more as a Ranter than a Digger. I hastily arranged another rough cut showing and invited Sid. 'Fantastically good,' he said. 'It brought it all back. That scene of the family sheltering from the rain, eating their bits of bread, that could have been us, soaked to the bloody skin, waiting till the clothes dried on you. That's just the way it was.' Over lunch, Sid held forth and a man sharing our table grew more and more hostile. We ordered, there was a long wait, and instead of food, the menus arrived again. Sid grabbed one and began to eat it, to the horror of our neighbour. 'Waiter!' shouted Sid. 'This isn't very tender.' And he tossed it back on the table. It landed in front of the seething gentleman, who picked it up and threw it back at Sid. Now Sid became consciously provocative, and one could see in his behaviour the stuff that Ranters were made of. I asked him if he would consider playing the role, and he said he'd love to – and he would find someone else who would be ideal.

'Bill Dwyer's the man you want,' he declared, in a voice that echoed across the restaurant. 'He's working with us on the Windsor Free Festival. He believes we should all eat together and fuck together…'

The hostile gentleman left immediately…

The idea of the Diggers moving their commune was carefully considered by Andrew, but the more he thought about it, the more opposed to it he became. 'The commune is symbolic to the audience,' he said. 'If you move it, just as they get used to it, they won't know where they are.' I agreed with him, although admitting that we gave ourselves extra problems. For their first site was on land owned by Francis Drake. Their second, across the parish boundary, was on Platt's land. But authenticity would have to take second place, for once, to the convenience of drama.

When Ernie wrote to say he would be back at the beginning of August, I set up a session for the weekend of the 5th and 6th. Andrew said this would be a mistake; Ernie would be exhausted. He had been in Ceylon throughout the whole of July, working on a very demanding documentary. I pointed out that Ernie had written to say he would be ready to work that weekend, we had a desperately pressured schedule because of this long sojourn and we had to get moving. Who were we to judge whether he would be exhausted or not? Ernie knew his own metabolism. In any case, he was coming back via Paris, and so may take a break there. Andrew proved horribly correct.

Assembled at Larchfield, we called Ernie, and Lynn, his wife, said he had been delayed in Paris, and wouldn't be back till late that evening. Late was right. A strike at Heathrow delayed Ernie for 16 hours. We called him next morning and Lynn said he hadn't woken. I was in a quandary; I said it would be awful to drag him down after such a flight, but so far 20 people had arrived, and I didn't know what to do with them. If he could come even for a short time, it might save the day. Outside it was pouring with rain. Virginia was ill with a severe migraine, Nick Nascht was also ill and David Bramley was suffering from appendicitis.

On *IHH*, I used to have a recurrent nightmare; turning up for a session with dozens of people and forgetting the camera. Well, here it was in reality. Thirty people had by now turned up, including a group who had never been on the film before. And worse than no camera, there was no cameraman. Andrew and I explained the position and we rehearsed the Digger song. Community singing was fun for a while, but it quickly began to pall. The rain lashed the fir trees outside. Late in the morning, Ernie rang up: 'If you've got 20 people down there I will have to come. I've a few things I have to do, but I'll be down at two o'clock.' I thanked him profusely, warned him of the heavy traffic and returned to the front room to try to raise morale. We went through the song until we were sick of it, and broke for a long lunch.

Rehearsing the song was more of an achievement than it sounds, for although the words of the Digger song were available, nobody knew the music. But a musician called Vic Gammon had contacted us; he specialised in traditional and popular music – broadsides, ballads – and offered his support. He managed to trace the tune for the Digger song, and he accompanied it on pipe and tabor.

When Ernie arrived, he was looking not pale and exhausted, but tanned and exhausted. Furthermore, he was suffering from a tropical bug he had picked up in Ceylon. He had been working in temperatures of 120 degrees, filming religious fanatics suspending themselves from hooks and walking through flames. Suddenly, he was transported to the dank atmosphere of an English wood, in the pouring rain, in temperatures well below the seasonal normal. The light was very low, and despite the intensity of the rain, you couldn't see it on film. So we added to the actors' discomfiture by pouring yet more water on them from a watering can. Accustomed to greater drama before his lens, Ernie complained that the setup was empty and dull, and he roamed the commune trying to find an alternative, while the extras stood around, getting wetter and wetter. Despite the rehearsals, no one had conscientiously learned the song except for Peter Wood, a singer friend of Vic Gammon's, upon whom we depended for the closeup. But by the time we had ground ourselves miserably through the establishing shot, push-

Singing in the rain

ing the actors deeper into the huts as we realised they couldn't remember the song, the light faded.

Vic Gammon heroically withstood the storm sitting in the centre of the commune playing his pipe while not only rain but several canfuls of water soaked him to the skin.

We paid a visit to our field to see how the crops were doing. Bill Petch came too. The field was full of weeds and bracken, and the stunted barley was badly beaten down. Andrew and I looked at it in dismay. Bill Petch laughed uproariously.

Remembering a desperately cold session on *IHH*, when we had made the cast sleep in an unheated coach in the snow, and how a letter had mollified the most rebellious, I sent a note to everyone who had

Vic Gammon (musicologist and actor)

attended the last session. But they regarded it as another experience, and were in no danger of storming off the picture.

The rushes of the rain session were fine, but they consisted of material which had not been scripted, nor planned, but merely improvised to save the day. (Of all the reviews we got for the film, I treasure the one from *Valeurs Actuelles* in Paris: 'The sequence where the Diggers, crudely sheltered from the rain, strike up a hymn to alleviate their despair, belongs to cinema at its greatest.')

We were now seriously behind schedule and Andrew and I talked to Ernie. He said that while he'd hoped Ceylon would enable him to give us the whole of August, it hadn't – he'd just seen his bills. We asked him directly if he was confident that he would be able to finish the film. He said: 'No.' Granada had made overtures to him about directing the next Disappearing World, and when Lynn had read him out our revised schedule, she had overlooked September. I told him of my recurrent nightmare and Andrew told us his; he is fast asleep on the set and wakes up with everyone crowded round staring down at him. Anyway, Ernie said nothing to subdue our anxiety.

General gloom enveloped both Andrew and me, and another grim session followed. For the sequence of the beating up of the Digger and the boy, we had selected Jeff Cornish and the son of Chris Wicking, Mitch. It was one of those occasions when the elements of a good sequence are totally lacking. Neither Andrew nor I had a clue how to shoot it and various runs through looked stereotyped and dull. We were both preoccupied and distant, and the partnership did not work. The action was stodgy, and I knew I didn't have the scene, and Andrew wasted no time in telling me I hadn't. Chris Wicking, a professional scriptwriter himself, kept talking of choreographing it and rehearsing more. Rehearse was all we could do, because two men playing soldiers had yet to arrive. Gradually, the long shot began to take shape. When the soldiers had been costumed, and shown the action, we tried a take. Things were beginning to gel when I told Charles Rees (playing a soldier) to rip the boy's shirt off. The Digger pamphlet described how the boy was left naked and the image seemed powerful and unexpected. The camera turned and Charles did as instructed – but in tearing the shirt, he swung Mitch against a hut. He was a fragile boy, and was shaken by this. On the next take he grazed his knee. I noticed his expression and hurriedly changed to closeups to give him a rest. Mitch was so red-eyed that I thought a break for lunch might cheer him up. We had shot practically nothing. Chris Wicking said his son was very upset. He was sitting on the lawn sobbing. Chris said he was so frightened, he couldn't face carrying on. What the hell do we do? Scrap the morning's work and do it over with Nicky instead of Mitch? Nicky was younger than Mitch, but he was sturdier and considerably less tragic. Mitch wouldn't say anything; he just sobbed. I felt like doing the same. I kept thinking: 'This is the son of a fellow who writes horror films?' Andrew thought we should start again with Nicky, but oh, the cost in time and stock! I talked to Mitch and suggested he just do some running. He said something at last – 'I don't want to be chased.' So I had an idea.

'Why don't you take charge of the scene? You direct it, and we'll do just as you say.' Eventually, he agreed and timorously we foregathered at the commune. It became plain that Mitch wouldn't let us rip the shirt from his back, let alone his breeches. So the scene dropped in effectiveness. And we were forced to shoot it subjectively, with the soldiers roughing up the camera rather than Mitch. (After a press show, critic Tom Milne said that while he liked the film very much, and he

Mitch Wicking ambushed by soldiers

particularly liked the style, we departed from it inexplicably in one scene, the soldiers beating up the boy…)

The soldiers set fire to a hut as they left the commune, and the thatched roof produced such impressive flames that the huge pine tree, which dominated the commune, was in real danger. For several minutes I watched sparks float into the treetops, imagining headlines as the fire caught the tops of the trees, and spread out of control across the county.

Remembering Sid Rawle's advice about discord in the commune, we shot two scenes. One, suggested by Virginia, showed a young woman chatting to one of the men, forgetting all about the cooking. The men return from the field and stand around the cooking pot glumly, while the young woman is berated by an older one, who scurries around trying to rescue the meal. The second scene, suggested by Andrew, showed a furious fight breaking out inside one of the huts, a wife ejecting her husband and throwing after him the contents of the hut. Both scenes worked well, but when we cut them into the body of the film, they failed to integrate with the rest of the material.

Mrs Platt's climb up the hill, which we shot the following day, was climaxed by her glimpse of the smoke from the Diggers' campfire. Andrew lit a smokepot in the wood at the back of our hill and from the camera position it looked excellent. Then we heard a strangled shriek. 'Kevin!' yelled Andrew. 'Fire!' We rushed down and Andrew was hopping about in open sandals, kicking a canister from which flames were belching. Smaller flames were licking up from the grass. Andrew's footwear was not ideal for the control of red hot smoke-bombs, but he had succeeded in controlling it. We beat the flames into submission with branches, and another Surrey conflagration was averted.

If fire and rain wasted stock, nothing consumed it more than animals. Prevented by an outbreak of cattle disease from bringing rare-breed longhorns to the barn at Larchfield, we had to go to Drusilla's, Alfriston, Sussex, and shoot the longhorns in their own barn. Andrew cunningly disguised the concrete walls with tarpaulin, and Ernie kept the shot of the longhorn, named Delilah, as tight as he could. All we wanted was for the cow to look round. We shouted, cajoled, roared; the cowman hauled her by the tail, but it took a lot of stock before Delilah obliged us with a baleful look. Miles, with his dislike of animals, was instructed how to milk, and since his hands were out of shot, we got away with an approximation. Trying to control them in an open field

was a different matter. The cowmen, playing bailiffs, had to pretend to beat the cows. Winstanley runs up to restrain them. While the men are arguing, the cows wander off. On the first take, the cows thundered into shot at a fantastic gallop, like a stampede from a western. On the second take, the cows went in different directions. On the third take, they very slowly ambled into shot. But we discovered that Delilah hated the screech of the walkie-talkie, and shied away whenever she heard it. Andrew switched his on full volume, and kept me talking into it, while using the distorted words as a long-range stick to keep Delilah, and thus the other, on the move.

Cecil Fennell telephoned in an uncharacteristically aggressive mood. 'The first rolls of rushes I've seen are totally unusable.'

'What's wrong with them?'

'They're veiled.'

'Veiled?'

'I can tell you it's nothing whatever to do with us. I don't know what you get up to over there. The tins arrive with only one piece of tape on them.'

'But tins only ever have one piece of tape wrapped round them.'

'I can't imagine what it is.' He said he would call with the news of the other rolls. I spent a nasty couple of hours writing off the cow scenes, when he called up to say the other stuff was all right – and he took back everything. He said: 'It was entirely our responsibility and I regret it from the bottom of my heart. A relief developer – he's an old chap, done hundreds of thousands of feet of negative – not used to this fast stock. He uses a torch – a correct pan torch, green, because he has to develop by eye. It's the only way he can do it. Well, I was watching as the first strands came off and he comes running out of the developing room and says: "How are the other rolls?" "Oh, they seem all right." And I happened to say: "It's very fast, you know, this FP4. You can't even use a torch."

'"Oh, Christ," he said. "Then it's my fault."'

The closeups of the bailiffs were wrecked, making it almost impossible to cut the sequence properly, and out of the question to use the best takes, since these vanished in a cloud of murk. We could have retaken them, but we had neither the time, nor the money, nor the inclination. The sequence never worked as it should have done, but we hoped that having found their gremlins, Hendersons would operate rather more smoothly.

Chapter Nineteen

Mamoun Hassan considered our rough cut lacking one important feature: the relationship of the villagers to the Diggers. We explained that we intended to shoot these scenes as soon as we could find a village. A couple of sites, such as the farm in Wales, had appealed to Andrew, but they needed a great deal of hard labour before they could yield even a single street.

What we needed was a real village we could take over for a couple of weekends. With Nick Rowling, we scoured the files at the Historic Monuments Commission and toured dozens of villages. But however many ancient buildings clustered round the duck pond, when we got there, either the demolition men had desecrated the site or it had been ruined for our purposes by fresh paint, tarmac or telegraph poles. The old photographs at the commission showed that as late as the 1930s, rural areas in Britain were relatively unspoilt. In the area architecturally correct for the film, every village had been cleaned up and prettified since the war; how we cursed the Best Kept Village competitions!

Driving through Hampshire, we spotted a group of buildings crowned with rat-eaten thatch and drove in to investigate. It was a former racing stable, belonging to Run-Run Shaw, the Hong Kong film producer, which had been allowed to fall into a state of decay. Thoroughbreds were still kept in part of the stables, but the remainder was empty. The thatch was perfect. Andrew was less enthusiastic about the buildings themselves because of the amount of work needed to convert them. But I was delighted. I could see many more angles than the Welsh farm would have given us – and the thatch was a magnificent bonus. Weyhill Stables became our village.

A couple of days before the session, Andrew rang up to say, despondently, that he and Nick Rowling had done a lot of work, but it still looked what it was. 'The trouble is,' he said, 'it's impossible to alter those sharp verticals.' He was referring to the aggressive Edwardian brickwork, expertly pointed, which refused to adopt the less disciplined line of the seventeenth century. Sarah's husband, Mike Ellis, drove me down and the place did look rather mournful. The walls had been daubed, and some bars put in the window, but nothing had been done so far to change the atmosphere. Andrew turned up in the truck with Elizabeth Dampier-Child, a former primary school headmistress, and a student on Nick's Open University course. She was amazingly energetic for her advanced years, and had been racing from knackers' yard to abattoir to public health inspector to try to get meat for the butcher's shop. In the seventeenth century, such merchandise was displayed outside the shop; we wanted to show the Diggers being refused meat by the butcher. Eventually they located a real butcher, who agreed to bring a load of meat on the Saturday.

I went round Weyhill and the local farms, rounding up extras. We needed entirely new faces, and Mike Ellis and I encountered some marvellous characters. Despite their assurances, however, all we got on the day was one boy and a kitten!

The centrepiece of the village was to be the Ranters. We planned to have them outrage the villagers before proceeding to St George's Hill to join the Diggers. Sid Rawle was holding his Windsor Free Festival, and Charles Rees drove Ian Sellar and me down to Windsor Great Park to ensure he would be available on the Sunday.

We hunted for the Cavalry Exercise Ground, where Sid had guaranteed he would be. A huge sprawl of multi-coloured tents gave the place the atmosphere of a medieval crusade; it was quite exhilarating, without that sense of aggression that accompanied a Sealed Knot muster. We asked a man selling *Socialist Worker* where we could find Sid Rawle. Was there a headquarters area? 'The people are organising this festival. You could find him anywhere.' Eventually, we found him carrying a blanket full of money – 'Collection for food,' he explained. He looked grim; his eyes were yellow and he said he had jaundice. There was no hope of his being free on Monday – they intended the festival to last nine days.

We drove on to Newbury, where the Sealed Knot was encamped. The tents were bigger and the officers had caravans; there was even a camp commandant. We relayed information about our session at Weyhill, and then returned to the stables. Terry Higgins had arrived and pitched his tent. 'It was a stroke of genius to find this place,' he said. 'There shouldn't be buildings like this.' The place was beginning to look rather good, but Andrew was content to leave the finishing touches until the first day of the session itself.

One of the first actors to arrive was the butcher. He pointed out that his meat was liable to go off in the fearsome heat. We had to do his scenes rapidly. The meat was gruesome – pigs' heads and other unmentionable morsels. Andrew created a splendid butcher's shop from old timber and the 'village' began to come alive. The butcher himself looked convincing in costume, but he had never acted before and had not the same amount of experience as the Diggers. The scene was sluggish. The flies clustered round the meat, and the sun grew hotter and hotter. We moved to a scene suggested by Elizabeth Dampier-Child involving village women and 'rough music'. This was practised in the old days to show the community's dislike for such interlopers as gipsies; one woman would bang a pot, the next would take up the rhythm until the whole village was pounding away like massed tom-toms. (Belfast women used the same technique with dustbins in the recent Troubles.) While we were shooting this scene, Ernie said he thought it was very bad, and couldn't understand it. No amount of explanation enlightened him. He shot it as though under protest.

The next day, he was equally obdurate. Dozens of extras turned up from the Sealed Knot camp, but when the rain came he refused to shoot anything more. There was obviously something wrong and Andrew and I had a long conference with him. It turned out he had been offered a feature.

We pointed out that since he had to work for money, then the BFI should pay him.

'I wouldn't take it,' said Ernie. 'I think that would be morally wrong. Not when everyone else is working for nothing.'

'But by taking money,' said Andrew, 'you would enable us to finish the film. On the other hand, if it isn't money, and the other film is more important, then nothing we say will make any difference.' Andrew emphasised that he, too, had an overdraft, children to feed, etc. The prolonging of the film meant that he could do no other work.

Ernie said he would take Sundays off – and that he could therefore give us one day a week. 'But there are 20 shooting days left. That would mean, at one day a week, six months.'

Ernie said he was sorry to be 'buggering us up' but warned us if anything came up in the meantime, he would have to take it – meaning we may lose those weekends already available before he took the feature. He made it clear he would not consider giving up the feature, which was *Got it Made*, directed by James Kenelm Clarke.

The unkindest cut of all occurred when Andrew left the game fowl hidden in their crate in one of the buildings, in order to visit a local village. Upon his return, he found the chickens stolen and only the crate remaining. Not a place we remember with great affection, Weyhill...

We received some wry amusement from a local newspaper cutting, sent by Elizabeth Dampier-Child:

'Although Weyhill could never be compared with Hollywood it did do its own little bit for the film industry at the weekend. A London film unit had searched most of the country for a setting which could be converted to a seventeenth-century town square before they eventually found the old racing stables at Weyhill, which they felt could do the job.

'But the stables were not enough, for the unit also needed people to fill the square – and that is where 30 locals came in. And our butcher Mr Albert Stevens was one of the 30. "They asked me to take them some meat for one of the stalls in the square," he explained. "And before I knew it I was dressed in a period costume playing a butcher."

'The 90-minute Government-sponsored film is about a religious sect called "The Shakers" who were outcasted by those who followed the more conventional religions. They eventually settled in America, where their belief is still in existence today.'

The rushes of the village were disappointing, but it was hard to know precisely why. The impact came when we cut them into the film and organised another rough cut show. This was an unmitigated disaster. The village scenes popped on to the screen without any establishing shots, in a kind of neutral mid-distance. The film had been conceived in terms of extreme long shots and extreme closeups, and yet here was a series of vital sequences photographed in mid-shot. The mid-shots were the best that could be done in those surroundings – the camera was prevented by solid brick from moving further back. The trouble was that they revealed the anachronistic texture of the original buildings, and largely excluded what had attracted us to the place – the rat-eaten thatch. The village was not a village, and although brave efforts had been made to conceal that fact, they had failed under the merciless scrutiny of high quality 35mm film. On top of which, the staging of the scenes was seldom convincing. Incidents which should have been glimpsed from a distance were played as though on a pro-scenium, especially for the camera. The whole experience was the undoing of two filmmakers who specialised in documentary conditions; once those conditions were removed, we were working to all intents and purposes on a studio backlot, but without the resources that a studio would provide. Directorially, the experience was similar to that first session, when Ernie was deprived of his zoom lens. Now we were deprived of our mobility and forced into setups we didn't really like, simply because they were convenient. We shot about ten separate sequences – Diggers selling brooms, encountering resentment, finding one sympathetic villager...and that villager being evicted by Platt...Diggers trying to get food...and the triumphal return of Parson Platt after the destruction of the commune on St George's Hill. While the Diggers should have been seen from far away, lurking hopefully on the edge of a little cluster of shacks, we had to show them stomping through the village itself. And thus we created for the film one of its major defects.

The villagers' point of view was so involved that it required length. They were, after all, in an even worse situation than the Diggers – at the mercy of tyrannical landlords, they were equally insecure, and they were forced to pay a tenth of all they earned to the church. Exploiting this insecurity, the landowners encouraged them to attack the Diggers, the very people who would have supported them. In trying to suggest their latent envy and fear of the Diggers, we needed to give the villagers equal screen time. Otherwise, we would have been left with little more than the end result – the violence – and the villagers would have been more villainous than they really were. By removing them completely from the film, Andrew felt the villagers would be transformed, not ineffectively, into the unknown enemy beyond the forest.

The failure of the village gave us problems with the Ranters. Their entry into the village would now have to be absorbed into the commune. The Windsor Free Festival was arousing furious headlines, so we fixed a session when Sid Rawle would be clear of that and perhaps his jaundice.

Sid brought down Phil Byfield, who had spent ten years in the prop department at Shepperton, Tex, a retired Hell's Angel about to go to jail, and one wild girl and a sombre one, with baby. Andrew spent a great deal of time on their costume, and when they reappeared, there was no doubt what kind of people they were. Their appearance in the

Phil Byfield, Sid Rawle and Ranters

commune disturbed the Diggers, who reacted just as the original Diggers must have done; they froze, and then recoiled in suspicion and alarm. It was not hard to get the right atmosphere. The first rehearsal was fine, and we began shooting. One take on the long shot – everyone seemed satisfied. The atmosphere remained icy and it took most of the day before Sid Rawle had melted the hostility.

The Ranter scene was an excellent example of the Brownlow-Mollo partnership, and a clear answer to people who asked us 'why co-direct?' The scene of Sid Rawle 'inspecting' the commune worked adequately in rehearsal but it needed directorial flair. Andrew provided it. As he checked Sid Rawle's costume before the first take, he whispered something I didn't catch. And when the Ranter confronted Winstanley, he walked up to him and kissed him like Judas. It took me by surprise and shook Miles rigid. The scene worked like a charm. Afterwards, Miles murmured to Sid: 'I think I ought to point out that I'm really quite straight!'

The rushes were startling; Ernie had captured some wonderful patterns of light and shade, and the languid sense of a summer's day

Sid Rawle confronts Winstanley

came across perfectly. Sid Rawle, however, complained about the well-washed hair, the healthy teeth and the polished skin of the children. These elements had worried me from the beginning (at one point we considered importing some down-and-outs to the commune). Terry Higgins's hair always looked freshly washed and Jeff's was like a Silvikrin ad. We bullied them constantly about this, and they used to brush a few pine needles into their locks, hoping they might help. Finally, we eliminated the most blatant of these shots with judicious editing, cutting out the healthiest children completely. When Sid saw the final film, he was quite satisfied.

Chapter Twenty

The courthouse was no problem. Andrew had come across an old photograph from *Ilustrated London News*, showing Malmesbury, the oldest courthouse in the country, and still in use. We went down to visit it and found it almost the same, except that electricity had been installed, cables, fuse boxes and a clock defaced the ancient walls, and an anachronistic coat of arms dominated the room.

The court scene, however, was a problem. As written in the script, it ran to three and a half pages of dialogue, allowing Winstanley plenty of room for rhetoric. Court scenes can kill a film; as soon as you see the set, you know you're liable to be stuck there for a reel or two. Malmesbury courthouse was very small and cramped, so there was little hope of creating striking camera angles. How could we treat the sequence in a fresh and unusual fashion?

First of all, find out exactly what happened. We managed to secure in photocopy form the court records, written in Latin. I found further evidence in the British Museum, and it quickly became apparent that the court scene in the script was completely at odds with the facts. Far from listening to colourful rhetoric, the recorder never let Winstanley speak.

He was driven to writing his defence and sending it in separately after three appearances in which they refused to hear him without a lawyer. Three appearances! Why not shoot it the way it happened, the attorneys droning in Latin, Winstanley becoming more and more frustrated?

We set up the Malmesbury session, with the cooperation of the Athelstan Players, who agreed to provide the extras. The courthouse itself was guarded by two old men who refused to let us touch, move or even breathe. We waited until boredom overtook them and they left. Then Andrew worked like a whirlwind. The black electric cable along the wall had to be camouflaged; he ran lengths of sticky paper along the cable and painted it the same colour as the wall. The cable vanished. (The guardians of the courthouse later approved of this and Andrew muttered: 'Just as well. The plaster would have come off if I'd taken the sticky paper down.') Then he slammed a ladder up to the roof, and although he loathed heights, he clambered up and removed the electric lights. A vast, fake chandelier he dealt with by concealing it behind the trapdoor to the roof. The ancient and very heavy coat of arms behind the judge's chair was a magnificent relic, but it had to go; it was a hundred years too late, and anyway, royal symbols were not permitted during the interregnum. I pointed out that it was impossible to move, so much so that the decorators had repainted the walls with the huge wooden block still in position, as could be seen from the drops of paint on the frame. The more I tried to dissuade him, the more determined Andrew became. I was sent up the ladder, despite protests that the thing was far too heavy for us, and couldn't we wait until Ian arrived? Against my better judgement, Andrew cajoled me up to the very top of the ladder. (I hate heights, too.) He started firing orders, and I found I had the whole appalling weight in my sweat-soaked palm, and what would happen if the ladder swung backwards with me on it? I was utterly petrified and carefully followed Andrew's steady orders – 'keep your nerve'. Mercifully, he took the weight and eventually the damn thing was on the floor. I was festooned with cobwebs blackened by two centuries of dust, and the wall was blank except for a large patch where the coat of arms had been. Andrew liked this, but I felt it was too scruffy, so he painted it. The courthouse was now fine, except for one last hurdle – the wall clock. How were we to unscrew it clear of its wires and workings on the wall? Andrew climbed up and picked it off the wall – it was held by a single nail. With such a triumphant victory over

Stanley Reed as Recorder at Malmesbury Court

the odds, who would have worried about the fact that we had only one power point?

That one power point proved our undoing. At Chastleton, Andrew had arranged with the Electricity Board to give us a direct hook-up to the mains, and that had worked perfectly. For some reason, we forgot that technique, with the result that every time Ernie had lit the set, the fuses blew. It was raining outside, heavily overcast, so there was no chance whatever of shooting by available light. Delays were endless, but the cast was very patient. No sooner had we one shot in the can than the lights blew again, sending the crew scurrying around for another source to spread the load. Soon, the three neighbouring cottages were wired up, and just as the occupants were watching the televised climax of the 3.00 race at Chepstow, we blew all three of them.

The journey back from Malmesbury to Churt in our truck was exhilarating; both Andrew and I felt a great sense of achievement, for despite everything we had the scene in the can. Lightning flashed across the sky and a mist rolled over the M4, a huge moon shining fiercely on wild, scudding clouds. I craned my neck out of the cab, gazing at the magical effect, wishing it could be captured on film. Andrew talked so optimistically about the film that despite my growing conviction of disaster, the thought broke through the dark clouds in my head that perhaps it would be all right. My euphoria was deflected momentarily by the odd feeling 'funny if something shot out from nowhere and crashed into us', which something promptly did. The crash was not very serious, and the argument between Andrew and the driver ended swiftly (perhaps because our truck was untaxed!).

Now the film had passed its midway point we could rely on certain groups turning up regularly; the Gowers, in their splendid Volkswagen van, were always equipped with flasks of coffee. Peter Gower, an architect in his fifties, had a distinguished face which was utterly out of character with the roughness of the Diggers. The one time we put him in costume, he looked like a Soviet scientist in the Gulag archipelago. Ann, on the other hand, looked ideal for the seventeenth century, with her aquiline, patrician features. Their daughters, Jane and Louise, in their middle teens, were also beautiful, but looked very seventeenth-century in costume. They were also excellent actresses. The two small Gowers, Alice and John, had to have their blonde and exquisite features concealed before they could convey malnutrition.

Pat Kearney, the *IHH* veteran, brought an excellent group which included Ginni and Oisin Little, Bill Brooke, Phil Dunn and his brother Pat. Ginni found all the suffering Digger-woman parts falling on her shoulders, once it became apparent from the rushes what a splendid actress she was. Bill Brooke I remember with gratitude for all the occasions he produced our breakfasts. Phil Dunn became a staunch member of the commune, as did Pat Kearney whose knowledge of the subject and knowledge of film sparked a rare enthusiasm.

Terry and Muriel Higgins (and Don) were now featured in the picture as much as anyone and their acting had improved tremendously. Terry's humour kept us going on many occasions. I remember particularly his description of the week following a session weekend: 'Sunday night, you get in exhausted, you can't move a muscle. Monday, you're crawling into work, and crawling through the day. Tuesday, you begin to get a bit of feeling back. Wednesday, the aches and pains have gone. Thursday, you're about back to normal. Friday night – you're off again.'

Chapter Twenty-One

Through both accident and design, we had departed so far from the script that it became necessary to provide ourselves with detailed descriptions of what we had to shoot. Andrew and I took care not to be too dogmatic about these 'typewritten suggestions'. Script-writing was not our forte and nor was script reading – as we had shown by our nonplussed attitude to Caute's original. Andrew once admitted that he couldn't read scripts, and it was only when he saw scenes being enacted that he responded to them properly. This could be maddening, when he had apparently agreed upon a scene, and turned against it during rehearsals. However invaluable spontaneity and improvisation, written scenes still provided indications of props and backgrounds, and if you hadn't got the correct elements to hand, no amount of improvisation could save the scene. Besides which, no one could improvise seventeenth-century dialogue. [We tried it once in a scene with Jeff Cornish. 'Say something Biblical,' I said, hopefully. Jeff shrieked: 'Jesus Christ.'] Seventeenth-century dialogue had to be researched, written down, duplicated, sent out to the cast and thoroughly learned. But quite often, in battling for one of my scenes (or, as was happening more frequently now, one of Virginia's scenes) I would spur Andrew to invent one of his own – which was sometimes better. Virginia had thought up a good scene involving a small child wandering from the commune. Andrew didn't take to it. I vigorously defended it and he came up with a scene of two villagers hunting with a musket. A movement in the heather brings the musket up – but the movement turns out to be a Digger child. The musketeer is about to shoot anyhow, but the other villager slams the barrel down, and the child scampers off. (We shot it, but it hit the cutting room floor along with the other village material.) 'I expect you're saying why couldn't he have thought of this when I was writing the script; but I don't think like that.'

Despite the hair-trigger suspense, script conferences became more and more important as we neared the end of shooting. One element surviving strongly from David Caute's original was the figure of Mrs Platt. She existed, but nothing is known about her. David Caute created a character for her in the novel: a strong, crazy and somewhat repulsive lady who falls for Winstanley and, in doing so, helps to wreak havoc on the commune. Alison Halliwell's screen presence suggested an altogether different kind of person. Andrew and I felt the fictitious elements had become more and more alien to the film, and yet we could not now drop Mrs Platt.

The trouble was that Alison's performance was very good; her scenes had been among the best in the picture. And she suggested strongly the middle-class woman, romantically inclined towards revolution, having not the slightest idea of what it entailed. The love affair with Winstanley in the script did not appeal to me, but then such scenes in films seldom do. We thought it advisable to hint at her infatuation, and concentrate on her distaste for Platt, and her image of the hill as some kind of utopian escape.

David Caute had written a subtle scene to turn her against the Diggers once and for all; she came up the hill, possessed with the idea of Winstanley as her lover, and sees the interior of a hut:

As we hear the violin playing, we first see Winstanley's books and papers stacked on the floor. Pan to show Robert Coster, sitting on the floor in a corner, playing the violin. Pan to show a woman breast-feeding a baby. Track forward to show locks of hair falling on the floor. Finally, pan up to show, very close to the window, Winstanley contentedly seated while Judith, staring behind him, cuts his hair. The restrained pleasure on Winstanley's face is evident. Judith now recognises her attraction for him, but more we cannot tell.

Andrew was fond of the scene. I wasn't. But in any case, the characters of the Costers had fallen from the film weeks before when the boy cast as Coster failed to show up. Besides which, the interiors of the huts were far too cramped for such a scene to be feasible; Mrs Platt was to interpret the idyllic vision as the end of her romantic hopes. The baby was Winstanley's. The girl was his also. 'During her flight down the hill we never come close to her, but the camera tracks in pursuit of her and we hear her ghostly moans and howls.' She then declares to Platt: 'I have seen the Devil! The Devil is married to a witch! And I gave him money! He must be hanged! The witch must be burned! You have neglected your duty!'

We needed a turning point, too; one that would fit the far cooler accents of the film. Marina and I sweated over the problem and she came up with the idea that Mrs Platt should still climb the hill, but she should join the commune – or try to. Yet she should insist on a rest after her exertions. When she got up (her appearance greeted with amazement) she should turn her literary leanings to the writing of a pamphlet, only to be greeted with blank stares. And the outrageous behaviour of the Ranters should trigger her exit, and her rejection of the Diggers.

I went round to Andrew's for a script conference, hoping to condense the rather long scene that resulted. 'I think it's illogical that Mrs Platt should get up and go straight out to a pamphlet meeting,' he said. 'She should go out and see Bill Petch eating with dirty hands; she should work hard in the fields and then come back, exhausted, to the pamphlet scene.'

'I came here to buy a watch, and you sell me an alarm clock,' I said. 'I didn't want to lengthen the scene – although I admit you're probably right.'

We shot the scene the following weekend, bringing over from Ireland 80-year-old Dorothy Phipps, the newly acquired mother-in-law of Virginia's sister, Sally. She was one of the most extraordinary people I had ever met – very strong, very funny, with a marvellous, deeply-lined face, and she never bothered to wear any teeth. In any situation, she was the centre-point, and I knew she would be superb in a cameo role as an old Digger-woman. She responded instinctively, and was very patient, despite the long, cold period of waiting in the barn, where we shot the interior of her keeping Mrs Platt awake by coughing. Besides Bill Petch eating with dirty hands, we shot Mrs Phipps removing nits from a child's hair, before giving the unhappy Mrs Platt her breakfast.

The scene in which Phil Byfield, one of the Ranters, shocks Mrs Platt by hurtling out of a hut stark naked was a tricky one. We didn't explain what was to happen to the Diggers, some of whom were as Puritan as the originals. When I described the scene to Ernie, he dragged me aside. 'Surely you don't want a full frontal?' he said, horrified. 'Surely you want it from the side?'

I explained that he didn't have to do a Compton Cinema closeup, but the shot had to have impact. Phil, despite his Ranterish attitudes, was very unhappy and he insisted that I told Terry what was to happen. 'I don't want a broken nose,' he said. I told Terry, and he, too, was taken

aback. 'Not starkers, surely; he can have his shirt off, but not the whole thing – give him a loincloth!' I explained Mrs Platt had to be shocked and this was the only way we could think of doing it properly. 'Have him come out of the hut with an axe – that would be more the sort of thing...'

I have always felt the shot a little too discreet. But the effect upon the Diggers was hilarious; Bob Davies captured it in a still which showed them equally divided between broad grins and horrified stares. Mrs Phipps's reaction was just the one you see in the film – a roar of toothless laughter. When Charlie Ware asked her anxiously: 'Were you upset?' she replied: 'Oh gracious, no. I never expected such a pleasant surprise.'

George Barrett, the thatcher, who played one of the Diggers, told me later: 'If you wanted a startled reaction, you got it.'

Andrew was slightly worried about a tattoo he spotted on Phil's body. 'It's all right,' he told me, after due examination, 'although it's not exactly in period. It says SPQR!'

The restrained conflict over the script reached a climax when we planned the March on the Village and the battle with Gladman's troopers. I always thought of this as one of the high points of the film – it was certainly an exciting passage in the book – and I had the comforting feeling that however slow and static the rest of the film might be, this scene would be an explosion of action. Being military, I was confident Andrew would give it special attention. But he rejected it out of hand. Part of the trouble was the village itself – the set at Weyhill – which he disliked intensely. But his main reasoning was that in every film of this sort, there is a march of peasants on a village, scythes held aloft, and such a scene had become a cliché. He felt the March should be dropped, and the scene should be played entirely on Winstanley standing on the hill and hearing the noise of rioting from a distance. The end, which I had envisaged as a furious montage, to echo the opening battle, he wanted changed. Instead, he imagined a series of long shots – long shots of the column of soldiers and villagers up the hill, and long shots of the fire on the hill. This, he considered, would be more moving. Instead of pots and pans and details, we would have an ethereal effect. While not doubting the need for a final long shot of the fire on the hill, I thought it a great mistake to destroy the commune yet not see it being destroyed. 'Why change the style right at the end?'

'We did with *IHH*,' said Andrew.

Andrew felt that my directorial approach was wrong. 'You turn up with a storyboard and do masses of shots and waste energy and time doing hundreds of alternatives, and you hope out of one of them you'll get something.'

I pointed out that I didn't shoot alternatives, but covered some of the main action in long shots and closeups in order to cut on action, to provide smooth transitions. Editorially, I liked to cut; I didn't believe in one-shot scenes.

'I don't like one-shot films either,' said Andrew. 'But it often pays to concentrate on one thing and not on hundreds of little things.'

We came to the conclusion that we should write an end sequence. He thought that as it stood, the end was dull and repetitive: 'We've seen the commune burn. We've seen marches on villages in other films. Now we want something unforgettable. Not a repeat of stuff we already have. We need more of Miles thinking, on his own…detached.'

A second discussion was on a less 'Here I stand!' basis. Following a viewing of the entire cutting copy on the Moviola, we adjourned to a back office and Andrew read his version. Mamoun joined us and seemed enthusiastic for Andrew's view. Andrew elaborated his criticism of my storyboard technique: 'I might be very unfair. But you force the film to match your drawings. It seems to me like a ladder with 500 steps – you take the first and you know how many more there are and you have great anxiety. You have too much to do on hundreds of shots instead of concentrating on the essence. I've worked with several feature directors and they never use them.'

'No,' I agreed. 'They have a script. I'd better explain the technique so you understand. They are my memory.'

'You should forget. It's a natural process of editing.'

'I do my editing in the cutting room. I am responsible for covering the scene as fully as possible; the storyboard is drawn when I'm calm, cool and collected. To indicate the setups I need. I can then see at a glance what I have left to do. If you want an example of a director who used it – Eisenstein.'

Andrew said that was a different kind of filmmaking, and stressed that he worked by intuition.

'I agree,' I said. 'If you come up with an idea that's better than the storyboard, I'll happily throw the drawing away. I think the flourishes

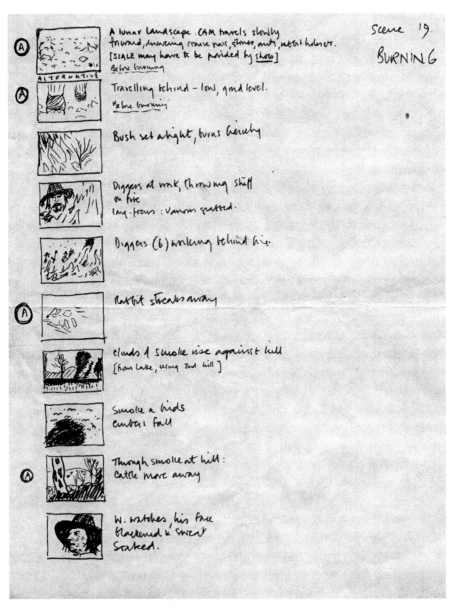

Storyboard

you have brought to the picture are great. When Phil Oliver spots a newly-arrived family, and you suggested he should weigh the child…'

'But he doesn't,' said Andrew. 'You haven't got the weighing, nor when he feels the child's arms. It's just manhandling.' (He's right, I admitted to myself, but he was there, and I do recall him saying 'Brilliant!' to Phil Oliver when we shot it.) 'You're too worried about the other shots which you don't need. You just needed the essence, which was that.'

We passed on to the other major problem, the March on the Village. Andrew had isolated Miles on the hill, while the Diggers battle off screen. He had taken up my suggestion of a gale, but still included the sound effects. I thought the storm and the sound effects were as much of a cliché as the march.

'Some clichés,' said Andrew, 'can be very good.'

The discussion ranged over the entire film. Andrew said the photography was not what he'd hoped for. 'At the beginning I wanted colour, and agreed to black and white only if it was very stylised. It isn't. It's realistic and straightforward.'

'I've been musing on this, too,' I said. 'Although I've studied film, and seen thousands, I have never been able to work out how certain stylised effects are achieved. I realise now I can't do it. It's not my style and that's it.'

We returned to the problem of the March. 'Are you sure you're not throwing it out because you hate that village location?'

'It's not because I hate the location,' he said, 'nor because I'm tired. I think it would be a great mistake.'

The value of the argument was to highlight in our minds Winstanley's predicament, for the Diggers' march to break the trading ban meant the end of the commune and the parting of the ways.

Remembering the similarly impassioned arguments which led to the creation of the Lidlington hospital scenes in *IHH*, I felt further research might help. At the British Museum, I looked up the broadsheets of the time and found that there had been no battle between the Diggers and the cavalry; just a petty riot…and a petty riot in those days could be the illegal gathering of more than 30 men.

From the broadsheet *Brief Relation*, 16 October 1649:

'Another sort who take a measure of the numbers of their party by the strength of their own affection to it, have made a petty insurrection at Cobham in Surrey, where being about fifty in number and so beyond the suppression of a Constable; and having had the impudence not to give over their Ryot at the command of a Justice of the Peace, thought they should be able to carry on the designs on the last years Diggers at

Saint George's Hill near the same place which was to level all things and begin with the hill first, and to introduce a new frame of government with an undistinguishing community for whom there is likewise order taken, and there is not likely to be further trouble with them, only to have them indicted and fined at the next sessions, and the fines will be levied without an army. There is known law sufficient to preserve the peace against such ridiculous attempts.'

In a period when men were hanged for theft, the imposition of fines suggested that no violence had taken place – certainly not the murder of Gladman, as in the novel.

I gave more serious thought to Andrew's idea, although I still felt the loss of the March on the Village would seriously impair the picture. One morning, Andrew, Miles, Ernie and I were walking through the woods at Larchfield discussing this thorny problem, and I asked Miles what he felt. 'I'm rather in favour of it,' he said. 'What about you?'

'I don't like the distant sound-effects,' I said.' If only someone would have a stroke of genius and come up with a single sound.'

Miles thought for a moment and said 'Church bell?'

That was it. A jigsaw was completed in my mind. Winstanley, alone on the hill, lashed by a gale, and all he hears, carried by the wind, is the church bell – ringing rapidly, in alarm. Andrew's plan was unanimously adopted.

The seasons were being very uncooperative. Autumn had officially arrived, but although we arranged a session to take place amid the falling leaves, the leaves refused to fall. Andrew brought out a 12-bore shotgun and blasted the leaves off the lofty branches. If it was funny at the time, it was hilarious at rushes, when leaves poured past the lens in a cataract.

Autumn turned to winter without a flake of snow. But time was running out, and we had to shoot the final scenes, snow or no snow. The last session was organised, with the widest possible range of publicity for extras – we needed at least 150, and while we didn't have that many costumes, we intended to shoot them like Fairfax's pony-club troopers – at a great distance.

On the Friday, Andrew called early and said, in a thick voice: 'What would it entail to call the session off until next weekend?'

'Impossible!' I shrieked. 'We've got 150 people coming!'

'Well, I don't think I'll be any use,' he said, miserably. 'I've got bronchitis.'

Waves of panic swirled around my head. 'The prospect is so appalling, I had better think about it and call you back.'

I talked it over with Virginia. What concerned me most was that Charles Kightly, of the Roundhead Association, had left for an unknown meeting in London in order to alert his Roundheads. Furthermore, Cedric Pheasant, convalescing in a country hospital, had lined up a coach load. And finally I had placed a bulletin on the notice board of Guildford Art School. Who knows who might have seen it? Usually, I have to mull over a problem like this for at least an hour before the balance in my head finally tips in one direction or another. But I realised at once that the only answer was to start the mass of phone calls that preceded each session, but this time put everyone off. I called Andrew back and told him. He was touchingly apologetic. 'It's difficult enough when one's feeling one's best,' he said, 'but I just don't see how I can be of any use feeling like this.'

Our record of illness was pretty good. I went down on one of the first sessions, and Andrew on one of the last. But whereas he could take over the direction from me on the battle scene, I couldn't take over the dressing of scores of extras from him. So the long haul began. Everyone I talked to was very pleasant about it and very concerned for Andrew. (Susie, Graham Samuel's wife, shrieked: 'How dare he!!' and Bill Petch, hearing from his farmer, thought he was joking. He sent a get-well card which said: 'A Mollo will never allow himself to be thrown by a bronc.') I managed to get hold of everyone except for some of Cedric's patients, who were unobtainable. (The Guildford School of Art had offered help, but never produced any – and fortunately they didn't change their ways this time.)

Peter Harvey, Virginia and I went down anyway, in case people got through the net, and sure enough eight people did. One or two Roundheads, the others from Cedric's hospital. We staged a sound effects session, and they were all very helpful, and promised to return the following weekend for the proper session.

Over the radio came forecasts of gales. I rang Ernie, but he said there wasn't a whisper in London and he didn't believe in radio forecasts. Charles Rees brought the camera equipment, Miles came over to the hill, and we were rewarded with a gale to end all gales. Peter Harvey

Girls cling to tripod

took over as cameraman for the sequence (and did a superb job). The rain turned into hail. The camera was so wet that the emulsion on the exposed loop of film turned to glue and two magazines jammed. Luckily we had a third. Virginia and Jane and Louise Gower clung to the tripod legs (as Griffith's assistants had done in the blizzard for *Way Down East*) and Peter Harvey strained to compose a picture through the rain-soaked eyepiece of the Arriflex. I wore my Spanish great-coat, Peter wore a sheepskin anorak and we were both soaked to the skin. Miles, in his seventeenth-century costume, was not, although he was desperately cold and wet. I commiserated with him and he gasped: 'No – I'm enjoying this in a masochistic sort of way!'

At the height of the gale, when he looked as red as a beetroot and was gasping as though drowning, I reassured him that those human guinea-pigs on Salisbury Plain exposed to cold weather for the benefit of science seldom caught colds – and so he'd be okay. 'It's all right, mate,' said Miles. 'I had a cold before I started and now it's much worse!'

By the time we had the sequence, and Peter had opened up the camera and poured the water out of it, we wondered whether we would have anything beyond liquefied emulsion. But the rushes were impressive; the water on the lens gave a thoroughly waterlogged view, which Peter Harvey later augmented with the sound effects of a raging storm.

For the final session, we sent out a flippant notice for the bulletin board of the National Film School:

'The picture may prove a write-off, about as memorable as *Old Mother Riley in North Africa*, in which case you can tell us what we did wrong. On the other hand, it

Peter Harvey in gale

220

might be staggering – another *Citizen Kane* – in which case you will be in a position to say to the Pauline Kael of the future "I was there". Either way – it's only a day. And when this thing's over, we'll do the same for you.'

But we never had much luck with film schools, and apart from the reliable Bill Diver, and a cameo role by Ben Lewin, we had to depend on locals, and groups like the Roundhead Association.[1] Since this was to be our last proper session, I will quote verbatim from my notebook, which gives some idea of the unexpected problems in an otherwise carefully-organised event.

'Last night, on television, we saw a *Hawaii Five-O* about two boys forming a partnership to make a film – about surfing – who have to steal to finance it. They get shot. A promised coach load of 'Overton's Foot' last night turned out to number four. This morning I lay in bed shivering as the rain battered down outside…I pretended to myself that it was the fishpond filler, which makes a similar noise, but this was far too heavy…I am still feeling pre-session nerves, but slightly more optimistic now because the rain has lifted and the birds are tweeting. It is 9am. In half an hour the first "crowds" start arriving. We hope for 150-200. We'll see. I reckon we'll be lucky to get 70 on a day like this. And what will the Roundhead Association do without a change of clothing? All day in the rain…it doesn't bear thinking about. And yet out of all the sessions, only one was ruined by rain, and we turned that to good advantage for the Diggers' Song.'

(Later) 'The big day was interrupted by periodic heavy showers, as predicted. Bill Petch, just before the big fire scene, said: "I smell rain" and ten minutes later, down it came. "It won't be a long one," he added. And it wasn't. It acted as a good fire precaution…'

We had an amazingly slow start, people drifting in casually. None of the promised coach loads turned up at all. At 10.30am, a head count showed we had a mere 34 – far too few to do the scene of the villagers and troops advancing on the hill. A few more drifted in. We started by

1. When Andrew directed a film for French TV, *The Battle of Naseby*, he used the Roundhead Association and discovered that their association with *Winstanley* had borne fruit. They had made new pikes to the correct length, changed their costume so that it matched what they had worn on the film, and expecting to muster 250, he got 500!

getting everyone we had into the wood (it promptly rained) to do a woodland fight for sound effects. The Roundhead Association did a mock fight for us. Then, having seen the technique on previous effects sessions, Charles Rees knew the value of realism, and he took a dive at George Hawkins, knocking him backwards over a tree stump. I saw what had happened, and rushed over to try and drag people off. They thought my yelling was part of the act and were all diving into the mêlée! Finally, George was freed, very shocked, and we put him to bed in the house, and rushed the doctor over. George had already been very ill after lifting a log and straining his back. A couple of medical men from Cedric's hospital took care of George[2] and before long he had made a full recovery and was back on the film.

Andrew organised the convoy of vehicles to the hill (and did it superbly – it was something none of the rest of us could work properly) and we found we had enough people for the long shots of the villagers and troopers advancing. I have no idea where they came from, but the straggling column looked most impressive. And a huge crowd assembled to watch the burning of the commune. The fire scene was about to start when it poured with rain. Andrew had ordered extra straw bales from the thatcher, and we rushed these under cover. As soon as the rain stopped, we burned one hut, but the actors playing the villagers couldn't perform their orgy in front of the flames. We had two cameras, one operated by Ernie, one by Peter Harvey. Ernie expressed disappointment in the fire and Andrew set another hut alight. Lack of rigid camera placement made it hard to focus and impossible to follow the actors. Ernie said he had shot 200ft and got nothing usable. Peter said he was blocked by the smoke. So we brought up more bales and built them into a wall and lit that, having done two rehearsals of the action at Ernie's suggestion. We then shot it and Ernie said he had some usable material.

We then went for the difficult shot, the soldier giving money to Winstanley, which Ernie thought was 'corny'. He was very tired (he'd been shooting all week) and thus irritable (for which he apologised next

---

2. One of the them, Don Shaw, a huge, bearded veteran of two communes in America, told us one had been burned by the Ku Klux Klan and carloads of state troopers when a mixed-race girl came to live there.

223

Villagers squabble over Diggers' possessions

day) and angrily dismissed the fire so far. I was glad of this, because it spurred Andrew, who was understandably unwilling to destroy all his handiwork, into burning another hut. The soldier scene went well. But Ernie got very cross over the closeup of Winstanley's hand with the coins being dropped into it. He said he needed fifteen lights to do it properly. 'You can't tell me that, on the last day,' I said, 'after a whole year!' We shot it with a sungun.

Next day, Sunday, the cast relaxed over Bill Petch's Sunday papers. We were surprised by the number of people who had turned up. We used them for sound effects and Andrew came across from the house and asked, 'Why are all these people coming for costumes? We've got enough Diggers as it is.'

'It's the last day – it's fun for them.'

'I've got to dry them out and sort them out and it's a waste of time and effort.' Pause. 'Except – I've just thought – we could do a scene at the crossroads of the Diggers being scattered by horsemen.'

'That's why I got them to put the costumes on,' I grinned.

Andrew heaved a sigh and a wry face. Another thought struck him and he turned to Peter Korner and said: 'You know, Kevin would really like 300,000 Chinese painted black and wearing knee breeches around a 300ft tree, using it to charge the walls of Babylon. If I could do that for him, he'd be happy, and he'd sit there with a megaphone and riding breeches and his hat turned back to front...'

While Andrew directed the scene from ground level, I went up to the top with Ernie – for the last time. We had practically worn a track up the side of the Devil's Jumps, and we noticed how the trippers had grown accustomed to us and gave us a wide berth. After we had shot the scene, we had an exuberant lunch in the warm sun. It was delightful, just like the summer. We shot some individual Diggers being pursued. Terry Higgins fell under the hooves of a horse and failed to get up again. I rushed over to see if he was injured. He played up to my fears and only rose from the heather at the last moment. 'Yes, it hit me, but it didn't hurt,' he said. 'Now I've got your title. Are you ready for it? "The Stillborn Dream".' He looked at us while we absorbed the idea he had germinated in the heather. Then he added: 'Of course you could always call it "Brownlow and Mollo's Abortion"!'

The shooting was over. We consumed a birthday cake cooked by Ginni for her young son Oisin. There was lots of singing, and lots of goodbyes, followed by lots of hoovering and scrubbing, and few regrets that it was over. 'Remember this,' I said to Virginia, as we drove back to London. 'We did it. We were young enough. Soon we'll be too old to do it.'

'And remember that we staggered through it,' she said. 'We didn't stride and we didn't bound. We staggered.'

Virginia Brownlow takes a rest during a break in filming

Chapter Twenty-Two

As soon as Sarah Ellis had completed the rough cut, and the film was absolutely complete – barring the snow shots at the very end – we held a screening. Some of the cast and crew attended together with Doug Turner, of De Lane Lea, who was going to dub the film and Beryl Mortimer, who was going to post sync the effects, as she had done on *IHH*. The film was almost entirely silent, and I read out the important dialogue. Beryl had brought her mother. They had a very different idea of what constituted good cinema, and their reaction suggested that the film was unlikely to be a big hit commercially.

'How long is it, dear?' asked Beryl. I told her it was more than two hours.

'That's long, isn't it, dear?' replied Beryl. 'We're starving.'

A little later, the silence was shattered by Beryl saying: 'That'll look lovely in colour, dear.' I explained that while on most colour productions the rushes were printed in black and white, ours were shot that way. Beryl watched for a while and then said: 'How long did you say it was, dear?' Her mother fell asleep.

Cutting room trim bin

The editing of a film is a complex process impossible to describe satisfactorily on paper. My notebooks are no longer of any value; for documentation they list pages of hieroglyphics such as:
-cut to CU Gladman when F says he'll leave him
-F to say P/S barley
-W P/S line expl.
-Wickings up hill cut 2/3rds.

I remember the editing as an exhilarating process; editing is much more enjoyable than direction because with editing you are dealing with strictly limited alternatives. With direction, as with writing, you have limitless alternatives, and had you the ability you could direct like Orson Welles or John Ford.

The most demanding aspect was the sound. As soon as Peter Harvey was free of his other commitments, he came on to the picture as full-time sound editor. There is no need to run over the problems in detail; shooting a historical film underneath a direct flight path to London Airport meant the sound for every inch of every exterior had to be recreated – bird song, wind rustle, footsteps, dialogue. We couldn't afford more than a minimal use of the post-synch theatre (at £25 an hour), and anyway, non-professional actors can seldom concentrate on

Peter Harvey, Doug Turner and Kevin Brownlow at De Lane Lea

sync as well as their performance. So we worked out an alternative method. Since people tend to speak at the same cadence, we took the actors out to a field, or open space with similar acoustics but less aircraft, and had them repeat their lines again and again. Peter Harvey then faced the daunting task of fitting everything. The trouble was that a line that fitted the lip movements was not always the best delivered line. Sometimes we went back and tried again, but this wasn't always possible. Only those who worked on the sound track can appreciate what a brilliant job Peter Harvey did with it. But it took time. It was Peter's first attempt at sound editing on a feature and progress was understandably slow.

To check the birdsong, which so many films get wrong, we invited Anthony Clay of the Royal Society for the Protection of Birds to see the film with a mixed track roughly dubbed by Doug Turner. He was able to use an aural magnifying glass: 'The curlew does that bubble only in the very late winter or early spring…the alarm call of the falcon – you're better without it. No one would shout you down, but it's too early for the young, and therefore confusing. After the sermon – that skylark was marvellous. I loved the wren singing in the rain. But the nightingale, where you've used it, is criminal!' We were able to alter the tracks to meet all his criticisms, so the birdsong in the picture is dead right.

We had a major screening, to which we invited Christopher Hill; to our intense relief he thoroughly approved of it, describing it as 'very good history'. He made some minor points, most of which we were able to adjust. I felt that after his comments, we weren't worried about film critics. But next day, Andrew, Charles and Ian came into the cutting room and said they hadn't liked it as much as before.

The addition of sound changed the picture radically, as we knew it would. Shot and largely conceived as a silent film, the picture worked surprisingly well. Dialogue and effects changed the pace and, occasionally, the conviction. On one occasion, a typist at the BFI left out one line on a dialogue sheet, and the scene never recovered, for the rhythm was broken and none of us could work out why until it was too late.

But we were committed to a sound film – it would have been tragic to have lost those natural country sounds – and a sound film it would be.

What would it be called? A long list of titles had been drawn up since 'Comrade Jacob' was now obsolete (no mention of the Jacob and Esau legend survived into the final film): 'Winstanley; 1649'; 'The Diggers of Weybridge'; 'The Surrey Rebellion'; 'The Militant Pacifists'; 'Gentle Revolutionaries'; 'Attempt at Utopia'; 'Liberty of Conscience'; 'Back to Nature', 'Onward to Perfection'; 'Fresh Air of Freedom'; 'Swords into Ploughshares'; 'This Fire Will Spread'; 'A Sane and Gentle Life'...

One sad event occurred which had a serious effect on the film: Mamoun Hassan left for a new job as head of films with the United Nations Works Relief Agency. (And he went to live in Beirut!) This gave him the longed-for chance to make films, but it meant that the filmmakers were to be thrown to the wolves. No one else in the organisation cared as much as Mamoun about the films, or their fate. His plans for holding all the features back until they could be launched simultaneously came to nothing, and one by one the features were dropped into the bottomless well of public indifference.

Barrie Gavin, who took over, threw himself into the job with enthusiasm, but his enthusiasm, too, was ground down by the bureaucratic machinery of the BFI, and before long he left – and returned to the BBC.

Moya and Mamoun Hassan

Before he left, he saw the film with Peter West, the BBC editor who had cut Bill Douglas's *My Ain Folk*. Their wildly differing reactions were an indication of what was in store for us when the picture was released.

Both were impressed by the visuals. Peter West thought the first attack, with the battering ram, was too long. Barrie Gavin said: 'Don't make it shorter. It is very powerful because it takes too long.' Gavin said: 'Cut the eviction in the village', West said: 'No, don't cut it!' West said: 'Remove the baby from the birth scene', and Gavin said: 'Keep it in.' Barrie thought that pulling the odd sequence out wasn't going to alter the fact that the film was slow paced. 'Instead of a slow two hour film, it will be a slow one hour 50 minute film.'

The most difficult reel was the opening one. We called it, privately, the Movietone News of 1649, and regarded it as a prologue, in a style totally at odds with the rest of the film. Into this reel we had to pack certain essential information for an audience unfamiliar with the period; they had to know there had been a Civil War…that this was a period of radical political ideas…and that those who expressed such ideas were dealt with harshly. To make it easy, we tried putting commentary (spoken by Felix Greene) over the battle, the Putney Debates and the Mutiny at Ware, but when we next ran the film we realised our mistake. The commentary in the opening reel clashed with Winstanley's commentary in the second, and so similar were the timbres of the voices that some people thought they were the same person. We resorted to silent film subtitles and cut and recut the reel endlessly.

But a screening to some of our fellow directors at the Production Board was very encouraging. All of them were enthusiastic. Chuck Despins (*Moon over the Alley*) found the opening exposition a little hard to follow. 'I found the whole end part of the film very moving. The actual end is fantastic. I felt alienated from Winstanley at first, but the reality of him gets stronger and stronger until he dominated the film very powerfully. Photography superb and the sound!'

Peter Smith (*Private Enterprise*) liked the opening reel, particularly the battle, but his attention clicked off before the prologue was over. He found the film a bit slow in its two-hour form. 'The period feel is as perfect as one would expect. The fact that the picture doesn't wander over a great canvas is all to the good. I identified very strongly with the era and I grew to feel the area. Photographically it looks absolutely marvellous.'

Bill Douglas agreed. 'It is ravishing to look at. I loved the film. It takes a little bit of getting used to, because it is so unusual. It has a completely different approach to the Richard Harris-*Cromwell* treatment. I loved the battle – it conveyed so much, that opening prologue, partly due to the music. It set the scene very quickly. It put a lot of those big budget films to shame – they take an hour to say what you say there in a few minutes.'

Chapter Twenty-Three

View from cutting room,
Lower Marsh

Working at the Production Board was the next best thing to a good holiday. And after the nerve-wracking tension of production, the post-production period was a sheer delight. Not that we worked any less hard, but the pressure was off.

The cutting rooms were situated alongside the main office of the Production Board on the second floor of the BFI's building in Lower Marsh, Waterloo, London. We spread over two cutting rooms. Light and airy, they provided views of Waterloo which, on summer evenings, hypnotised us with spectacular sunsets. I watched a helicopter fly repeatedly towards the South Bank, only realising when I saw *Frenzy* that it was Hitchcock's camera plane.

Across the street was a splendidly and enterprisingly cheap restaurant called La Versilia. I mention these apparently irrelevant facts because they meant a great deal at the time, and it is hard to convey the atmosphere without them.

Nita Bird was Mamoun's secretary, and she kept the Production Board going. She was one of those people who give the impression they cannot cope; it is all too much. Whereas some people present a calm and responsible front, concealing chaos, Nita presented a frantic front, which effectively camouflaged her ability. Her sense of time operated out of sync with everyone else's; she arrived well into the morning but worked late into the evening, when the phone stopped ringing and she could concentrate. Late evenings became a habit at the board, and then one faced the spine-tingling walk through empty side-streets and down a sinister tunnel, straight out of Gustav Doré, to Westminster Bridge. While we were at Lower Marsh, a railwayman was murdered on a footbridge at the South Bank and a theatre director on Hungerford

P. Harvey, D. Turner, K. Brownlow, B. Gavin, A. Mollo

Bridge; while Lambeth had the highest incidence of street violence in London, we saw no sign of it. Lower Marsh was a street market during the morning, and was largely deserted, except for La Versilia's German shepherd dog, during the afternoon. We became fascinated by the area – Chaplin's childhood home – and I suspect everyone at Lower Marsh regretted the day the BFI moved back to Dean Street.

Although he spent some of the time recuperating from his illness, Cedric Pheasant was the third member of the Production Board staff, responsible for technical matters. He was a veteran of the BFI, having worked there for 30 years; a veteran, too, of earlier administrations at the board.

The new administration at Dean Street sacked John Huntley, a prominent member of the BFI executive, and the BFI came out on strike. This happened just as Barrie Gavin took over from Mamoun. We worked on through the first week, mainly because no one seemed to have noticed us. Then Deputy Director Allan Hill demanded that Barrie Gavin stopped being so equivocal. 'You are currying favour with the pickets, and yet supporting management by working. You must make a decision.'

'Oh well,' said Barrie. 'In that case I'll come out.'

Although we should have supported the strike, Peter Harvey and I were so involved that the interruption was infuriating. We organised a screening at De Lane Lea, and the technicians blacked us. We bribed a projectionist at another theatre, and managed to get the film on the screen, but after that we had to stop and wait.

When the Production Board returned to normal, we decided we would hold out no longer; the film had to be shown to David Caute. It had departed so far from his script that he could hardly approve of the film, and the screening was a black spot on the horizon.

Perhaps it was a Freudian slip, but Caute arrived without his glasses, and he could not see very well without them. We positioned him in the front row of the Coronet. I said: 'First of all, I must thank you for not hassling us over the years. When you've seen the film you may wish you had. The point is that while it is inspired by your book and by your script, and we couldn't have worked without them, about halfway through we began to diverge. It's the way we work; we have to find the film and feel around and you could see things changing in front of the camera. It's no reflection on the script that we have changed – it's just that we had forgotten how we worked.'

The lights went low, the projector whirred. Then stopped. The lights came up. 'How d'you like it?' I asked. 'It's the best we could do for the money.' Caute laughed good-naturedly, and I hoped the atmosphere was now more conducive. The picture began properly and we were launched into the battle. When showing the film before, I had feared it was a long and boring film. This time I felt: 'God, that's good.'

When the lights faded up, Caute didn't. He sat there, teeth clenched, face white for several seconds. Andrew and I pretended to be gathering up papers, but we were extremely anxious to know the worst. And it was the worst.

'I don't really like it,' he began, deceptively mildly. 'If you had changed the script enormously, but the film was frightfully good, I'd say fine – I'd have my name associated with it and be glad it worked out. But it is so bad in terms of dialogue and the way it tells a story…I think if it had been very different, that in itself would not have prejudiced me. But I cannot acknowledge that I wrote that.'

He found the film confusing: 'Quite often, you don't know who's who. When Mrs Platt defects, it's not clear why. In the original, she was disappointed by Winstanley's refusal to have anything to do with her.'

He realised we had gone back to the novel upon occasion, and this he felt was unnecessary. 'The film oscillates between very stylised language, mood and naturalism, and this doesn't work.'

'The most difficult thing in all of art,' he said, 'is to portray good people. It is much easier to portray bad people. Miles is such a good chap and somehow every time he says: "Do come and sit down," it doesn't work with me. I wished for a lot less words. You have such powers to express things silently, it is a pity there is so much dialogue. The occasional break into narrative doesn't work. I didn't like the captions. The battle is marvellous, but why did you put that awful music on? You outdo Hollywood, then promptly put a Hollywood score on it.

'The level of acting is established very early on, in the Debates, which are so short, no one knows what the hell it is. As it is very difficult to represent goodness, so it is very difficult to represent social radicalism. And it is too ham when the soldiers protest. You have an over-anxiety to fill in the audience on what is happening. Results in an over-didactic feeling.

'Miles is much the best actor – he is often very good, particularly his silent expression. But early on in his upper-class reading from the pamphlets and his confrontation at the crossroads with Platt, he is too much the Sunday school teacher. He is not rough enough, and lacks the necessary guts and fire. Platt comes across perfectly well. Mrs Platt is very good. Haydon is very good. Fairfax, too. Gladman fine. Generally you don't have a problem of acting in the main parts.'

He thought we had made a great mistake by cutting out the visionary aspect, the allegorical scenes which had been such a feature of his script, and the substitution of the pamphlets had not made good that loss. 'You've put in a great deal more social rhetoric which is superfluous. Particular social ideas can be put over, but it means cutting down what you have. And Miles reads the pamphlets in that goody-goody voice. Yet his reactions to violence or to cows being taken away are marvellous. And he has an extraordinary ability to attract love.'

He felt we had shot an enormous amount about life on the hill, but that, despite everything, the period had been well caught and he felt he was in the seventeenth century. He was still very enthusiastic about the photography: 'The composition of almost every scene is among the best things I've ever seen on the screen. An audience who loved the cinema would be riveted. But you see, you're back to your old problem of *It Happened Here*; you are supreme documentary artists. If you had gone back to a documentary on the period, it could live on its own terms. But you have always had a fidelity to the original novel much greater than I have. And *It Happened Here* had something going for it which this doesn't: people's interest in recent history. As it is, this is a very simple story of rich and poor. It's lost a lot without the mysticism – there's too much of life on the hill. The Ranters work well, and so does the Fairfax inspection. That's really rather good. I had a grudging respect for some of the lines. I thought it was just how he would have done it, and I hadn't thought of that when I wrote it.'

Now Andrew made an extraordinary remark: 'What did you think of the argument between Miles and Terry? All those lines were spontaneous.' I recalled the hours I sweated over them and the hours Miles and Terry sweated rehearsing and learning them. I pointed out that some of the lines were David Caute's own, but the incident was supplanted by something else.

And Andrew came up with another startling interjection: 'It would be profitable if you would go through the film again with us.'

'I'd love to. It is an awful lot of film to remember. I can listen to the readings from the pamphlets and I might think of something more suitable for him to say. I'd like to go through the film slowly. I feel more than ever that I would like the mystical visions back – I want the film to be about an aberrant nature – a disturbed mind of the seventeenth century. The Ranters work extremely well. They provide discord. Brilliant. There wasn't enough of Mrs Platt. There should be, and perhaps you have it, a long scene with her and Winstanley. I liked the coach scene, by the way. But the consequence of giving the money is not there. So many things are lost as you race along to the next piece of wood chopping.'

We agreed to hold a session in the cutting room, to go over his points in detail. Meanwhile, Andrew and I held a post-mortem, as we walked along the streets of Soho. I said I was amazed that he should have invited Caute to see the film again. 'We have just got ourselves out of one situation and we'll land ourselves in it all over again.'

'We-e-ll,' said Andrew.

I told him about my reaction, how I thought the film was converting Caute during the screening.

'I'll be quite blunt with you,' he said. 'I am absolutely indifferent to the film. Like *It Happened Here*, there are one or two good things in it, and a hell of a lot of crap. It lacks imagination in so many areas. On the whole, I agree with Caute. It's just too much like hard work to keep on arguing over every point with you. If you think it's right, let's dub it and get it over with. But if there's a chance of radical alterations, we should show it again to Caute.'

Andrew had been convinced for some time that I had been short-changing him as far as alterations to the cutting copy were concerned. We would screen the picture, he would make suggestions, and I would argue against them or I would implement them. But by the time we held another screening, Andrew couldn't see the slightest difference. As I was responsible for the cutting copy, he felt he couldn't win.

There's no sense in a partnership in which both sides agree all the time. But this scathing dismissal of the picture suggested a lot more was wrong with it than I had imagined.

I said I was disappointed that he should feel so negatively after all we'd been through. Apart from half a dozen alterations, I felt the film was as right as I could ever get it. I tended to take more notice of other people's reactions than he did – and I would welcome a completely opposing view. But not Caute's. Andrew modified his remarks slightly by saying he was never satisfied with anything he did. But to be dissatisfied and to be indifferent are conflicting emotions. I suspected after 19 years, this would be the last work we would do together. I had never thought that before.

David Caute went through the film on the Moviola, and stopped at a line spoken by Miles. 'Are the poor so large in your thoughts, then, Parson?'

'That's absolutely impossible outside school drama,' he said. 'It is the quintessence of amateur acting. The way he delivers that line is the way I would say it, if I were doing it.'

He then began to dissect the line itself, but first produced his script. 'What was the line again?' I told him. He found he had written it, so he passed on.

Of the coach scene, with Winstanley remaining silent as Mrs Platt pleads to be allowed to join the Diggers, he said: 'This scene is an excellent example of the kind of clarity and economy as to who these people are. You emerge from the scene several steps ahead.'

He stopped at the catechism scene, with Platt and his children. 'It is irrational for me to stop at any particular scene. I'll reserve my comments for the end, but the spirit moves me to make a comment. This scene here you say: "It's Platt time." You have devoted the time to an illustration of the way Platt regarded children. But the children are not of any consequence.'

Andrew explained that Platt was an archetypal villain, and we were trying to make him more sympathetic. 'Then my point is not that it's superfluous: it is an extremely well done scene which has exactly the impact you want.'

He carried on, making notes which he didn't read out, until Mrs Platt was frightened out of the commune by the Ranters.

'One of the things which was so strong about *It Happened Here*,' he said, 'was that you followed one woman from beginning to end. One person we could empathise with. What you're doing in this – you move to so many characters, there is never any time to get to grips with any of them. The practical problem you are going to run into with audiences is that they'll ask: "Who the hell is this?"'

'I think you have done something absolutely impossible: bringing her up the hill, moved by her obsessions, and the Diggers look at her suspiciously (she's only the Parson's wife) then we see a woman getting fleas from straw (part of the sequence excised from final version), she quotes a bourgeois remark from Milton, sees a Ranter take his clothes off – and turns against them. You will find the audience baffled.'

I explained that Mrs Platt was a romantic, and her case was typical of the middle-class person who has a romantic idea of helping people less fortunate than themselves until they actually try it.

'If you're going to shift the whole burden of alienation to just the bourgeois being disillusioned, you've really got to dramatise that. You're prepared to spend long minutes showing people whittling wood – but you get through moments of crucial and very formal human conflict in seconds. One can't do that. You can't be implicit and understood. So there is a very curious thing here; if you take the most conventional notion that the plot is the interaction of main characters, you have made the foreground the texture of life and you have fragmented the plot into a sub-plot of several characters. But if Mrs Platt were sexually attracted to Winstanley and if she gets to the top of the hill, sees though the window of a hut another woman cutting his hair – you've got it in one shot.'

Following the viewing, Andrew broke the inevitable long silence with: 'As I see it, there is one major problem – Mrs Platt's relationship with Winstanley. That would be most difficult to put right. There is nothing we have shot, and there would be problems about re-shooting. I haven't seen Miles or Alison for some time and their appearance might have altered. The location isn't available, and the best we could do is a two-shot dialogue scene, head and shoulders.'

'The problem is your scope,' said Caute. 'Even if you were to see it my way, your practical scope is very limited. The problem for me is one of mixed emotions. While I think you can believe me that I've understood that a script in the world of filmmaking is just a skeleton – especially on a small budget film – it was very essential to me that I wrote the script. We had lots of discussions about what would happen – all of which seem farcical in the light of the film. Perhaps 20 per cent of my words are still there. What were important to me were the structure and the use of language. That is all a writer can hope for. The director is the king of making a film. He is the artist. On many occasions, following the script hasn't been practically possible. On occasion, you have the same scene but you have changed the words and gone to the pamphlets. From the literary point of view, the script has been mauled and disparaged. There is nothing more pointed to me about the whole thing than the decision to go off and read the pamphlets and put the voice over.

'If one takes the long, long view, one can see that, to put it as neutrally as possible, you were always going to make your own film in the end. I am not accusing you of bad faith – when you talked with me, you seriously thought of the script as the basis. I don't want to say anything to make the blood run to your eardrums. You are directors of strong personal style. But it has got so far from anything I authored, I realise we are on a completely different wavelength. If I thought I could advise you, and the result would be a substantial movement back, then I would do so. But I don't see it. The problem is mainly one of language. A writer stands or falls by the language and the dramatic structure. And the film has taken too great a departure.'

We decided to hold a screening for friends of David Caute, to which we would invite some impartial viewers. When Caute had gone, both Andrew and I acknowledged how impressed we had been with his cool, almost detached judgment. It was an ironic thought that harsher words had passed between us than between Caute and us.

A propos of his attitude to the film, Andrew said: 'I ought to elaborate on my remark about feeling indifferent. I agree completely with David Caute – about Miles's character and his relationship with Mrs Platt. He should have been very conscious of other women and I have always stressed this. But there is nothing of it there.

'The commune is very one-dimensional. The only element I was dead against that works is the Ranters. But if we had agreed about Miles's sexual infatuation, that would have created the necessary tension. The roughness, bawdiness and discord are missing – not only among the Diggers, but in the tavern between Drake and Platt [a scene from the novel]. We were going to make much more of a character out of Gladman. I expected the film to be something it's not, so I'm a bit disappointed about it. I have got to reconcile myself to the elements. There are still a lot of details in the film that I don't like. All the emotional scenes are stereotyped. The arrival of the Wickings [the second family to reach the commune after the Higginses] is so corny. Is there no other way one can get over togetherness but by biting lips and holding hands? I seem to have seen it all before.'

Andrew still found the end a problem. Having given him his March on the Village alternative – playing it on Miles – I got my way with a furious Abel Gance montage for the end, showing the villagers burning the commune and fighting over the sticks of furniture. But what bothered Andrew was the progress of events towards the end. There was another attack after the March on the Village, in which a pregnant woman was kicked. Platt is told that she had miscarried her child and he seems taken aback. He suggests that if the Diggers can justify their cause from the scriptures, he would not pull down their houses. Naively, Winstanley and the others put together a pamphlet and Winstanley delivers it in person. Platt seems mollified. The Diggers broadcast seed upon their field and prepare for another year. But Platt leads soldiers and villagers in a final assault upon the Diggers. They are dispersed and their huts burned down. Andrew felt the attack in which the pregnant woman was kicked dissipated the pace and was repetitive.

We held the show. None of the current Production Board committee attended except the chairman, Michael Relph. The audience sat there at the end with the silence that accompanies embarrassment. Fitfully, the comments came; Relph objected to the music for the battle coming from *Alexander Nevsky*. Critic Eric Rhode said the attacks were repetitive and the film was far too long. 'It is a very weighty film, and a very fine film, very concentrated. But it is too long to take in at one viewing. Up to half way, I found it very moving. Then I found it a slog.'

'We shouldn't have shown it in the lunch hour,' I said.

'Perhaps that was it,' said Rhode, consuming his last sandwich. 'My stamina.'

Another critic, Philip French, said: 'I was greatly struck. I found it visually stunning. My only point is whether Winstanley is sufficiently established and placed, politically and socially.'

Andrew asked if anyone had any comments about the accent of Winstanley. Stanley Reed said it was the only thing in the film that gave you his background. Melvyn Bragg, who had been invited by Caute, said: 'Winstanley grew on me. I started impressed but not moved. Later on, I was both impressed and moved. I found the first reel too cluttered – too many titles. You could do it more simply. Not that it wasn't terribly well and dramatically done. But cluttered.'

After the show David Caute telephoned to say that Melvyn Bragg and his agent Elaine Greene had got in touch and both had thought the film marvellous.

'But they think the same things need to be done. No criticism has yet been made that I didn't have in my mind – which may sound self-congratulatory, but which is nonetheless true. The most important point is the end. There are five attacks and by the end I fear people will giggle. After a while, one gets a Donald Duck feeling – how does he get dry so quickly after falling in the pond? One is amazed at how the Diggers survive all these attacks. The attack by the Diggers on the village would have been far more effective than the succession of scenes you have now.'

The film had had its first exposure to an audience, and was not entirely unbloodied. Andrew said that I now had the film the way I wanted it. What about the way he wanted it? Sarah Ellis was at work on another Production Board film. But Peter Harvey volunteered to assist Andrew, and I left the two of them to recut the picture.

Chapter Twenty-Four

Our problems with the film were put in perspective by a letter from Mamoun describing conditions in Palestinian refugee camps in Lebanon. This was before the Civil War, when the camps were being bombed by the Israelis, and he was obliged to film the aftermath. He quoted in full one of his interviews, which was very tragic and very moving; a woman who had lost both her husband and her eldest son. (The film was eventually released as *Some of the Palestinians*.)

Andrew's recut was full of surprises. Inevitably some of the surprises were shocks and others were thrills. He attacked the opening of the film proper, after the prologue, and threw out a sequence of the Diggers clearing and burning the land. He tore out yards of Winstanley and Everard getting up on a cold morning, and started with Winstanley outside the barn in extreme long shot. It worked. I have since regretted the loss of the burning sequence, which had a slightly mystical quality about it, and brought the film full circle, beginning with a creative fire and ending with a destructive one. But there was no denying the new shape was neater.

He also threw out a sequence of Everard climbing the hill to join the handful of Diggers at the top. 'And Gerrard?' calls one. 'Scribbling,' replies Everard. 'We owe much to his scribbling,' says the Digger, quietly. This established Winstanley as an isolated character, but indicated what the others felt about him. However, apart from being visually attractive, it had nothing else going for it and I agreed to keep it out.

Some of the sequences were thrown against each other in startling and sometimes stimulating juxtapositions, setting up ideas for rearrangement which would never have been suggested without such brutal recutting. It was a refreshing procedure (although my hair stands on end at the memory of it) and one which I thoroughly recommend.

One area where none of us could agree was the build-up to the climactic fire; certainly, there were too many attacks, but I felt that since the last days of the commune had been so well documented by Winstanley, we should shoot them exactly as they happened. Andrew felt we should cut it all, once Fairfax had signed the document permitting Platt to use force, and race to the end. My defence was that the events, as described by Winstanley, were unexpected and strange, and the phrase I kept using was 'we don't know how good they are'.

Peter Sainsbury, soon to be head of the Production Board, came to our rescue when we were totally stuck. With a simple cut, in the middle of a line of dialogue, he enabled us to keep the order of events, and yet lose that final attack and thus a great deal of footage. By the time the purge was over, the picture ran for 95 minutes.

Now we had to lick the problem of the title. Dozens more had been suggested and we whittled them down to two: 'Echo of the English Revolution' and 'Winstanley'. For a plain, simple film, 'Winstanley' was a plain, simple title. David Caute came up with 'God's Brief Visit to England', which he said would be long enough to be remembered. I favoured 'Criminals of Want', a quote from the Internationale. But we finally settled on 'Winstanley'.

Peter Harvey now had the colossal task of dubbing the picture. We loaded the tracks – more than 20 per reel – on to the BFI's hand-operated lift at Lower Marsh and broke the brakes. Doug Turner at De Lane Lea mixed the tracks, and to Peter and he (with hard work from assistant Charlie Ware) can be laid the credit for the superb track that resulted.

As the dubbing got under way, I heard from a Professor Lutaud at the Sorbonne, author of a two-volume work on Winstanley. He came to London, saw the film, and said he would include reference to it in his book. (He proved very helpful with the exploitation of the film in France.)

The five days allotted to dubbing the 13 reels went remarkably well, apart from occasional cut-outs in the dialogue tracks, where Peter had endeavoured to remove camera noise from sync-dialogue tracks. The worst moment came with the scene of Mrs Platt resting in the hut of an old woman. 'I thought we were going to have a really revolting cough over that,' said Andrew, listening to the effect.

'Well, where are we going to get anyone to do that now?' I snapped.

'I will,' said he. So into the commentary box he went, and exploiting his asthma for all it was worth, he coughed until he made me heave. Peter Harvey rushed round to the projection box and laid the tracks. To me, it sounded like Andrew coughing…but no one has ever drawn attention to the discrepancy.

The dark cloud hanging over us was reel one. Having been shot on 16mm, it was blown up to 35mm by Kays (who had done the same for *IHH*). Everybody opposed the music, *Alexander Nevsky*. David Caute had been especially critical. 'The music not only romanticises the battle: it de-realises it. By putting music on you make it choreographical – instead of a nasty, grim struggle. It becomes a ballet to symbolise great hopes, and the rest of the film is laid low.'

Andrew said that he couldn't have put his view more eloquently than Caute did. 'It is very exciting, but it is just a piece of romantic cinema.'

Doug Turner converted him by sheer dubbing skill. Peter Harvey had provided effects and Turner balanced these against the music, and brought the music back at just the right level to contain the entire prologue.

When the dub was over, there was a great sense of anti-climax. It had been fun; no fighting, no real tension, no rows – not a proper dubbing session at all!

A screening of the finally cut film with dubbed track was held for the BFI distribution department. To settle the music copyright question, we invited the Soviet cultural attaché, but he failed to turn up. (He failed

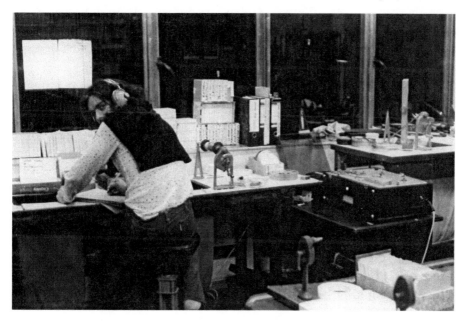

Peter Harvey

245

to turn up on every subsequent occasion, too, and we finally paid a lump sum to a Czech record company, Supraphon.) The distribution department was represented only by Gerry O'Halloran, who played in the picture. So I called a few more people to fill the vacant seats. A surprising number turned up. Colin McArthur, head of the BFI's Film Availability Service, arrived and said: 'I can only stay for an hour.' I was sufficiently irritated with the lack of interest from the BFI to say: 'Would you mind waiting until you have time to see the whole film? We are very hard up for seating.' Michael Relph, Chairman of the Production Board, arrived and said he could only manage an hour. But then he'd seen it already. Off he went. Another member of the distribution department, Diana Curnick, had also seen the picture, although she put it in a disconcerting way: 'I've seen the rushes; shall I go too?' I was delighted to accept her resignation. Two girls from The Other Cinema grabbed the last two seats and a few latecomers sat on the floor.

After the show, I overheard some members of the cast reminiscing. Nostalgia already? 'We had this scene riding up the hill at quite a lick,' Dawson France was telling a girl. 'I was the only one who could ride. When we got to the top, I looked back and they'd all fallen off!'

The reaction was enthusiastic. Eugene Mollo, Andrew's father, was quite eulogistic: 'Very sad and very beautiful. The casting is perfect. These are real people, not film people. There is less entertainment value for ordinary filmgoers than the last one, but a much deeper message.'

Dawson France: 'You really recaptured all the discomfort we went through. Visually, it's what every cameraman aims for – it's a cameraman's ideal. Directorially, a director's ideal. Every camera position is a pure painting. It has the most superb sound track I've ever heard.'

The curious thing about private screenings is that if anyone is critical, you automatically accept their sincerity. But praise is acutely embarrassing, and the more heartily expressed, the less one believes it. People expect you to say something in reply, but you want to shrink into your shoes. I always remember Josef von Sternberg's dictum: 'In Hollywood, you can attack a man's wife, you can rape his daughter, you can wipe your hands on his canary bird – but you cannot call his picture anything but "great".'

And however genuine the enthusiasm, at the back of one's mind is a cynical voice: 'You got away with it this time – but wait till your next movie!' As I scribbled in my notebook: 'Let's hope we won't be rushed into something like *The Breaking of Bumbo* that we don't believe in.'

The visuals of *Winstanley* aroused rapturous comment, and it was a pleasure to pass them on to Ernie. But Cecil Fennell deserved his share of the credit, for his grading had been flawless, and the cutting copy was the most beautiful I had ever seen. Keith Lucas asked for the film to launch the London Film Festival – it would have been the first British film to do so, and we would have been grateful for the kind of publicity that went to the eventual choice, *Akenfield*, directed by Peter Hall. But Cecil Fennell warned us against rushing. He had been rushed before for a festival booking, on *My Ain Folk*. I wrote to reassure him:

'We took note of your reaction and turned down the Festival. We consider it essential that you do the grading of the final print – and that you don't find yourself rushed. You are without doubt the finest grader for black and white in the business – and we have put up with all the disasters in the developing room simply because of this. It would be a great shame if we were forced to look for another lab now.'

Virginia Brownlow files trims on last cutting stage of *Winstanley*

However, I said I was very concerned for the safety of the negative, and that the disasters we experienced were too frequent to be exceptional. So we would have the negative cut by specialist neg-cutters (Mike Fraser).

I am glad I sent that letter, because Cecil was brilliant at his job, yet greatly under-rated. Sadly, he fell ill and, on 14 March 1975, he died. The laboratory was thrown into disarray, for Bob Henderson, the manager, had himself already died. Hendersons asked us to take the film away – they could not cope with it in the foreseeable future. Once again, the film received a blow from which it would never recover.

I decided to give Studio Film Labs a second chance. I had a meeting with John Sears and Sid Wilson, and told them the hard facts: how good their original test had been, how we selected FP4 as a result, how we put in our first rushes, how awful the result had been. How we nearly fired the cameraman. How we finally pulled the film from SFL. They were both rueful. I also told them that the BFI had blamed SFL for handing over an Irish film the Production Board were involved in to the Ministry of Defence. 'That's something we'd rather not talk about,' they said. They brought in an old grader, shortly to retire. He showed no enthusiasm for the job, even after I raved about the test he had done for us. Sid Wilson all but ordered him to take the job on, saying: 'I want to get our reputation back with the BFI.'

But when we got the test, the result was simply…blah. It was several points too light and absolutely lacking in guts. We turned to Humphries.

Their grader, John Williams, was outspoken from the start. He said he wasn't interested in duplicating someone else's work, and he thought his grading better than Cecil Fennell's. But it wasn't. It was heavy and dead, without the subtlety and range we were used to. Part of the problem was in the developing, of course. He agreed to make another test – and Andrew, Peter Harvey and I raced down to Churt to take advantage of a brief snowfall for the final shots. We got them just in time; it was the only occasion I can ever remember hearing the snow melting. The sound was similar to a giant bath being drained.

Humphries' first print was hardly encouraging. The first reel was totally grey, and when I said it was NG, John Williams replied: 'It's got to match the rest of it. That's all you can do.' I said that if the rest looked like that we'd better stop right away. The rest looked like SFL's original test. 'Then this should match that.'

'No, it can't,' said Williams. 'It's not original material. It's blow up – different kind of negative. This is the best you can do.' So it went. Some of the print was spot on, some way off.

'It's all very well saying it's right in the cutting copy,' said Williams. 'They probably spent a long time getting it right. It's a special thing. Once the neg is cut in with a lot of other stuff, you're never going to get the same effect.'

At the very end, noticing my dispirited expression, Williams said: 'I know what you're after, but you're never going to get it.'

'No,' I thought. 'Not with you grading.'

I suggested I took the reels and worked through them, marking up each shot so he would have absolute guidance. He agreed.

A day or so later, Nita called to say John Williams was acting very strangely. He told her that his supervisor, Bill Bush, had instructed him not to send the print out for me to work on.

Bill Bush was aggressive when I rang him. 'I have reports from grading that you are taking the answer print, but you won't pay for it. Now is it a chargeable commodity or not?'

'The grading is very erratic,' I said, and explained what I intended to do. 'It depends which way round you want to do it,' I continued. 'According to standard lab practice, you pay for an answer print and get a second free if you don't like it. Or the answer print is thrown away and you pay for the second. We don't mind which way round it is – we just want to end up with an acceptable print.'

'Fine,' said Bill Bush to my surprise. 'Then there's no problem.'

I ploughed through each reel, marking every shot with camera tape '2 points lighter', '3 points darker' and hoped that the effort would be rewarded. No sooner had I returned the print to Humphries than I was rushed into hospital with appendicitis and lost interest (temporarily) in the proceedings.

Chapter Twenty-Five

Upon my discharge from hospital, I discovered that nothing had been done. I fixed up a meeting with the production manager at Humphries, John Lucas, and gave him the background. I tried to spark some enthusiasm for the work by making it sound challenging.

'It's not worth the bother, frankly,' he said. 'We haven't got enough black and white work to keep our baths going. We have to make up a special bath when we get enough in – and that bath has to be standard. The same for everyone.' I said I realised his position, but he might attract more work if the lab gave better service. There were liable to be quite a few 35mm prints ordered by the BFI. But if there was no sign of improvement, then we might as well wait until Hendersons were back to normal. 'Why is there no one at Humphries one can talk to who knows about such things as developing time?' I asked. John Lucas said there was; he got his secretary to telephone down for Ernie Gower. 'I am very concerned about doing anything unusual with baths,' Lucas warned me. 'It'll result in chaos. You have to understand we only have machine operators; they switch on and they switch off. And that's that.'

Ernie Gower was a veteran, and he understood at once what I was trying to say. He realised that five minutes in a 'pos' bath would merely increase the contrast. But six minutes in a 'neg' bath would produce the effect we wanted. He persuaded Lucas that there would be no problem and I gratefully staggered out into the sunlight.

The following morning, I called John Williams to learn that he had only vaguely heard of the procedure. I told him the vital thing was to get the new print out as fast as possible.

'I don't know when I'm going to get round to it.'

I said it was essential he did it right away. We had lost too much time.

'I can't do it, old son. I'm on reel five of a nine-reel feature and I'm plodding away and I don't see any end to it.' I said John Lucas saw no problem. 'Oh, that's nice. Sit behind a nice desk and see no bloody problem. I don't care who knows it – I'm bloody well cheesed off. I can only do one thing at a time.'

'Well, do *our* thing,' I said, impatiently.

'You'll have to talk to John Lucas.'

'I don't see why I bothered to drag myself off my hospital bed to go and see Lucas if it was for nothing. Let me tell you why it is so essential we get that print. We have been invited to the Berlin Film Festival, and we have to get the print over there immediately.'

'Well, I've got news for you. The film I'm doing – that's been invited to Berlin, too.'

I could only think of one other picture, which a friend had edited – *Overlord*, directed by Stuart Cooper and cut by Jonathan Gili. Williams agreed that was it.

I called Jonathan Gili and he said that poor John Williams had to plough through the negative looking for scratches – it wasn't a grader's job and it was driving him nuts. The film was due in Berlin in two weeks for subtitling – and it was the official British entry. (Our film wasn't going to the proper festival, but to the Forum, which was non-competitive.) Jonathan said he'd make sure that John Williams put our print through – at least he could do a test.

Sure enough, the test was done, and John Williams phoned me with the glad tidings that I could see it whenever I wanted. 'But I want to warn you,' he said, 'that it isn't any good.' He was right; it was milk pale, and there was no sign of that rich, almost sepia tone that Hendersons achieved.

'That was a waste of time,' I murmured.

'I could have told you that,' said Williams.

'Would you mind running it to Ernie Gower,' I said, 'since neither of us understands the neg-bath situation.'

'I do,' said Williams.' I'm not an idiot.'

I couldn't resist asking why he had never told me in the first place. This sparked a catalogue of complaints, culminating in the confession: 'Because I'm like you. You're not the only perfectionist. It annoys me when it's wrong and it annoys me more when I have to tell you about it. But basically if your story's good, you can let the labs have a certain tolerance – a certain amount of sparkle – and the audience won't notice.'

'Quite true,' I said. 'But I made one film ten years ago. Since then, I have tried to make another – without success. This one is a non-commercial picture. Very simple, very specialised. It isn't going to appeal to many people. So it's going to be as right as I can get it. It may be the last film I ever make – so when it hits the screen it's going to be dead right.'

John Williams took me to Ernie Gower, who drew a graph to explain why I would never get the effect I was after. But he helpfully offered to try a type of stock called Agfa-Gevaert, which had higher contrast.

I suggested that Gerry O'Halloran telephone Humphries in his official capacity, to see how things were going. He was passed to John Williams. 'If you hand me another of those bloody things,' he laughed, 'I'll hand in my notice!'

O'Halloran was supposed to keep after John Lucas, not only to make sure that the Gevaert stock was in, but to explain that if it wasn't, he should proceed with Kodak stock to get the print out by our Berlin deadline. But he didn't ring, and the result was that the print wasn't done.

'Disaster,' said John Williams. A familiar word by now. 'We put the print down and reel 12 went.'

'I'm sorry. I don't understand.'

'We put the negative down to the printers, and while they were printing it, reel 12 went – the splices went.'

'Oh.'

'So I joined that up and reel 13 went. I took that away and joined it up but the printer said: "Here, what are these frames in the gate?" And there were four or five frames stuck in there. So we've got to get a synchroniser and wind through and find out where they came from before we can print it again.'

I suggested we took the reels back to the neg-cutters, Mike Fraser, and he said: 'Yeah, but if all he's going to do is the same as us, we'd rather do it and make certain.'

He made certain and reel 13 broke three times. 'It's just a miracle it broke cleanly and no damage has been done,' said John Williams the next day. 'A girl worked all day on it and still it broke. I can tell you what's wrong. The emulsion is not scraped sufficiently. I could flip my fingernail under each join. I won't, but I could…'

At long last, the print was ready. I wondered, when I phoned John Williams, why he sounded so odd. We ran it at Preview One, and even though the theatre had installed a new lighting setup, it looked grim. Reel one was adequate, but the titles were far too light. From reel two onwards it was disastrous. Unfortunately, not being forewarned, I had invited distributors and other interested parties – Richard Craven (who later formed the Association of Independent Producers), Susan Raven, Tony Gruner, a television man, Mike Kaplan, a distributor from America, working here. The photography had no quality at all, and as a result, nor had the film. Mike Kaplan did an involuntary imitation of an American distributor bewildered by what he had just seen. 'Great job,' he said, and raced for the exit. We adjourned to a coffee bar.

'What terrible weather they had,' said Susan Raven. She added that she had enjoyed the afternoon, but wished she had known it was all based on fact. 'Perhaps a great illuminated scroll at the beginning?'

Kaplan kept putting his hand across his face, as though to exorcise the non-commercial images he had just seen. 'You may not like the picture,' I said, 'but we have a terrific poster.' He wasn't amused... He said the picture would depend on its exploitation. 'Yes,' he said slowly, and with great deliberation. 'It might go this way and it might go that.' I began to build up the film's chances on the college circuit in America – a very lucrative area. 'I tell you what I'll do,' he said, as we walked into the street and he hailed a cab. 'I'll think about it.'

Deeply upset by the miserable print, I telephoned John Williams.

'Was there anything wrong with that print?'

'No – nothing that I know of.'

'Did it go through any unusual process?'

'Well, since you ask, I noticed the cans as they came up and there was the wrong numbers on the lid. Instead of 122 there was 9 something, which means the whole thing is two or three points too light.'

My sympathy for Humphries was further strained by the news, next day, from John Lucas, that both he and Williams knew about the problem in advance. I sent a carefully worded memo, and when I next spoke to Williams he was rebellious.

'Quite honestly,' he said, when I mentioned the memo, 'I'm not going to touch it. I'm not doing any more grading – no more "one point here and one point there". I've had my fill. What with two other people after me...'

I bumped into an old friend, director Peter Smith, who said he would never have anything more to do with Humphries. 'Why not?' I asked, innocently. His grader, John Williams, had apparently told him: 'I'm not going to do any more grading – that's it!' on a Children's Film Foundation picture. Peter also said that he had done a film about a painter and the greens had come out red. When he objected, John Williams had said: 'There's someone here who knows that bloke's paintings – and the colours are right!'

Before Berlin, there was the Cork Film Festival. We had premiered *IHH* at Cork, and many members of my family and Virginia's family lived there. So we felt nostalgically inclined to let Cork have the so-called 'world premiere'.

When I discovered that this 'world premiere' had been scheduled at 3.15pm on a Wednesday, I was furious. Hardly anyone could manage that time. 'Is this your last word?' I demanded of the organiser, Dermot Breen, over the phone.

'Well now, Kevin, that was not my decision but was democratically arrived at by our selection committee. We finished at five this morning. We jockeyed the position, but you must understand that Wednesday is a very popular day and as the film was of particular interest, we put it in that slot.'

'3.15pm isn't much of a time for a world premiere.'

'We threw out seven world premieres. But when you've got 26 features in seven days, what can you do?'

'I realise you have problems – but we have problems too. Not every director has 13 cousins and God knows how many uncles and aunts in Cork. It means it's not worth our coming over.'

'I'm very sorry. I'm not up in all the details because I've been in hospital…'

'I heard about that. And this is the kind of thing that'll put me in there, too.'

We now had a below-standard print at Cork. It was vital we had a top-standard one at Berlin. I called my nemesis at Humphries.

'How's it going?'

'It's not.'

'Oh, for Christ's sake; what do you mean?'

'You'll have to have a word with my grading manager.'

'You'll have to explain a bit more. What do I talk to him about?'

'What I've got to do – how much I've got to do – and in what order I've got to do it.'

He transferred me to Bill Bush, who said: 'We're not moving on *Winstanley* at the moment.'

'Oh, that's helpful. What are the reasons?'

'I don't see why I should talk about it.' He advised me to talk to John Lucas.

'What's the matter with you all at Humphries?' I exploded. 'You're behaving like a bunch of children up there. Every time I ring up, there's a long pause and a whisper. Why can't you tell me what's going on? I'm getting fed up with it... there are other labs, you know.'

After a long pause, Bush finally admitted that *Winstanley* had been taken off and *Overlord* put on the printer.

'Thank you,' I said. 'That's all I want to know.'

'If you think we can take *Overlord* off, you just have a try.'

'I'm not going to insist that you take it off. I'm not going to be unreasonable. I just want to be told what's going on. I will now call John Lucas.'

'He's not in,' said Bush, triumphantly.

When I do manage to get hold of him, he is clipped in his manner.

'What news?' I ask.

'Nothing, really.' He breaks off to talk over the phone to someone called John. He returns to tell me he cannot put two men on a black and white bath during day shifts. 'It's throwing money down the drain.'

'I've heard so many reasons why things have to be made easier for you. I never hear anything about things being made easier for us. And we're paying. We've had a pretty rough passage at Humphries. You've had this material since March and we've had one print. It is now June the sixth.'

'I think you've had two prints,' he said. 'As I told you before, we cannot be expected to operate a service outside the normal. You say you've had a rough passage. You've already had two changes of stock – Fuji and Kodak – and numerous grading alterations...'

'They didn't make the slightest difference or require any grading alterations. We still haven't had the Gevaert stock we asked for.'

'Customers expect us to drop everything and produce it on their stock to their specifications and it can't be done.'

'We still haven't had the test on Gevaert.'

'Gerry O'Halloran said you didn't want it.'

'That was because of speed. We had to have a print and you didn't have any Gevaert. We still want it, and you agreed to provide it. Now what about our Berlin deadline – the last print should have gone to Berlin. How soon can we expect the next?'

'I haven't passed your note to John Williams. The negative has been cleaned, that I do know. We will check it for the specific problems you mention. We'll print Monday.'

'Can I have it Tuesday?'

'More like Wednesday.'

I told him that I knew *Overlord* was going through.

'I can assure you *Overlord* is not going through. There is no other black and white production.'

By way of an exit line, he blamed the wrecked print on a faulty printer light.

From Cork came a telephone call from Virginia's sister, Sally. The festival had gone downhill since we had last visited it. 'The big thing now is the dinner dance. They have a film called *Brannigan* on Wednesday night – obviously they felt they had to have John Wayne to get people off the streets of Cork to buy tickets for the film and the dinner dance. They'd hardly feel like dinner, let alone dancing, after *Winstanley*!'

12 June, 11am, John Williams on the phone. 'One reel is at the wrong light for starters,' he said, reviewing the new print. 'Reel 12 fell apart. And reel two's not so funny.'

The only reason we were able to secure any special treatment from Humphries was because of Stanley Kubrick. Just before we put in our negative, he had placed an order for a large number of prints of *Paths of Glory* (1957). The picture had never been shown in France, since the authorities had banned it for the image it presented of the French army in the Great War, and the ban had at last been lifted. Kubrick had the knowledge and power to order precisely what he wanted – and he insisted that they develop the film with ten strands less. This meant that the celluloid, snaking from roller to roller like a spinning jenny, would get a marginally shorter developing time. I imagined this would result in an adverse effect; that what was needed was longer developing time, as at Hendersons, but the test looked good, and we rolled through the developing bath in the wake of Kubrick and benefited from his expertise.

The *Daily Telegraph* carried a review from Cork by our old adversary Eric Shorter; he called the film 'dull, boring and confused.' The next night, Ruth Brandon of Kaleidoscope on BBC Radio 4 made up for Shorter's vitriol with an enthusiastic review. The BBC telephoned me to ask which actor had been the sole professional, and I had told them: Jerome Willis. So I was taken aback during a discussion of the 'very fine acting' that Miles was singled out as the only professional.

If the *Daily Telegraph* review was bad, it was only to be expected. But on 14 June there was a heartbreaking review in the *Guardian* – a big picture, splendid presentation, but a miserable sting in the tail, saying 'it lacks the kiss of life'. I kicked myself for not going to Cork. How absurd to have babied the film so carefully through every stage, and then to turn it loose to stand on its own feet the very moment it most needed support. Worse was to follow. In the *Sunday Telegraph* of 15 June, Tom Hutchinson wrote a piece saying it had left him cold and (once again) that it was boring.

If the critics say you have made a boring film, then that's the way it will pass into history. For historians are critics in disguise. The clippings file at the BFI, to which they all refer, will immortalise these words. And there is another, more immediate danger, too: potential distributors will be deterred. It was the worst period, for me at any rate, of the entire production. After all the enthusiasm, the one thing I did not anticipate was bad reviews.

David Robinson, critic of the *Times*, blamed me for not going to Cork. 'You brought it on yourself,' he said. 'The public read reviews to give them some background, so they enjoy the film more. They like to be told what to think. Critics are just the same.'

Curiously enough, the picture won an award at Cork – Andrew Mollo received the trophy for the outstanding art director. This represented a degree of consolation, for if anyone deserved recognition, it was Andrew. It was infuriating that Ernie did not win the cinematography award, for I cannot believe that better photography appeared on Cork's screen that year.

But the general barometer of opinion appeared to be clouded with disfavour when we held the Distributors' Show at De Lane Lea theatre. Twenty-five people said they were coming, and the theatre held eighteen. Somehow, a few kitchen chairs were conjured up, and 30 people crammed into the place, and several had to sit on the floor. This was not the ideal way to treat film distributors, particularly on a hot day.

Once the sound level had been adjusted – and this is a more important part of a show than you may think – I left, returning 90 minutes later. I was surprised to see through the projection port that no

258

one had abandoned ship. When the film was over, and I pulled the door open, it was like the Marx Brothers' cabin in *A Night at the Opera*. Some elderly distributors, discovering girls seated on the floor beside them, began to stammer that had they but known …

David Stone of the Gate made the standard farewell speech of the distributor to the filmmaker: 'Great, Kevin, I liked it very much.' Others streamed past without a word. Stanley Forman, importer of communist films, wrung my hand and said it was so good, so important – 'sensational' – which was a help since he would be on the jury at the Moscow Film Festival.

Charles Cooper of Contemporary, perhaps the most likely buyer, wasn't there. He sent his wife, Kitty, who in 1966 had denounced *IHH* as a fascist film. I heard second hand that she had said: 'Films should have a standpoint. This is like the last one – it has no standpoint.' When this was repeated, it brought a strong reaction from a German called Schlacke from Cinema Action who said: 'Then, she has no sensitivity. I know Kitty, I know she is sensitive. But she is totally wrong. This is partisan from beginning to end…' And an enjoyable argument broke out on the pavement outside De Lane Lea. 'I cannot emphasise what an important film this is,' said Schlacke. 'It should have been made 50 years ago. It is no reflection on the makers that it was not. The Production Board, in fact, should be proud that they allowed it to be made. It is a film of tremendous significance to the English. Now in Germany, with three social upheavals, it may be received gently. In France, with several upheavals, it may not mean so much. But it is tremendously important in this country. And it has so many levels. It is a wonderful work.'

A woman, who had been hovering on the sidelines, finally approached and said: 'I'm Rita Jarvis. I just want to say how much I liked it. It was a perfect film.' To which her partner, Mark Williams, added: 'The dubbing was incredible.' And Rita Jarvis, who at that time represented a distribution company with the name of Pleasant Pastures, said: 'But it is not right for us.'

Lekharev of Sovexportfilm emerged from somewhere with Gerry O'Halloran and the chief of the selection committee for the Moscow Film Festival. They had not been at the show, although invited. The chief of the selection committee was a woman, and when she heard Gerry talk about the film she fired a question at Lekharev: 'You have the telephone numbers and the lines of communication?' Lekharev nodded with confidence: 'Of course.' When her back was turned, he hissed: 'I haven't. Give me the numbers quick.'

Andrew and I were both invited to Berlin and Andrew went ahead. I had never seen the city and was immensely intrigued as the plane glided low over the heavily-repaired rooftops of Berlin, to land at Tempelhof, probably the only airport in the centre of a city.

The airport itself was a Nazi structure. Andrew, Carmen and a Greek driver met me and Andrew pointed out the huge eagles, minus swastika, still standing on the perimeter building. Nearby was a monument to the Berlin airlift. We drove to the Sylter Hof hotel, and then to the Europa Center to check in with the festival people. It quickly became apparent that there was a vast divergence between the main festival and the Jugendforum to which we had been invited. And it became clear why Humphries had had the skids put under them for *Overlord*; it was the official British entry in the festival proper (and was to win a Silver Bear). Michael Relph, chairman of the Production Board, was also chairman of the Film Producers Association, which selected official British entries, and we decided to make sure that we were selected for at least one more festival – hopefully Moscow.

Andrew and Carmen are shown over the Berlin Wall

260

East Berlin: bombed church with birch tree on roof

The Jugendforum screenings tended to begin with the appearance of a large number of mournful-looking students, who filed in front of the screen and delivered an oration to the audience about the misdeeds of the West German Ministry of Justice. No one tried to stop them, since the Forum specialised in radical films, but the lengthy speeches caused the last performance to run extremely late.

Our screening at the Academie des Kunsts was jam-packed. The experience of seeing the film with an audience was hard to bear, for they seemed to signal through some sort of osmosis precisely which scenes should be cut; certain quiet scenes, for instance, which were plainly leading to a drop in the temperature. The sound on one projector was misaligned, so I found a control knob at the back of the theatre and re-balanced the reels. From this position I was able to watch those who walked out – and there were plenty, including Jan Dawson, organiser of the Perth Film Festival (who quit during reel four and demanded a special screening later!). Other people walked in, which was equally distracting. The rest of the audience responded well to the film, which had been subtitled in German (thank God they didn't dub it!) and applauded at its conclusion. Most of the house emptied for the press conference and those that remained quickly followed when the Germans started their interminable questions.

The immediate reactions from people around me were encouraging. Tom Luddy, of the Pacific Film Archive, said he thought it was 'fabulous'. Another festival organiser shook hands and made the right noises. Then, David Robinson said: 'Get up there!' and propelled me towards a table on the stage, where I joined Andrew and the Forum organisers. So far as I could tell, the press had left the theatre to the students. The first question was from an American, who seemed surprised that we had bothered to make it: 'Why did you shoot this film?' I stumbled through an answer, making heavy weather of 'the first socialist manifesto, The Law of Freedom…how we started with David Caute's book…and gradually became immersed in this forgotten period of English history.' The second question involved the statutory two parts: first, why did we did not mention the enclosures, nor the wanderings of the many homeless people? I replied that to include such things properly would have converted the film from 95 minutes to six hours. The second part was 'a question of aesthetics'. There was too much 'weather phenomena'. Andrew answered brilliantly. 'Many of us who are politically active [an opening which surprised me!] demonstrate for their beliefs, then return to a centrally heated house, take some food from the fridge and switch on TV. Most communes today exist in California, where the weather is kind. We wanted to show that these people were not only demonstrating their political beliefs – it was *ein Kampf gegen die Elemente* [a struggle against the elements].'

Changing the guard near the
Memorial for the Victims of Fascism and Militarism (!)

Another member of the audience said he was struck and surprised by the way the film was made. 'Contrary to the tendency of recent years, it is not a work in which sequences are shot from one camera position – the editing is on the Soviet model.' I said I loathed one-camera sequences, a technique more suitable to primitive Edison pictures. Furthermore, amateurs could seldom sustain performances and consequently scenes had to be fragmented.

Despite the vaguely inimical air of the questions, the reaction of the German audience proved to be enthusiastic, as did most of the reviews. This surprised some of the BFI people, who disliked the picture. Richard Roud, who had turned down *IHH* for the New York festival in 1964, stayed true to form and protected his audiences from this one, too.

David Robinson reported an enthusiastic outburst from a woman director; she had spent an hour talking about the film and was especially keen on the Drake sequence, with the dogs. When I told him of the lacklustre BFI reactions, he said: 'I think it's just the English not catching on. I feel very inadequate writing about it at such length – just three paragraphs. I'm longing to do justice to it, and to its language. Gerrard Winstanley must take credit for the film as much as you – his ideas and his language.' He added that he thought Andrew 'a saint' for putting up with the film always being referred to as 'a Kevin Brownlow picture'. He went through the piece and made sure both names were credited.

His piece in the *Times* was the first appearance in the English press of a favourable review:

'Kevin Brownlow and Andrew Mollo's *Winstanley* was something new for the Forum, and was enthusiastically received in Berlin. It is indeed a completely original film, using traditional narrative forms to express an idea. Perhaps this is what foxed the local audience at the Cork Film Festival. Because they have created a spectacle out of a shoestring, and employed techniques of the story film, Brownlow and Mollo arouse expectations of a swashbuckler, which their film in no way intends to be.

'Based on the novel *Comrade Jacob* by David Caute, and with dialogue taken from the original writings of Gerrard Winstanley, who endeavoured to set up a commune on a seventeenth-century Surrey hillside, this touching account of the birth and failure of an ideal touches on many areas of social and political experience, while keeping its contacts within a simple and human level of experience...*It Happened Here*, Brownlow's previous collaboration with Andrew Mollo, and *Winstanley* are two of the most singular works to come out of the British cinema.' (*Times*, 14 July 1975)

A more ambivalent notice appeared in *Variety*. Last time, a good review in *Variety* won us a United Artists contract. This time, the review was the opposite of a sales review: 'A low-budget pic' was how it described the film. (*Variety*'s hard-bitten vernacular greatly amuses me.) 'In addition to the application of today's communal experience, the pic's sparse, ascetic visual beauty is an impressive throwback to the naturalism of the silent era, although the dialogue has a condescending theatrical ring.'

I had tried hard to make contact with *Variety*'s representative, in order to explain the picture to him, and to make sure he realised what we were trying to do. Seventeenth-century dialogue is difficult for modern audiences, granted, but people spoke like that in real life, not just on the stage of the National. Unfortunately, no one could tell me who was covering the festival for *Variety*, and a valuable opportunity was lost. As far as the United States was concerned, the film was sunk with faint praise.

Chapter Twenty-Six

The chairman of the British Film Institute Production Board was Michael Relph, an industry veteran. He was also chairman of the Film Producers' Association. The FPA selected the official entries for film festivals. We were anxious that *Winstanley* should be the official British entry to the Moscow Film Festival.

We were told that official entries were always purchased for distribution throughout Eastern Europe by Sovexportfilm, and as the film was concerned with the origins of communism, we thought it would be a natural choice. Usually, a film in competition at one festival is ruled out at another. Having been at Cork, we could not be in competition at Berlin. But Moscow had its own rules. We therefore requested, through Barrie Gavin, that Michael Relph be informed of our request. Relph did not reply; but, after Stanislav Lekharev of Sovexportfilm ran the film at his office, *Winstanley* received an invitation to Moscow.

Andrew was anxious to attend because of his Russian background and his intense interest in the country. He had already paid his first visit while I was in hospital; on this occasion, *IHH* had been invited to a Festival of anti-fascist films at Volgograd – formerly Stalingrad – to celebrate the 30th anniversary of the end of World War II. (The Russians would not have been amused to know that simultaneously it was being shown in Paris, without our knowledge, in a festival of right-wing films. A festival dedicated to a film historian shot by the resistance!)

As the official entry, we fully expected the Russians to pay our fares. I had attended Moscow once before, without representing a film, and my fare was paid; they had already covered Andrew and Carmen's expenses to Volgograd. This time, however, they refused. 'There are far too many delegates attending for us to pay fares,' was the gist of their excuse. I went to see Keith Lucas and he cleared the cost of one ticket. (The Russians covered hotel expenses.) I covered the cost of the other. Since this cost £225.20, neither of us would have gone had we not been certain that our film was the official British entry.

Our arrival in Moscow was enlivened by the beaming smiles of Viktor, our interpreter, who had made friends with Andrew at Volgo-

View from Rossia Hotel

grad. His enthusiasm diverted our attention from the fact that *Winstanley*, far from being the official British entry, did not appear in the festival schedule at all. We registered and we had our first meal at the Rossia Hotel with the English delegation. I loathed the critic of the *Daily Worker* on sight. (I later found her hilariously funny and one of the brightest aspects of the trip.) Virginia Dignam was large and she was loud and she kept telling everyone who asked about how ghastly everything was at Cork...with meaningful 'I'm sorry, but' glances at me. Also in the English delegation were *Daily Telegraph* critic Patrick Gibbs and Gerald Thomas, director of the Carry Ons. ('They showed *Nurse* in Russia,' he told me. 'Trouble is, they won't pay for them.')

We were sitting at the delegation table the following morning when Viktor broke the news: the film had not even been seen by the selection committee. 'They may reject it.' Most of the day was squandered in roaming the Kafka-like corridors of the Rossia in search of an official with the unlikely name of Mak-Mayevsky. He apparently held the key to our survival at Moscow. It took a long time to find him, and the conversation that resulted was strange. He told us the film had been seen ('all films are subject to special screening'). 'What did we do wrong,' I asked him, 'that the film is not in competition?'

Mak-Mayevsky gave a most peculiar reply. 'You did not send a special note saying that the film should be in competition.' (If the Russians have no answer, they will make one up.)

'Why do you think,' I asked, 'that we put the film into the festival in the first place?'

'I cannot answer your question,' replied Mak-Mayevsky. 'In any case, we are not interested in *Winstanley* but in *It Happened Here*.' At the request of the Russians, we had brought this film in our luggage – a very heavy 35mm print. It proved as hard to get that shown as *Winstanley*.

The following day we met Ian Mitchell, of the FPA, who tried to be helpful. Thanks to him, we learned that it was not a Russian we should attack for the fate of our film, but the chairman of the Production Board, Michael Relph. When we brought up the question of the official entry, Mitchell said: 'That's news to me. I wish I'd known about it. As it was, I was stuck. I finally thought of *Great Expectations*, knowing how all Russians love Dickens, but I'm dismayed. Russians keep coming up to me and saying: "David Lean?"'

The new version of the Dickens novel may have been made in England, but it was not a British film. It was directed by an American and financed by American television. We discovered that a special salesman, Ian Jessel, had been shipped out to promote it. Neither of us was invited to the trade talks with Sovexportfilm, nor to the press

Moscow street scene

conference for the British delegates, at which questions were asked about *Winstanley* which no one could answer.

Meanwhile, we made our own efforts to set up a trade show, and to invite members of Sovexportfilm. Michael Relph had by now joined the delegation, and when he heard about the projected screening, he murmured: 'Who arranged your trade show?' as if such extra-mural activities were somewhat infra dig.

Believing there must have been a genuine misunderstanding, neither of us took the matter up with Relph until well after the festival.

In between these frustrating interludes, we enjoyed ourselves thoroughly. At last a showing of *IHH* was announced, and we were assigned a huge car which we shared with a Portuguese delegation. One member of this was fed up with Moscow, hated the food, and moaned all the way to the cinema. Andrew warned me not to make jokes, and to keep my speech to short sentences. So I made him do the introduction. He did it quite well. We were introduced by Slava Kulisch, the young Soviet director of *Dead Season*. We had to wait hours to get the car back.

We visited the set of *Till Eulenspiegel* at Mosfilm studios, and saw how the vast Russian film industry tackled a medieval subject. Their set covered most of a huge sound stage. Curiously, two directors were at work on this one, too. They were asked how they worked together. 'He hates everything I suggest,' said one, 'and I hate everything he suggests.'

The better I got to know Virginia Dignam, the more favourable became her attitude to the Cork Film Festival. Eventually, she told me that *Winstanley* received rapt attention, with a gasp from the older members of the audience at the line 'The Virgin Mary is but a common whore' and a roar of laughter from the younger. She said there was applause and cheers at the end, which I know was merely Miss Dignam converting history into an act of generosity. However, I was relieved to think that she might review the film favourably. But she didn't; she merely gave it passing mention.

Winstanley was eventually shown at a cinema a long way from the centre called Illusion. Andrew and I introduced it – and to our surprise Michael Relph made a speech from the stage. Andrew remained to watch some of it with a Russian audience while I talked with a man from the Soviet archive, Gosfilmofond. Andrew reported disaster; at least 40 people had left in a great mass, halfway through, just as had apparently happened with the *IHH* screening. The rest gave it rapt attention, but the sound had been switched off to allow a commentator to translate the dialogue, and this had a deadening effect. The director of Illusion explained that people attended western films to see sex and violence, and once they realised they weren't going to get it, they left.

Our interpreter wrote in his notebook the slogan on a T-shirt worn by a festival delegate: 'I am frustrated, inhibited and nobody loves me.'

This would have described our own feelings had we taken the festival too seriously, but we had so much else to occupy our minds, the film's reception was merely a passing irritation. 'Your film *Winstanley,*' said a Russian journalist. 'Translate please.'

We began to think that perhaps Relph had been right to drop the picture. At any rate, we finally challenged him directly as to why it was no longer the British entry. 'That was due to the Russians,' he said. 'We offered it to them but they said it was too specialised. They wanted something more commercial. They wanted *Great Expectations.*'

'But that was made by an American director for American TV, wasn't it?'

'Yes,' said Relph, simply. We did not labour the point.

His indifference began to make sense in the light of his position with the FPA. On the other hand, Nina Hibbin of the Northern Arts Association (and previous critic for the *Daily Worker*), Tony Gruner of Talbot Television, and Stanley Forman, all of whom were extremely busy with their own agendas at the festival, took it upon themselves to campaign for *Winstanley,* and such success as we had in promoting the film was due to them. Michael Relph, apart from his speech, did precisely nothing.

I tramped the corridors of the Rossia, putting invitations under the door of every Sovexportfilm agent, from Bulgaria, Poland, and Hungary etc. At the theatre of the Film Market, I checked with the projectionist that the print was all right. This is essential practice, even though it is a thinly disguised way of saying: 'Do you know what you're supposed to be running?' As it happened, the projectionist said: 'What print?' and we had a Mack Sennett scramble. The embarrassing chaos calmed down when someone produced a print from a cutting room (a cutting room??!) and we managed to get it on the screen.

The interpreter confirmed my misgivings; there was no one from Sovexportfilm in the theatre. They must have assumed that their talks with the British delegation had covered everything. Three of them were in the restaurant below the theatre, and when I tried to corral them, one of them said: 'Go away. We are busy.' I took the interpreter aside and explained: 'We have come thousands of miles, and we spent three years making this film and it's running without a single member of Sovexportfilm present. Will you please ask one of them to do us the courtesy of attending?' The message was conveyed. No result. 'You have failed,' said the interpreter with finality.

Such a situation could never have occurred had *Winstanley* been the official entry or had it enjoyed the support of the Film Producers' Association. As a result, *Winstanley* was never sold to Russia, nor was it shown in the Soviet Union apart from its two festival showings. The Russians responded only to organisations, we found out, not to individuals. We could make progress up to a certain point, beyond which a few words of support from Michael Relph, as chairman of the Production Board, would have opened the right doors. Those words were not forthcoming.

However, we did better than the other film from the Production Board, *Moon over the Alley*, which was also Mr Relph's responsibility. That never got shown at all.

Chapter Twenty-Seven

Upon our return to London, I composed a memo for Keith Lucas. 'Since all the details I shall go into here reflect upon the attitude to the Production Board of its chairman I shall add my voice to the growing clamour for his immediate resignation. He behaved like a vicar at a flower show with the utmost decorum and absolutely no interest whatever in the exhibits. There was more concern for Production Board activities shown by Nat Cohen, who attended the festival as the head of EMI.'

Unfortunately, no move was made to oust Relph. Lucas explained that the FPA was an important source of revenue for the Production Board, and if Relph went, £40,000 would go with him.

Barrie Gavin, on the point of resigning from his position as Head of Production, wrote a sharp note to Lucas about the Moscow situation: 'Whatever the outcome of these enquiries, the situation is a disgrace to the British Film Industry and an insult both to the Institute and to the makers of the film. It is events like this which has made the post of Head of Production totally unworkable and unacceptable to me.' (28 July 1975)

Barrie Gavin

A Berlin television company offered £10,000 for the German rights to the film, but the deal seemed to be foundering. Or, in BFI parlance, 'it isn't going through as easily as one at first thought perhaps it might.' The distribution department, however, was confident they would secure it. They didn't.

Our morale was raised somewhat by a letter from Ken Wlaschin, Programme Director of the National Film Theatre: 'I meant to write to you earlier about how very much I enjoyed your film and how pleased I would be for the privilege of showing it in the London Film Festival in November. I understand that you were slightly perplexed by the reaction to the film in Cork, but I hope individual reactions like that will not affect you very much as the film is very fine indeed and you should be very proud of it.'

Our morale soared even higher when it was decided to open the festival with *Winstanley* in NFT1 and *Requiem for a Village* in NFT2. The first British film ever to open a London Film Festival had been *Akenfield*, the previous year.

London Weekend Television invited us over and announced their intention of devoting the whole of an Aquarius programme to the making of the film, with the theatre director Peter Hall, who had made *Akenfield*, as presenter. This delighted us, for it would encourage the distributors, like Contemporary, and arouse the publicity campaign for the festival opening. But early in October, London Weekend called me. 'Bad news, I'm afraid.'

'It's all off?' I joked. (I shouldn't make jokes like that.)

'Yes – forward, er, planning got a bit muddled.'

'You mean Peter Hall didn't like it?'

'Between you and me, I think it was a bit close to *Akenfield*. He commented all the way through – lovely, that's lovely – then at the end, he sounded a bit rehearsed. He said it was unwatchable…'

I happened to mention this to Lindsay Anderson, and was very startled by the direct action that followed. He confronted Peter Hall with this reported event in a letter. I received a postcard from Hall: 'Lindsay Anderson tells me that the current rumour is that I "blocked" *Winstanley* from Aquarius. This is, of course, not true. I saw your film and admired it very much. I believe [producer] Derek Bailey's reasons for excluding your film have been made known to you. I wish you luck with it.'

Since I had not heard from Derek Bailey, I rang him up, consumed with curiosity.

'Peter Hall had nothing whatever to do with the reason for excluding it.'

'What was the reason?'

'We didn't make a conscious decision to exclude it. We just decided not to include it.' He sounded somewhat hesitant, as if that remark was not entirely satisfactory. 'We saw your film and the production film [Eric Mival] and thought it would make a good item, but then we looked at the overall balance of the 13 programmes and decided that, well, we had put more money in films of our own. We had more material we had originated – and there was nothing more sinister about it than that. It was an editorial decision, and I realise we put you to a lot of trouble providing prints but I'm afraid that was what we decided.'

Akenfield was the first professional film to be made in the way that Andrew and I had made *IHH* and *Winstanley*; Rex Pike, the producer, had worked with me in the cutting room on Lindsay Anderson's *The White Bus* (1966) and, unlike most professionals, he was only too willing to explain how his film had been put together. He and Peter Hall realised that they couldn't possibly make the film with a full profession-al cast. They felt it would be an impertinence to go around researching what farm workers say to each other, picking out the best bits and giving it to actors. 'Why don't we get real people?' said Peter Hall. 'Put them in the situation they are in all the time and see what happens?'

Five hundred people wrote in after an item on the film appeared in a local newspaper. They asked for agricultural accomplishments, but wanted young men – instead they got veteran horsemen and old ladies expert at cake-baking. With a video camera, they made recordings of the most promising applicants. Pike said:

'One only had to speak to a couple of distributors and merchant banks to find out that with no murder or rape, ordinary Suffolk people and Suffolk accents, there was no likelihood of finance. Instead of approaching one source for £100,000, we asked lots of people and spread the risk. Labs – Technicolor let us down, but Samuelsons sup-ported us, Twickenham Studios…The technicians were enthusiastic and felt that this is the way films ought to be made, and they invested in the picture. Every pound invested, as salary or cash, was equal. We formed what was basically a co-operative, with all union demands built in, together with cassette sales, record sales, etc.

'The people who screwed it up were the union (ACTT), who blacked it and did everything to wreck it they possibly could. I ap-proached them long before we started, explained, made all the right noises and they let us start. We began shooting at weekends. The technicians could work in commercials or documentaries during the week, and work with us at weekends. As soon as we were involved in filming in a big way, ACTT said: "Right, no investment." We said they want to invest. But they wouldn't allow a technicians' meeting; every individual had to write to the union separately. In retrospect, it turned out that they were about to launch their nationalisation drive, and here was a practical alternative which was a reality.

'What we did was to say: "We will pay everybody". If they still wanted to invest, they would pay income tax on their salary, and their investment would be taxed as unearned income, instead of being salary and earned income. Yvonne Richards, of ACTT, said: "We thought of that, which is why we did it. We hope they won't re-invest." We gave the union all the cheques and said: "You send them out." Ninety per cent were returned. As a result, the Features Committee began talks on co-operatives.'

Other innovations on *Akenfield* included a new lens, developed in Germany by Wolfgang Trauer, which meant they could shoot without lights. They used Techniscope, a wide-screen process with a picture area of half a frame, which was thus as economical as 16mm. Cameraman Ivan Strasburg (like Ernie Vincze, a television documentary man and former assistant to Chris Menges) dispensed with a tripod and substituted an Elemag dolly with a jib arm, so the camera could be mobile and there would be the suggestion of a hand-held look. The unit consisted of half a dozen people – the rest were paid to stay in London.

'One costume girl dressed 130 people in wartime uniform. "Here are eight racks," she said. "Pick something that suits you." She found that former officers chose officer uniforms, former privates chose other ranks, and the casting was therefore done by the cast. We took over a cottage in which an old man had died, and we didn't dress it in any way. Souvenirs from a day at the seaside in 1923 were still on the mantelpiece.

'There wasn't a single written line. We ended up with 254,000ft with no line the same.'

Perhaps the most daring innovation was to premiere it on television and in the cinema at the same time. London Weekend Television had put up about £40,000. Instead of putting ads all over London saying: '*Akenfield* – a real experience,' they put nothing in the budget for advertising. 'We would let everyone know overnight that it exists, if it's a lousy film it will kill us overnight. But we hope that the eight million who see it will tell the 46 million who haven't seen it.'

That *Akenfield* was a commercial failure was one of the saddest events of recent British cinema. Had it succeeded, the way would have been clear for more films made in the same resourceful way. Both Andrew and I were pinning a great deal of hope on its creating a new climate for the financing of British films.

Rex Pike was as honest about the film's financial failure as he had been about the production. He gave me the figures for the Paris Pullman, the cinema owned by Contemporary Films, which provided a dismal picture for the makers of independent British films.

Akenfield played seven weeks at the Paris Pullman and grossed £6,536

    Contemporary passed to Rex Pike, as distributor: £1,467

    Pike's company had to pay for advertising: £1,221

    Which left him, as producer, with £246

Rex Pike then told me something significant: 'The only money *Akenfield* made was in the regional theatres of the BFI. They paid promptly, and if they were given sufficient notice, they worked hard for the film. I wish we'd gone with them in the first place. On the other hand, we heard that Portsmouth Regional Theatre had kicked up a fuss about showing *Emmanuelle* and *Last Tango* and were demanding good British films. So we put on *Akenfield* and in one week we got nine people. Two of them were friends of mine that I'd told to go.'

I am detailing the fate of *Akenfield* in such detail because it was an extremely important British film and the lessons it taught us should not be forgotten. *Winstanley* was even less of a commercial proposition; before the London Film Festival, we still had no offer from a major British distributor. From the very first show, the Other Cinema said they wanted the picture. I was fast coming to the conclusion that they were the right people to handle it, but the Other Cinema was a charitable organisation – literally – and we could never make our production costs back through them. But at least they wouldn't waste money, nor would they (how shall I put it?) deflect the money. So in the back of my mind, I decided upon the Other Cinema, but meanwhile I was very unfair to them. Confident of their offer, I nevertheless carried on a campaign against the other so-called art distributors, who had made no approaches whatsoever. I did this as much to help the other BFI features as to help our own. And the London Film Festival gave me an ideal opportunity.

Chapter Twenty-Eight

The press reception for the London Film Festival was held at the top of a tower block in the Haymarket, with a dazzling view over London. The festival notices had, with a couple of honourable exceptions, totally ignored the Production Board and its achievements. Keith Lucas was the first person Andrew and I met at the reception and I put this point to him. 'I think one should take up gardening,' he said (he was probably thinking

Kevin Brownlow and Andrew Mollo on the stage
of the 1975 London Film Festival

of a scurrilous document that was doing the rounds of the BFI). 'At least the flowers don't bite.'

When Ken Wlaschin asked if I could say a few words, I thought he meant that night, at the opening. Suddenly, I found myself in front of a microphone, without the slightest idea what to say. Wlaschin said that *Winstanley* had received some adverse reviews, but he thought it would outlive its criticism. 'Whether we will is another matter,' I muttered. Seeing the assembled press, I felt a surge of indignation and let fly: 'Since all the press is here, I must say I'd like to take you by the throat. None of you [and this was an unpardonable exaggeration since David Robinson and Alexander Walker had written about the BFI] have mentioned the BFI Production Board and the extraordinary work it is doing. Now I'm a historian. In years to come I'll look back at the clippings to see what trends you've observed – and there'll be nothing.' I plugged as many of the BFI films as I could think of, and made the point that all these films had received the ultimate in praise and the ultimate in hostility, which was very healthy.

When I rejoined Andrew, he was berating George Perry of the *Sunday Times* for not doing anything to help us (the *Sunday Times* had rejected all our stills as below their required standard). 'What is the use of friends like you?' said Andrew, in a good-natured way. Then we got involved with Derek Malcolm of the *Guardian*. I tried to put Mamoun's policies over, but oh, how I wished he had been there. I did get one point out that I considered important – that the people who provided the money to the BFI, the Department of Education and Science, knew nothing about films and could only judge the work we were doing from the printed word. Andrew interrupted: 'Absolute rubbish!' at which I lost my temper (and my feeble hold on the subject) and Malcolm smiled at this sign of discord.

The party broke up as a waiter ostentatiously drew the curtains across the amazing high-angle of London. We went to a nearby salt-beef bar and Derek Malcolm continued his explanation of why his review was so ambivalent. 'I don't give a fuck if you have the right pigs, and I don't give a fuck if you have the correct costumes. I just wish you had invested that amount of care into the drama.'

'But we deliberately avoided the dramatic.'

'I accept that,' said Malcolm. He enthused about *Kaspar Hauser* by Werner Herzog and said that this set a high standard. One critic,

Elizabeth Sussex, thought our film empty and facile – a battle with a bit of story stuck on the end.

So the Big Night began with our morale in our boots. I discovered that at one press show, the reels had been shown in the wrong order so I checked them at the NFT. We had printed 2,000 copies of Winstanley's pamphlets as a souvenir. At each of the two shows, I told the audience, but requested that they left them if they weren't really interested. There were 500 people at each house. Eighteen hundred pamphlets were taken!

I learned that Tony Benn was in the audience for this first show. Andrew and I had to go on stage to answer questions – usually a gruelling experience because of that inevitable silence when no one comes up with any questions, and you stand on the stage feeling idiotic.

Which was precisely what happened this time. After a pause, a hand was raised and I recognised David Widgery of the Socialist Worker. 'At last a British political film,' he said. He brought up the subject of Portugal, and the role of the Army, so similar to that of the New Model Army, in the Portuguese Revolution. 'General Fairfax, touring the commune, was exactly like Wedgie Benn. Although, if it had been Wedgie Benn, he'd have made much more of a mess of it...'

Before any more damage was done, I stepped up to the microphone and said: 'I ought to point out to you that Mr Wedgwood Benn [as he was then known] is actually in the audience.' (Ian Sellar told me that Widgery sat down as though shot, and buried his face in his hands while his friends tittered.) We met Tony Benn afterwards, at an NFT reception. He was very enthusiastic about the film. 'I thought it was so good – marvellous – and I want to show it.' He explained that he was to lecture on the Levellers at Burford, the town where three of the Levellers had been shot by Cromwell. His American wife had heard that we were giving a free show for members of communes and wondered why: 'The film isn't about communes, or only incidentally – it's a really important political film.' Tony Benn said his wife had tried to make him get up and reply to Widgery's remark, but he wouldn't. 'He's quite right. If I'd been there at the time, I'd have had to put them down. I'd have been a member of the Establishment...' I asked him if what I'd heard was true, that he came to socialism through Winstanley. 'I was a

Andrew Mollo, Hugh Jenkins (Arts Minister), Tony Benn, Kevin Brownlow

member of the Labour Party at 16,' he replied, 'then I discovered Winstanley.'

Soon it was time for us to return to the theatre. The applause was more prolonged and louder than at the first house, but the questions included a tough one: 'Why does Winstanley talk with a twentieth-century middle-class accent?'

Andrew answered that we had written to an authority to find out how people spoke in those days, and nobody knew for sure.

'We know,' said the questioner with icy authority, 'that people spoke with regional accents. It would have been perfectly possible for you to find regional accents even today.'

I had to agree. I explained that we had been aware of this – Platt, one of the first to be cast – spoke with a Wiltshire accent. Unfortunately, some of the others could not manage to imitate regional accents convincingly. Winstanley's voice should have been North Country, and we were at one time going to post-sync it so that it was pure Wigan.

But we decided that Miles's voice was so sincere, so compelling and so sympathetic it would have been a crime to change it. Ken Wlaschin asked the audience if they felt the same way as the questioner and there was a chorus of 'No.'

After a few more questions – whether we used a detailed script, how we worked together, why non-professional actors – I made the point about the pamphlets. 'If you hate the picture, please leave them alone because they cost us 10p each.' Later that evening, Scott Meek, the NFT manager, came up with two 10p pieces, saying an elderly couple had insisted on paying. So Andrew and I split the first takings of the film.

As we went up the stairs, we encountered the audience coming down. 'As an ordinary member of the public, may I say how much I liked your film?'…'I really appreciated your film'… 'I loved your film'… 'Thank you for making it'… I wished we could give something back to the well-wishers, who were like something from a delightful dream. 'The care and accuracy showed in every frame. It was superb,' said one young man. Someone else raved about the costumes: 'Is the costume lady here? They were the most convincing and beautiful costumes I've ever seen.' There were so many of these remarks (and a number of cross comments at our tough questioner) that we could hardly get up the stairs. Although one lady congratulated us on our wonderful film about Gerard Manley Hopkins…

The evening was an amazing experience, even more gratifying, because of this direct contact with the audience, than the Festival screening of *IHH* back in 1964.

The flood of publicity led to some extremely good reviews and some extremely bad ones. At this point, the critics were equally divided and I toyed with the idea of publishing an advertisement on these lines:
'Rather confusing' (*Daily Telegraph*)
'Admirably clear' (*Financial Times*)
'Awkwardness in the acting' (*Financial Times*)
'Distinguished by very fine acting' (BBC *Kaleidoscope*)
'Slow and dull' (*Daily Telegraph*)
'A fascinating story' (*Guardian*)
'Lack of narrative drive' (*Guardian*)
'Gripping narrative' (*Financial Times*)
'The whole left me cold' (*Sunday Telegraph*)

'Intensely moving' (*Observer*)

The evening papers were both excellent. Felix Barker in the *Evening News* led with a teaser that made it sound as if he was describing recent events at the Windsor Pop Festival (which was relevant since Sid Rawle was currently in jail for attempting to organise it). He called it 'an outstanding piece of filmmaking' (November 6 1975).

Alexander Walker helped our distribution campaign no end by running a marvellous review, with picture, under the headline 'Not for the Public Gaze': '*Winstanley* strikes me as a simple, hard and beautiful film to watch and to listen to. It is really so original an undertaking that you feel like banging your head against the wall in despair at the thought of some of our native British distributors who (up to now) have fought shy of playing it in their cinemas.' (*Evening Standard* 5 November 1975)

Tom Milne in the *Observer* was equally enthusiastic: 'Marvellously photographed in luminously frosty black and white by Ernest Vincze, it is an intensely moving film, and one not without considerable contemporary relevance.' (16 November 1975)

These reviews helped us immeasurably, but they were not enough to allow us to follow the example of *Akenfield* and premiere the film on television.

The BBC turned it down shortly after the London Film Festival. All we ever heard from inside was that the controller of BBC2, Aubrey Singer, disliked the film and felt one of their own junior directors, given the same facilities, would have made a better job.

I recalled that the BBC turned down *IHH* too, for several years, finally showing it some time after they had made their own version, *If Britain Had Fallen*. Shortly after *Winstanley* was rejected, a photo appeared in the papers of a family clustered round a camp fire, surrounded by thatched huts, which I thought for a second was from our film. It was an announcement of a new series, *How We Lived Then* (eventually shown as *Living in the Past*), which BBC2 was embarking upon. It would take two years. It would be filmed throughout the seasons...

Perhaps the roughest review was in *Time Out*, the one paper I thought we could rely upon:

'It seems unfair, if not reactionary, to kick independent British features at a time when it's a miracle any get made at all,' wrote Andrew Nickolds, 'but the truth is *Winstanley* isn't much good…overriding solemnity crushes the sympathy that is clearly demanded for the story's characters, almost inviting a shrug. *Winstanley* looks much better seen with a documentary about the making of the film, a good-natured account of the enormous and lengthy difficulties involved. Unfortunately, all the spirit and effort seems dissipated when the material is finally brought to the screen.' (14-20 November 1975)

But when the Other Cinema screened it at a benefit performance, *Time Out* printed the following review:

'Films which come into the world without ready-made marketing labels are usually damned before they start, which may help to explain why the most beautiful and original English narrative film of the past decade lacks a distributor in this country. If *Winstanley* had been made in another language with subtitles, it probably would have garnered all the necessary raves in a flash; but alas, this black and white study of the seventeenth century is English to the core – as intransigent and idiosyncratic as its title hero. A love for the purity and textures of the silent cinema works hand in glove with a mania for period accuracy, so that history is neither seen at the wrong end of the telescope, nor converted into fashionable agit-prop, but recreated at the roots in all its mysterious ambiguity. Like *Barry Lyndon*, it is s-f about the past where a vanished era becomes the focus of the same sort of curiosity, awe and wonder commonly reserved for the future. It refuses to pander to simplistic demands for "contemporary relevance" (rather than let this emerge naturally from the material) betraying a respect for the audience that is all but anachronistic.' (Jonathan Rosenbaum, 20-26 February 1976)

This review drew an irritated letter from Charles Cooper of Contemporary Films, who had at long last tendered an offer for the film, following press notices of the London Film Festival. We answered:

'Distribution is such a desperate problem for the independent filmmaker in this country that we decided to use *Winstanley* to focus attention on the subject. We showed it to the Independent Film Distributors, including a representative of Contemporary Films, in June 1975. No offers were received. The Other Cinema had already seen the film, had already asked for it, but we decided to make an issue of the general lack of interest – as much for the benefit of the other BFI Production Board films as for our own.

'After the Board was reinvigorated by Mamoun Hassan, it was responsible for a remarkable series of pictures, and became the nearest thing we've got to a national cinema. It is profoundly depressing that these filmmakers should sweat their hearts out for next to nothing, to be greeted upon completion with a shattering display of indifference from the distributors.

'During the London Film Festival, our campaign helped to bring this matter further into the open. It also created a lot of publicity for *Winstanley*. As a result, we received an offer from Contemporary. It was a good offer. But it came seven months after the original show. The managing director, Charles Cooper, had not seen it earlier "because of the difficulties I have experienced trying to obtain distribution of films made by the BFI Production Board." We realise the problems. But we filmmakers have to overcome much greater problems to make the pictures in the first place. Do we have to take on the burden of distribution as well?' (*Time Out* 5-11 March 1976)

Phil Hardy, in a paper called *Street Life*, provided us with the most amusing reaction to the film: 'An awesome historical epic whose commitment to historic authenticity rather than the contextualizing of historical ideas is best seen in its acknowledgment of the assistance of the Rare Breeds Poultry Association.'

However, in January 1976, the British Film Institute voted for *Winstanley* to receive the Special Award of the Year; the main prize went to *Travelling Players*. We had won this award before in 1964. Even though we never saw any proof of it, we were greatly encouraged.

But as the right hand giveth, so the left hand taketh away. We were summoned to Colin McArthur's office to be interrogated about our poster. Before the LFF, Ken Wlaschin had said that a feature of the festival would be a display of posters. Could we supply ours? We hadn't got one, but enlisted John Harmer's help. At the distribution meeting, it was agreed we would have a poster, although no final decision about cost was arrived at. Harmer came up with a striking design, and with a surprising lack of hitches or delay, we had 500 posters.

Now we had to suffer for evading bureaucracy. Colin McArthur gave us a moral lecture; he pointed out the promotional budget of £5,000 was for 40 BFI films (£125 each??!) and a great deal of it had gone to making posters for *Requiem* and *Winstanley*. *Requiem*'s poster had been completed and then totally redone, but *Requiem*'s director, David Gladwell, retained his characteristic silence. Gerry O'Halloran also remained silent; since he had passed the arrangements, he was responsible to the Institute. Andrew brought up the occasion on which we were instructed to spend BFI money as fast as we could. 'You'd think there'd be some leeway now.'

Peter Sainsbury tried to pooh-pooh this as being just the way Mamoun's production flow was oriented. I said it gave us the kind of attitude to finance which had brought about this situation.

'You were a governor,' Ted Heath said to me. 'You're surely not saying you didn't get a true picture of the way the BFI organises its finances.' I replied that when I was a governor, I had been shocked by the way the BFI organised its finances. Colin McArthur, dark glasses, tight-lipped: 'A lot of us have been shocked but the BFI is not a monolith. There are people who think differently. We are trying to do something about it and this meeting is one of those things.'

John Harmer was told he would receive nothing for his work, although his printing bills would be paid. But no other budget had a penny to spare, and the BFI could not accept responsibility for the £200-odd we had spent. I explained that the Archive had recently refunded the money I had spent in the restoring of *Napoleon*, and if the worst came to the worst, I could always pay for the poster myself.

Peter Sainsbury said he would see if any of the films had any money left over, and he delivered another moral speech about taking money from other filmmakers. I said perhaps they could take it out of our salaries, as we hadn't been paid to make *Winstanley*. It occurred to me that since the responsibility rested with the distribution department, whose representative had passed the poster, it would not have hurt those highly-paid employees of the BFI to contribute a small amount each and cover the debt, but no such suggestion was made, and the atmosphere was hostile enough as it was.

'Let's talk about our successes,' I said. 'What about the BBC?'

Sainsbury said their letter had been a straight refusal. I told them of a Canadian filmmaker, Teri McLuhan, who had made seven approaches to the BBC, the last one of which had succeeded. 'We must keep trying.' I also told them about Rex Pike and the regional theatres – the only places which gave him prompt payment and good exploitation.

'So here you have a circuit of your own and you're paying other people to distribute the film.'

'We don't have a circuit,' said MacArthur. 'That is one of the things we're striving for – an overall policy. The regions plan their own programmes three months in advance.'

'We must keep the impetus started by the festival going. We've had hundreds of pounds of free publicity and it'll be wasted unless we can keep going.'

They protested. Production Board programmes were planned for the future.

'That's too late. It'll all be forgotten.'

'You have censorship fees for the RFTs,' said Heath. 'That'll cost a lot of money we haven't got.'

'Isn't there a way round that?'

'Only by showing the film to each local authority, in each region. It's very difficult.'

I made some dismissive remark about these difficulties, and Colin McArthur became thoroughly riled.

'Look,' he said, 'you may think we're mindless bureaucrats, but we're actually your allies.'

And so the meeting ended. But the amount for the poster was found in our budget; we had come in £1,000 under the figure Mamoun had anticipated.

Chapter Twenty-Nine

The National Film School is the toughest place imaginable to preview a film. The training ground for future filmmakers, it harbours some of the names who would be world-renowned in a decade or two. I remember director Jack Gold screening reels of his uncompleted *National Health* and sparring with some of the most breathtakingly aggressive criticism I have heard. One student, John Lind, informed Gold that his film was merely an inflated *Carry On Nurse*.

Ernie Vincze persuaded us to go, since he had a teaching post there in between photographic assignments.

We arrived at the old Beaconsfield Studios, once home to British Lion, in driving rain, and went straight to the canteen. In the queue, we were greeted by an Egyptian girl who said she had seen our film at the festival, liked it very much and, touchingly, insisted on buying us lunch. I thought perhaps the experience might be more pleasant than I had anticipated. However, a student asked: 'How long is your film?'

'Ninety-five minutes.'

'Oh, that *does* take a chunk out of the afternoon.'

As Andrew joined the queue, he overheard this snatch of dialogue:

'Are you going to see *Winstanley*?'

'You must be joking!'

The school's theatre must have been designed by someone who hated the cinema. There was a phone inside the auditorium, which never stopped ringing. A door with a fire-escape bar which clanged with dreadful emphasis whenever anyone walked out. And two 35mm projectors, aligned neither for vision or sound, one at least six points lighter than the other.

At the end, Ernie dragged us to the front and then said nothing. Nor did anyone else. 'What do you say on these occasions?' I asked. 'Are you still awake?'

A Magnum photographer, veteran of the Vietnam war, Philip Jones Griffiths, kindly eased our predicament by asking how we cast. Howard Sharp asked us about our reaction to the critical response. Someone else asked how we would have done it had we had a regular budget.

Afterwards, Ernie introduced me to Mike Radford, who would go on to direct *1984* and *Il Postino*. 'You obviously gave the people who worked on it a marvellous time – and that was worth £20,000 of anybody's money.' I was so taken aback by this remark that I paused and balanced the cans, picked up from the projection box, on a seat. 'You must have really enjoyed the film,' I said, ironically.

'I did,' replied Radford. 'I quite understand why you used those faces. Of course, the playing without exception was rotten. But I quite understand why you chose Miles Halliwell – he had a marvellous face; of course he was limited to one expression, but one has to put up with that.'

'Are you connected with acting, by any chance?'

'I was, of course, an actor – but that is completely irrelevant.'

'It's just that many people connected with acting object to the playing in the film.'

Radford said when it came to a choice between authenticity and beauty, we'd chosen beauty. He quoted some line about the space behind the camera being as significant as the space in front. 'One knows that behind the camera you have people watching and waiting to go on. Bodies passing the camera do so too perfectly. The children on the slide – all that was just too perfect. The negative comments I've heard all say the Diggers have nothing to do – I appreciate this. The film explodes into life when one person is hitting another over the head. But in one sense you lose interest when you have two people standing up talking to each other. One never knows who these people are – or where they come from.'

Andrew said no one knew, and we weren't going to add a fictional framework.

'The strongest scene,' continued Radford, 'is the battle. It's beautiful. But what does it add to the rest of the film?'

I said I thought it added something when Haydon says: 'Fairfax understands. He is a soldier. We were all together once.' He disagreed. 'It's the script. There's a big hole in the script. A fatal flaw.'

'The odd thing about this film,' I said, 'is that we get a totally different reaction from everyone. The only consensus is that most people find it moving – that's all that bothers me.'

'Oh, I don't think you should take any notice of what I say…But I enjoyed it very much,' he added, as we were leaving.

Chapter Thirty

I had had my fill of festivals and had no intention of accompanying the film to Rotterdam. Nor had Andrew. So I was unprepared for a phone call from Rotterdam Festival organiser Hubert Bals, pleading with me to come, for he had a press conference at 11.00 the following morning and it was essential I be there.

Gullible me! I flew out at 21.25 and was met at Rotterdam airport and taken to an office to meet a harrassed Hubert Bals. 'The print has not arrived. It was sent from Berlin and I'm sure it's here. Let's hope it will be through by tomorrow.'

Next morning, I turned up in good time for the press show, but there wasn't a press show because there wasn't a print. I was anxious to return to England, but Bals asked me to wait until evening, when they would put on the press show for sure. I reluctantly agreed, and spent the day visiting Amsterdam, which was very pleasant, and returned to be told there was still no print. It should have arrived, but they had sent it by truck instead of by plane, and it had gone back to Berlin, having been refused at the border. Would I please stay until Saturday afternoon?

Bals said he had spent two hours on the phone, and I felt sorry for him. I was behind schedule with my own work in London, but having come all this way, I agreed to stay.

Early on the Saturday morning, checking in his office, Bals told me that the print was almost there. The audience gathered at the advertised time to see *Winstanley* and the print was still almost there. The delay was agony. I discovered that yes, the print had arrived, but it was on spools, and the projectionists had to take it off the spools and wind it on to a platter. This took, and I can scarcely believe it as I write it, one hour. No one bothered to inform the audience. I rounded up a festival official and persuaded him to make an announcement.

Three hours late, the film came up on the screen. The projectors were equipped with poor quality lenses, and Ernie's lovely black-and-white looked as if it had been shot through an aquarium filled with seaweed. I departed, to fix my ticket back to London, and returned to the theatre for the discussion – which, evidently, was what I had been brought from London for. The applause surprised me, but virtually everyone left before the discussion – hardly surprising in view of the delay.

Paul Jarrico, blacklisted producer of the American communist film *Salt Of The Earth* (1954), asked if the English weather was the cause of the dampening of the revolutionary ardour. I expected more than a patronising joke from such a man. A colleague of Fassbinder made a speech about the commercial and the non-commercial filmmaker, and asked why we wouldn't make a film for both kinds of audience, as did Fassbinder himself. I said Andrew and I wished we could.

An Englishman got up and said the introduction was staccato and hard to follow. 'Interspersed with your amateur soldiers making speeches. When the film got going, I thought it tremendous. In retrospect, do you feel the introduction to be a failure?'

To my surprise, some Dutch people had read Christopher Hill's book *Winstanley and the Law of Freedom*. One of them said he loved the film, but missed the village and the villagers' point of view. An Indian castigated me for my naïve faith in 'museum documents', saying the violence should have been fictionalised 'because museum documents deal only in effect and never in terms of suffering.'

'What do you want the audience to take away with them?' had been one of the questions from the auditorium.

'I would like them to feel they had visited the seventeenth century, and to feel they know something about Gerrard Winstanley.'

A film cannot achieve very much in implanting ideas, for moving images are as common as tap water, and one film quickly displaces another. But if I were to answer that question more fully and perhaps more honestly, I would add that I hoped they derived aesthetic pleasure from these moving images. Unfortunately, at Rotterdam, with the lamentable projection, that simply wasn't possible. The film was never distributed in Holland.

A brief review appeared in a historical journal *Past and Present*, which had not previously reviewed a film. It was written by Christopher Hill and counts among my favourite reviews:

'Good historical films are sufficiently rare for it to be worth drawing attention to *Winstanley*, directed by Kevin Brownlow and Andrew Mollo. Although made on a shoe-string budget, the film's detail is meticulously accurate, down to the shoes which the Diggers wear, the agricultural implements they use, the breed of animal they farm. The film was shot in Surrey heathland, not far from St George's Hill, now absorbed into the stockbroker belt. But more important than this convincing background is the imaginative reconstruction of the world in which the Diggers lived – still torn by social conflict, but one in which fundamental reform still seemed possible. This film can tell us more about ordinary people in seventeenth-century England than a score of text books. All but one of the actors are amateurs, but the critics stressed "the very fine acting" as well as "the simple, gripping narrative". *Winstanley* is never likely to be a commercial success, but it is a film that readers of *Past and Present* should go out of their way to see if they get a chance.' (Balliol College, Oxford, Christopher Hill)

Thanks to Tony Benn, *Winstanley* was shown at Burford. The historical connections were with the Levellers rather than the Diggers, but the film attracted two packed houses at a school just outside the town. Any euphoria I might have had about its reception was shattered by the projectionist. He tested a reel of the brand new 16mm print and ripped it to shreds.

'Who made this film?'

'I did.'

'Why didn't you say?'

'What difference would it make?'

'All the difference in the world. I thought this was just another film. It didn't bother me, leader ripped – didn't worry me. Now I realise you made it and it's your property, well, it puts it on an entirely different footing.'

Tony Benn quoted from *Winstanley* in his speech, referred to 'the marvellous film we saw this afternoon' and gave us some splendid publicity.

Burford was a fascinating occasion in its own right, but far too often I found myself meekly complying with a request to introduce the film in a distant town to an audience who gave no indication of interest. These were depressing experiences; I attended as many as I could out of a sense of duty. It was the attitude suggested by some of the questions that cast a certain gloom over the proceedings: 'Why was there so much wind?' was one I remember travelling several hundred miles to be asked.

I not only became involved in personal appearances, but, in the pre-release stage, in wheeler-dealing. With the major distributors taking no notice of the film, Simon Crocker, brother of agent Julian Seddon, produced a fascinating idea of tying in *Winstanley* with concert-style promotions around the universities. I was still determined to go with the Other Cinema, but suggested to their director, Nick Hart-Williams, that he should consider this new idea. He said he would. The Other Cinema was planning to open its own theatre in London for which they needed £15,000 to match a BFI grant of the same amount.

I never heard any more of the concert-promotion idea. But the Other Cinema announced that when their cinema opened, it would open with our picture.

That seemed to both of us the ideal answer. A cinema, when it opens, spends the maximum on publicity, even if it draws in its horns later. I was taken aback, however, when the Other Cinema committee objected to John Harmer's striking poster and insisted on a new one, to their specifications. I couldn't stand the usual run of Other Cinema agit-prop posters and told them so. It took several meetings before Andrew took the project over; he produced a photograph of an early tapestry, showed it to the artist, the Argentinian Oscar Zarate, and between them they concocted an excellent poster, incorporating letter-

ing from the original pamphlets and a stylised, tapestry-like 'engraving' of peasants and soldiers. I was delighted with it.

I was even more delighted with the programme that the Other Cinema had arranged around *Winstanley*. They included not only the films that had inspired and influenced us – *The Emigrants*, *The Parson's Widow* – but also the films we had reacted against – *Witchfinder General* and *Cromwell*, for instance. I never met anyone who had seen the full programme, but it was a brave and imaginative experiment and I was sorry it was never repeated.

Chapter Thirty-One

Winstanley was at last shown publicly in London on 16 October 1976. The opening night saw a long queue and a capacity house, and it drew a quiet response. The *Times* gave it the lead review: '*Winstanley* is a film I can see again and again with increased pleasure' (David Robinson, 29 October 1976) and Alexander Walker in the *Evening Standard* called it 'a hearteningly apposite choice with which to open London's new club-and-public cinema...it is shot in black and white tones of amazing beauty and often astonishing loveliness that lets the story be permeated by emotions as relentless and English as the weather. The fine old directness of English common speech is like an extra turn of the dagger finding its home in the enemy's bigotry. Miles Halliwell plays Winstanley with the radiance of a quiet zealot. The film is certainly the best thing the British Film Institute's Production Board has funded to date.' (14 October 1976)

On the other hand the *Daily Telegraph* and the *Sunday Telegraph* gave it poor reviews and the popular papers didn't bother with it at all.

The Other Cinema about to open – 1976

A thoughtful notice appeared in issue 13 of *Undercurrents*, the magazine of radical technology, written by Martyn Partridge:

'The Diggers failed to achieve their aims, and they failed abysmally. After less than two years on barren heathland, harassed at every turn by the authorities, their spirit was broken and the movement crushed. The film sets out to show the human elements that underlay this short, sad fact...how the unity of the movement was imperilled by lunatics (Ranters – "self ended spirits") and by the simple pragmatism of those with families to support, who could not live up to Winstanley's standards of self-denying honesty. And, more than anything else, it demonstrates the cruel reality of living by the land...the dirt, the hunger, the unremitting toil, set against a background of -changing weather. The most memorable scene is the recurrent prospect from the hilltop, a leitmotif depicting all the seasons, sometimes assailed with storms and at other times shimmering beneath the hot sun. Anyone who wants to live closer to the earth must love it in all its moods.

'*Winstanley* is a didactic movie of great importance...a typical piece of our history featuring poverty, property, gentleness and power. It asks questions which were put into cold-storage in the seventeenth century and are, this day, still waiting to be answered. The words of

Winstanley, and Miles Halliwell's remarkable voice, still linger: '...here I end, having put my arm as far as my strength will go to advance righteousness. I have writ, I have acted, I have peace.' How many of us will be able to say as much?'

The film ran at the Other Cinema for five weeks and, in accordance with their promise, they brought the film back from time to time. At the first run, it was seen by 4,935 people. (A single television screening could have been seen by four million.) And that was it for London. The total net earnings were £3,897.89, which, for a film costing £24,000, was hardly encouraging. Which is why there were so few independent British features. *Akenfield*, with all its publicity and its pre-sold audience from the book on which it was based, did better – it made £6,536 in seven weeks, together with a television screening – but with its £100,000 budget it had much further to go to break even.

So *Winstanley* had been to festivals, it had had its good notices and its bad notices, it had had a respectable London opening. It had nothing to do but float around the provinces, to film societies and regional film theatres. Its release would have been a monumental anti-climax had it not been for France.

In France, its distribution was handled by two women, Pascale Daumont and Annabel Herbault, who had formed themselves into Paris Films. I had asked that the subtitling be done by a friend, Bernard Eisenschitz, who, in collaboration with Professor Lutaud, worked on it with infinite care and patience. Much of the film's success was due to those impeccably translated subtitles. And what a success! When Pascale and Annabel asked me over to Paris, I turned them down, imagining a repetition of Rotterdam. They persuaded me to fly over for a day, and wickedly, I made them drive me round the secondhand film stalls so that my time was not completely wasted. But they had arranged meetings with a number of critics, and in discussing the film with them I was startled by their enthusiasm.

Reviews kept arriving from the French opening, but my French was not good enough to cope with them. I sent them to Sarah Ellis, and when she had translated them I could hardly believe my eyes. I thought perhaps she had rewritten them.

In a surfeit of self-indulgence, I am going to end this account with the French reviews. I cannot offer any explanation for their eulogies, nor for the fact that the film ran for months, and at one time was running in two Paris cinemas simultaneously, nor for the award of the 1976 Georges Sadoul Prize. Andrew and I are simply grateful that the film, involving so much effort, so much sacrifice and so much public money, found a genuine response somewhere. We were sad that it was not in England, for the film is very English and it celebrates some very English characteristics.

These reviews will also help the people who worked with us feel that their effort was recognised. When I look back on the period of shooting, it is to those people that I feel a surge of gratitude, not only for the excellent work they did, but for the remarkable spirit they brought to the film. The film may well prove to be the last film Andrew and I will make together, and possibly the last feature either of us will have a chance of making. A sobering thought! But I would never want to forget the experience, and I would never want to forget those extraordinary people who shared it.

Kevin Brownlow
London, 1976

Reviews from Paris

November 1976, translated by Sarah Ellis

Ecran 76, Marcel Martin

Brownlow and Mollo have illustrated this page of history with totally convincing realism. Their reconstruction of seventeenth-century England is a model of the form. It presents total credibility based on absolute verisimilitude in all the aspects (sets, costume, speech). The use of black and white adds considerably to the authenticity; whether the filmmakers were forced to use it for economic reasons or whether they chose it for aesthetic ones does not invalidate the choice, and for me it was with a real sense of enchantment that I watched this superb work in black and white (stark, yet at the same time subtly varied in the range of greys) after seeing so many multicoloured daubings.

Though they adopted an essentially simple approach in the direction (the style is more or less that of a documentary) the directors have achieved a sequence for anthology. It is the battle sequence that opens their film, which has excerpts of *Alexander Nevsky* for its sound track, and is, by virtue of the mastery of rapid cutting, worthy of Eisenstein's masterpiece. Often static, the camera behaves in an 'I was there' manner which makes one think of Peter Watkins' reconstructed newsreels. The sound track is particularly carefully done, picking out natural sounds (wind, rain) with a stunning sharpness; and so the film, which was almost completely shot exterior, reveals a marvellous sense of nature in both the physical sensation of space and in the path of the clouds' shadow across the land.

This extremely beautiful film is not only a delight for the eyes – it is also a celebration for the intellect; we must heartily welcome this 'return' (unfortunately late as it is) of two filmmakers whose first film *It Happened Here* (1964) was already an event.

Les Nouvelles Littéraires, Michel Perez, 5 November 1976

A wonderful reconstruction of English peasant life in the time of Cromwell, *Winstanley* is the work of two passionate cinema-lovers who possess the huge merit of not using their knowledge of cinema to bedazzle with subtle quotes and pastiches. Gone scandalously unnoticed and foolishly deemed reactionary and nostalgic for Nazism by superficial minds, their first film *It Happened Here* already testified to a mastery rare in young filmmakers and to a professional precision that is extremely difficult to find today. This precision we find again with *Winstanley* – a film the two men have taken four years to make [sic] without being afraid of taking on a historical reconstruction with only the smallest of budgets. In black and white, conceived with a knowledge of editing that immediately makes one think of silent films, and Russian in particular, it is a film that's a million miles from giving way to the easy ways of aestheticism and one in which the personal and original tone is unfailing. This no doubt comes from the fact that Brownlow and Mollo have always known how to keep the balance between the fervour of the cinema lover, and the political engagement into which their subject leads them – a history lesson of no mean importance and which finds an echo in the social reality of today – a record of failure but also a poem of the love of the land… *Winstanley* is above all a marvellous piece of cinema on which advocates of the slapdash, or the 'mis-construction' and of the so-called Brechtian distancing would do well to meditate a bit.

France-Soir, Robert Chazal, 6 November 1976

The incomparable greatness of masterpieces of the silent cinema in black and white – that's what strikes you from the very beginning of this film, with its sense of actual modelled beauty and perfect understanding.

Winstanley's merits are numerous, and first of all cinematographic. The film opens with a battle supported by Prokofiev's music for *Alexander Nevsky*. It has an extraordinary beauty and underlines the kinship between the film and the great Soviet productions. From this piece of bravura the historical accuracy is already evident and through the work the quest for truth achieves the simplicity and effectiveness of documentary.

But *Winstanley* is an epic work served by powerful direction and a cast as perfect as it is numerous. This film really transports us to Cromwell's England.

This film is one of the most perfectly realised period films – a genre which is so often betrayed.

L'Express, P.F.
...in front of Kevin Brownlow and Andrew Mollo's camera the history lesson becomes fascinating – humble in its purpose and of a rigorous plastic beauty. In black and white images inspired by the silent films, history adorns itself with the steel charms of *Alexander Nevsky* and the white-hot will of a libertarian ballad. *Winstanley* is to cinema what Robert Mandron's works are to the study of history – a look at the mentalities...

Valeurs Actuelles, N.M.
...if their sympathy for him as a person limits somewhat the import of the philosophy of the film, that isn't to say that their style doesn't have a stunningly persuasive strength...Directed with a sober and touching realism...a sort of successful 'retrospective documentary'. Voluntarily didactic, the story systematically sets aside the picturesque in favour of a dense and often poignant vision of characters of the time, with the radiant sweetness of some episodes contrasting with the dark violence of others. With *Winstanley*, Kevin Brownlow and Andrew Mollo have quite clearly contributed to the renaissance of the historical film in Europe – which breaks with Hollywood conventions in favour of a historical consciousness founded on a rigorous approach to the past which is circumspect and quasi-scientific.

...among its qualities one admires particularly the beauty and mastery of the photography whose role particularly consists of dramatically expressing the importance that atmosphere, in the strictly physical sense of the term, could have on history. The sequence where the Diggers, crudely sheltered from the rain, strike up a hymn to alleviate their despair belongs to cinema at its greatest.

Hebdo Politique, R.D., 8 November 1976
In the wilderness of the English cinema, this film should be blazed with a white stone. A model of historical reconstruction, this film, with a sense of moderation and rigorousness, illuminates a particularly signifi-

cant episode in the English class war. The battle that opens the film will remain a piece for anthology.

Le Nouvel Observateur
In order to achieve the perfect reconstruction of Cromwell's England, Kevin Brownlow and Andrew Mollo have drawn on their rich intelligence to compensate for their modest budget. Each shot in this exemplary film is a jewel of research, rhythm and lasting quality. A model of thought at the boundary of precociousness. [Sarah Ellis added: 'Haven't a clue what that last sentence means!']

Le Monde, Louis Marcorelles, 7 and 8 November 1976
Brownlow and Mollo have 'set up' in both the cinematic and historical sense, the most extraordinary game of patience ever thought of in the cinema. Shot in black and white, on 35mm, with £24,000 (about one eightieth of the cost of *Barry Lyndon*) in seven weeks, but seven weeks spread over four seasons, it is a film which at one and the same time denounces the sectarianism of the puritans and affirms the virtues of ideological and cinematographic puritanism. *Winstanley* is a monument to individual revolt as much through its method of production as through its hero.

L'Humanité, Bernard Eisenschitz, 6 November 1976
Winstanley is an exceptional film for more than one reason – the subject matter and the nature of production. The film represents the result of a huge task of reconstruction nearer to *La Marseillaise* than *Barry Lyndon*. As in Renoir's film, the spoken word is generally historically accurate. Fiction is only made use of to focus the film more precisely on historical facts and events. Not only in the introduction, which summarises the revolution and the sharpening of social conflict in the Civil War, but also in the plastic representation of space – be it that occupied by the Diggers' settlement or by the houses of the powerful, *Winstanley* is a rigorously conceived and masterful spectacle.

Télérama, Michel Lenghney
In spite of a small budget, the directors have known how to bring to life a vigorous, authentic seventeenth century, so different from the usual

period concoctions entangled in their shiny costumes. The camera attends to the details, scans the faces and piece by piece recomposes the puzzle of an epoch with impressionistic touches. Each image, each shot, is marvellous, reaching a rarely equalled level of visual beauty. This film, shot in black and white, risks passing unnoticed. It must be discovered. It is a masterpiece of the genre.

And here I end, having put my arm as far as my strength will go to advance Righteousness; I have Writ, I have Acted, I have Peace: now I must wait to see the Spirit do his work in the hearts of others, and whether *England* shall be the first Land, or some other, wherein Truth shall sit down in triumph.

Gerrard Winstanley

Index

312

313

Printed in the United Kingdom by
Lightning Source UK Ltd., Milton Keynes
140904UK00001B/10/P

9 781905 796229